Expert Systems in
Data Processing

Expert Systems in Data Processing

A Professional's Guide

Jerome T. Murray

Marilyn J. Murray

McGraw-Hill Book Company

New York St. Louis San Francisco Auckland
Bogotá Hamburg London Madrid Mexico
Milan Montreal New Delhi Panama
Paris São Paulo Singapore
Sydney Tokyo Toronto

Library of Congress Cataloging-in-Publication Data

Murray, Jerome T.
  Expert systems in data processing.

  Bibliography: p.
  Includes index.
  1. Electronic data processing departments.
2. Expert systems (Computer science) I. Murray,
Marilyn J. II. Title.
HF5548.2.M87 1988   658'.05633   87-37859
ISBN 0-07-044088-3

1234567890 Doc/Doc 8921098

ISBN 0-07-044088-3

*The editors for this book were Theron Shreve and Nancy Young,
the designer was Naomi Auerbach, and the production
supervisor was Dianne L. Walber. It was composed by the
McGraw-Hill Book Company Professional & Reference Division
Composition unit.*

Printed and bound by R.R. Donnelley & Sons Company.

Many view technology as a juggernaut moving inexorably forward in accord with an inscrutable karma. The circumstances of technological development, however, reflect a much less esoteric reality. Technology advances at the pleasure of its employers—those true pioneers of progress. Technological growth depends upon this special breed, sadly diminishing in ranks, willing to stake both future and fortune on technology's leading edge. It is to one of these very few that we dedicate this book:

MR. WILLIAM RICHARD ROSE
President and Chief Executive Officer
Rose Packing Company, Incorporated

Contents

Contents

Preface

A systems analyst working late in his office hears the sudden wailing of an alarm over the rumble of thunder from an approaching storm. The sound is coming from the electrical room down the hall—the high-voltage room. The Uninterruptable Power Source (UPS) is installed there, but he has never had the occasion even to look at it. He runs to the room, opens the door, and there on the UPS display panel is the message: UPS—ALARM.

He recalls that before the UPS installation storms would knock the system down and, for days afterward, the department would be the focus of users' complaints—no recovery is perfect. His project is off schedule now and a recovery effort will only exacerbate the situation. There beneath the message panel he sees a small sign, PASSWORD: UPSGO.

He returns to his office and signs on his terminal with UPSGO. A screen appears directing him to the UPS room to read the message—he has already been there. He chooses the option matching the message he saw there—UPS—ALARM. The system returns, presenting a graphic of the UPS control panel. It directs him to press the highlighted keys in the sequence specified. He returns to the UPS room and does as directed—a new message appears on the UPS panel.

Six minutes later, after four trips to the UPS room, the situation is stable. A prolonged utility power voltage fluctuation had caused the inverter to trip. This caused the UPS to place the critical load on bypass power. The UPS was no longer protecting the computer configuration. With a storm raging there was the risk of a computer crash if the utility's power failed. Indeed, immediately after the UPS was stabilized, the power did go off. The building blacked out, but the now stable UPS was supporting the computer. A recovery effort was averted that could have been costly not only to the project but to user relations.

Is this story a thriller? No, it is just an example of an expert system in action. The system was written by a novice, in 4 days, while referring to an equipment user's manual. It was ultimately used by an analyst who was totally unaware of either expert systems or the intricacies of UPS. He was not about to read the 1½-inch-thick UPS manual. Had he attempted to master the user's manual, the storm would have won the evening before his new knowledge had a chance to function. Instead, the expert system saved the department's image and many hours.

Why would anyone create an expert system from a manual? In this case, trouble with the UPS was so infrequent that each occurrence required a rereading of the manual. It quickly became clear that this reinventing of the UPS "knowledge wheel" was not only dangerous but foolish.

Artificial intelligence (AI), at least in the form of the expert system, has invaded the domain of data processing. Reactions do not differ much from those that greeted the advent of computers themselves. Responses have run the gamut from "Let's set up a budget and look into this," to "Our company is just not that complicated." The worst-case scenario sees a separate department established outside of the data processing department for the creation of expert systems.

The fact that many expert systems require only microcomputing equipment for their creation and delivery may mislead some data processing professionals. They may conclude that, like spreadsheet programs, expert systems belong elsewhere. To the contrary, data processing personnel have implemented expert systems on personal computers solely to support the data processing function. Mainframe expert systems are becoming just as numerous. The system illustrated above is but one of many.

The adage "He who chops his own wood is twice warmed," certainly applies to the development of expert systems for use internal to the data processing department. The resultant system brings with it experience that is employable in broader expert system development.

Even if we disallow any immediate opportunity to implement an expert system, the significance of the intrusion of AI remains undiminished. Computer professionals are in only one business although they may work, at one time or another, in any number of industries. They have repeatedly demonstrated that their first loyalty is to computer technology and their mastery of it. Maintaining this status requires a relentless study of the field, thus presenting their current employers with major benefits. It is the computer professionals who are best able to introduce novel technology to the organization and thereby contribute to profitability. Certainly, an understanding of expert system technology is necessary in today's competitive environment.

There are a number of excellent books that introduce the reader to artificial intelligence, and they should be read by anyone interested in understanding the full spectrum addressed by this field. AI is multifaceted and addresses areas such as natural language processing, pattern recognition, theorem proving, problem solving, game playing, robotics, computer vision, and automatic programming. Unfortunately few, if any, of the current introductions address the details of expert system development in a way most likely to satisfy the data processor's need for practical knowledge. It is our hope that this book will serve that need.

The chapters ahead provide the computer professional with an introduction, familiarization, and, finally, enough involvement in the building of an expert system to constitute "experience." We have gone to some lengths to avoid the creation of a book without compromising in those areas that require due rigor. Consequently, the professional familiar with at least one procedural programming language (Cobol, Fortran, PL/I, APL, BASIC, C, Pascal, or Assembler) will find trouble-free travel on the journey at hand.

Chapter 1 discusses the many expert systems in current use or under construction. We then describe the several differences between expert system technology and traditional data system development technology.

Chapter 2 investigates the expert system application opportunities that are found in the data processing department as well as those in the company at large. Payback is the primary consideration. The professional data processor should come away from this chapter with many ideas for the creation of immediately profitable systems. Risks present in the implementation of expert systems in user departments are identified as well.

Chapter 3 turns our attention to the expert. We consider the specifics of expertise and discover the credentials required of an expert. Because experts change and grow, we learn that expert systems must afford ease of modification. We delve into expert system psychology.

Chapters 4, 5, and 6 look directly at the components of expert system technology. It is important that the data processor understands the fundamentals of this technology. We describe the algorithms for forward and backward chaining as well as the design of a frame-based system. The programming languages LISP and Prolog are introduced and explained in some detail. Chapter 6 turns our attention to expert system shells and their role in the creation of expert systems on both the mainframe and the PC.

Chapter 7 addresses the implementation issue. What tools should be used? Should every system be written in LISP or Prolog? Are expert system shells equivalent to application generators? The professional data processor will see that both high- and low-level development facilities are available for expert systems, just as they are for data systems.

Chapter 8 deals exclusively with the IBM Expert System Environment. This software offering from IBM allows the user access to a mainframe database. In association with an expert system consultation (user session), the expert system may be designed to invoke processing programs written in the programming language of the system designer's choice. This IBM offering makes expert system technology available to a huge segment of the computer-using community.

Chapter 9 applies everything presented earlier as we proceed to build an expert system. Interviews with the expert are seen to be tedious, repetitious, and, yet, challenging.

Chapter 10 crisply summarizes the earlier chapters. Where applicable, we present additional material that is meaningful from the perspective of the newly knowledgeable reader.

Chapter 11 is a collection of sources for expert system programming languages, shells, hardware, consulting aid, and further education and training. The list is certainly not exhaustive. New AI organizations are appearing daily. For this reason we include publishers whose periodicals offer to keep the reader abreast of the ever expanding marketplace.

Welcome to expert systems—the future is now.

Acknowledgments

There perhaps was once an era in human enterprise when men and women could single handedly reach their goals. If that time truly did exist, it has certainly vanished in the mists of antiquity. While the writers's task is a solitary one, it does not go forward without the aid of many. To them we are indebted.

Ms. Julie Ulbrich, IBM Systems Engineer, and Dr. Eva M. Mueckstein, Manager, IBM Expert Systems Programming, together with others at IBM, too numerous to name, afforded us insights and technological details of IBM's offerings in expert systems technology.

Mr. Ted Jernigan of the Texas Instruments Data Systems Group and TI's cadre of expert systems specialists have contributed information not only to us but to thousands through the Texas Instruments Corporation's Satellite Symposia.

Mr. Mark Turner, Consulting Knowledge Engineer, Digital Equipment Corporation Technology Center, Hudson, Massachusetts, heavily influenced the creation of Bob Haynes in Chapter 9. Mr. Turner was but one of a number of those at Digital Equipment Corporation who shared their views and expert systems technological information with us during the creation of this book.

Ms. June Donath gave unhesitatingly of her time and expertise by volunteering to be our expert in the development of Chapter 9. Without her contributions, Chapter 9 would not exist because without an expert there cannot truly be an expert system.

Mr. Alfred Vaza diligently scoured the contemporary literature and forwarded every bit of information he could find dealing with expert systems without knowing that he was contributing to this work. He, like Ms. Donath, is an expert in his own right. He offered his aid not only through friendship but through an interest in the advancement of knowledge.

Finally, there is that vast army of AI researchers—professors, graduate students, and industrial knowledge engineers—who daily toil to breathe intelligent life into the microscopic chips that we call computers. Their victories have not been addressed here in any detail because our effort addresses only a limited area of AI and its accomplishments in commercial applications.

That expert systems are saving uncounted dollars is important. How expert systems will save uncounted lives and perhaps humanity itself is the story yet to be written. When that story is completed, it will be to these and the nameless thousands of contributors to whom we will all owe a debt of gratitude.

Expert Systems in Use

It was November 13, 1985—a typical bone chilling autumn day in Chicago. The gray sky was shedding mist and the University of Illinois' Circle Campus was anything but cheery. A number of respondents to both published and mailed advertisements had been invited here to attend a satellite symposium on artificial intelligence (AI) presented by Texas Instruments, Incorporated. Upon arriving, they were directed to a drab basement lecture hall in the School of Pharmacy.

Unknown to them at the time, 30,000 others across the United States and Canada were filing into similar lecture halls for the same purpose. They represented nearly 500 government installations, corporations, and universities. Ironically, in this inauspicious environment, AI was making its commercial debut. Artificial intelligence, in the expert system, was stepping into the board rooms of major corporations, the data processing departments of schools, hospitals and small manufacturing firms, and most important, into all of our lives.

Less than 1 year later, on June 25, 1986, more than 50,000 people filed into over 900 locations in North America, Central America, South America, and Western Europe to attend Texas Instruments' Second Artificial Intelligence Satellite Symposium. Clearly, an idea's time had come.

Expert systems technology had been developed by university AI researchers much earlier and was, indeed, being profitably applied in a number of major corporations and by the government under the auspices of the Department of Defense. Until the Texas Instruments' Satellite Symposia, no major electronics manufacturer had elected to expend the resources necessary to bring these facts to the attention of the general data processing community in a dramatic way. Texas Instruments made that commitment and proceeded to support it in the best pioneering tradition.

The symposia brought together personnel from industry and academia. Representatives of companies that had successfully implemented expert systems described the development process, their results, and plans for additional projects. Academicians discussed the genesis of expert system technology, its current state, and directions for future research. Questions and comments were accepted from the symposia audiences across the network.

In the computer arena a major development tends to follow a maturation trajectory that sees its announcement followed by the development of a mystique, then broad vendor support, and finally acceptance as a staple. Whether Texas Instruments' public commitment to expert systems will hasten the journey through this trajectory remains to be seen. It is certain, however, that the publicity garnered by the Symposia for the expert system development efforts of its panelists, among them, Campbell Soup Company, Ford Motor Company, Corning Glass Company, DuPont Company, and Arthur Andersen & Company, has intrigued their competitors—a fact not overlooked by the presenters or their audiences. Secret expert system development is accepted as part of the technology's application environment.

The Expert Systems Mystique

It is, perhaps, intrigue that has shaped the expert systems mystique. Never before has the professional data processor been confronted with a software technology whose applications are so specialized that they approach trade-secret status. Alternately, those expert systems given wide publicity often seem so specialized that they offer little incentive to organizations not faced with identical problems.

While data processing applications are also specialized, their unique qualities grow out of a company's special requirements in order entry, inventory control, and so on. Data processing applications may contain secret formulas but rarely does an application itself constitute a trade secret that might offer its user a competitive edge. Consequently, it is the highly specialized nature of an expert system that is intriguing and at the same time confounding.

The definition of an expert system that describes it as a computer program that manipulates knowledge to solve problems in a specific area in the same efficient manner as that of a human expert explains the basis for this specialization—expert knowledge. We depend upon our expert controllers, engineers, market analysts, and schedulers to keep our enterprise viable. In each capacity, the knowledge is specialized.

The mystique is dispelled as soon as we review the fundamentals. Data processing applications manipulate data and output information. Information is processed by experts who output problem solutions. From this perspective, expert system technology is seen as the next natural extension of the information system. It is certainly within the purview of the data processing professional.

We see expert systems, then, as information processors whose applications address highly specialized and restricted areas of expert human knowledge. Because the expert system's function is problem solving, we would expect that an expert system, such as a financial advisor, would require specific information about existing financial conditions before rendering a recommendation. The question of information acquisition arises: Must an expert system be integrated with a data processing application?

The Applications

Many of the expert systems we will review are stand-alone applications. While those integrated with data processing systems are quite impressive because of the synergistic effect, it would be false to require integration as a prerequisite to the data processor's involvement. As we shall see in later chapters, many profitable stand-alone systems may be implemented on personal computers.

The Campbell Soup Company

Perhaps the grandfather of expert systems in commercial use is Cooker. At the very least it is among the best known and most frequently referenced expert system. Anyone familiar with the canning industry is familiar with the huge retort cookers into which canned products are conveyed. It is here that the products are cooked. A failure in the retort cooker affects the entire canning process, thus qualifying the skill of the maintenance engineer as a key ingredient in the plant's production.

Faced with the coming retirement of its leading retort cooker maintenance engineer, the Campbell Soup Company undertook the creation of an expert system that would capture his knowledge. The system that was to be developed was of the stand-alone variety. Problem information was to be entered by lesser-skilled maintenance personnel, whereupon the expert system, using its knowledge base, would provide solution recommendations.

Cooker could not completely replace the expert, but it was hoped that the expert system would shorten downtime in the face of the diminished skill availability that would result from the primary engineer's retirement.

The effectiveness of Cooker's performance is measurable in terms of the Campbell Soup Company's current publicly announced expert system development activities. An ambitious expert system development program now exists at Campbell addressing real-time control, scheduling, marketing, and financial applications at a number of locations. Already completed are six expert systems performing services similar to those provided by Cooker.

It is said that at the Campbell Soup Company engineers do not retire; they become floppy disks. Looking beyond the levity, we see, from the announced areas of interest, that integrated applications are due in the near future if some have not already reached completion.

The Ford Motor Company

The Ford Motor Company trains many of its maintenance personnel at its robotic center in Dearborn, Michigan. It was there that the development of a maintenance and servicing problem was detected. Because the company employs a number of highly sophisticated devices in its production facilities—machine vision systems and programmable logic controllers as well as a variety of robots—it is necessary to retain personnel trained in the repair of a diversity of equipment.

Although maintenance engineers are routinely sent to vendors' service schools for training, their knowledge is difficult to maintain because of the reliability of the equipment. High reliability leads to prolonged periods between failures, resulting in an engineer's need to relearn because of his or her lack of frequency with the particular item of equipment. Relearning usually involves perusal of nearly 1000 pages of support documentation before trouble-shooting may begin.

Personnel at the robotic center envisioned the development of an expert system that would act as a diagnostic aid in support of the engineer's maintenance efforts. They chose a specific robot that was widely used and began development of the expert system with the limited goal of addressing only a subset of the possible problems, albeit a subset containing the highest-frequency problems.

It became apparent that the effort was successful when, while the system was still in the prototype stage, it was determined that the expert system could reduce repair time by several orders of magnitude. A problem that required 1 week for traditional solution was submitted to the system, resulting in the production of the same solution within 5 minutes. Ford Motor Company has proceeded to distribute this expert system to its plant locations and has requested that the vendors of robots with whom it does business develop similar expert systems to support each of their offerings.

On the face of these activities one might conclude that the Ford Motor Company has a limited interest in the development of expert systems. The evidence belies such a conclusion, however. Ford has interests in the Carnegie Group, Incorporated, and in Inference Corporation. Both companies are specialists in the development of expert systems and artificial intelligence systems in general.

Arthur Andersen & Company

Arthur Andersen & Company is an accounting and consulting firm whose operations address a number of major divisions: audit, tax, and systems practices. This company is deeply involved in the development of internal expert systems in support of each practice. Simultaneously, their consulting efforts are directed to the development of expert systems that will produce a competitive advantage for their clients.

While the ethics of client-consultant confidentiality preclude the possibility of learning details of the expert systems created for clients, Arthur Andersen personnel have selectively discussed systems made public by clients such as the Securities Exchange Commission (SEC). The Financial Statement Analyzer was created for use by the SEC.

This expert system computes ratios from filings that are sent to the SEC in text format. Because these filings are unformatted, their analysis requires in-depth knowledge of accounting procedures as well as SEC policies that specify the ratios of interest. The system's task is largely the location of the required information which, as familiarity with financial statements will attest, may be qualified in footnotes and parenthetical remarks.

It takes little imagination to appreciate the competitive advantage that a similar but modified analytic system would offer a chief executive officer faced with declining margins and diminishing market share. While expert systems development may be shrouded in some mystery, those systems that do reach public disclosure give us more than an inkling of the rewards that may be gained from judicious use of this technology.

Corning Glass Company

At the Corning Glass Works in State College, Pennsylvania, there is an annealing furnace that is over 160 feet long. Such furnaces, called "lehrs," are common to glass makers—Corning uses a number of them in various of its plants. The temperature within the lehr is controlled by burners situated in approximately the first 10 feet of the device, with dampers and louvers along the remaining length. The goal of the lehr's operation is to eliminate internal stresses that are present in newly molded glass products. The glass products are conveyed through the oven where they are initially heated to a near molten state and held at this point until the stresses are relieved. The subsequent controlled cooling obviates the re-creation of stresses, thus producing the resilient, long-wearing product for which Corning is so popular.

Imprecision in the temperature curve along the length of the lehr results in unrelieved strain in the product or the creation of stresses caused by incorrect cooling with consequent excessive breakage. Excessive breakage reduces yield and negatively affects profitability. Because glass constitution varies by product, the lehr's operation is far from routine and expert skill is called upon in the set-up and damper control. Three factors influence product quality: the amount of time for which the product must be held in the near molten state, the subsequent cooling rate, and finally, the exit temperature.

An expert system was developed at the Corning Glass Works that captured the skill of Corning's lehr expert. Ultimately the expert system became a lehr planner-simulator. Information describing the three control factors is input to the planner which then consults its rule base. Having developed solution recommendations for the lehr's control settings, the simulator is called to predict how these settings will affect the temperature curve. The expert system then evaluates the effectiveness of the proposed solution. If the temperature curve has not been approximated, another iteration of the procedure follows.

Texaco Corporation

Reports are that Texaco is using an expert system in a process control application that has not been widely publicized. The difference in price between a barrel of toluene and one of benzene may be as much as $10. Because hard-wired process control does not respond effectively to optimizing this type of separation, the use of a real-time expert system has proven to be an appropriate solution. Once more, detailed information on the system is not readily available, but it is clear that the profit incentive is not difficult to determine.

Truesports

Truesports of Hilliard, Ohio, quietly saw its March-Cosworth race car cross the finish line at the 1986 Indianapolis 500. Few were unaware of Bobby Rahal's performance in piloting the car to its first place win.

Almost none, at the time, were aware of the role played by an expert system in achieving this goal.

Strategically located in various parts of the car were sensors that recorded the car's engine rpms, suspension activity, ride height, gear shifting, and the aerodynamic pressures. This data was then manually transferred to a remote expert system for analysis. The team of race mechanics used the system's output in fine-tuning the car, resulting in its final victory.

Westinghouse Electric Corporation

Research metallurgical engineers at Westinghouse are using an expert system that evaluates the critical points in steam generators. Water impurities often result in corrosion that pits, dents, cracks, and thins a generator's parts. The expert system accepts information input that produces alternative alloy recommendations.

The Honeywell Corporation

Honeywell's customer services division employs at least two expert systems which are available to its customer engineers via telecommunications in dial-up mode. One, Intelligent Software Configurator, automatically configures the Honeywell DPS 6 minicomputers, performing a service in minutes that formerly took days. Software support specialists use the configurator for fine-tuning the DPS 6 line of products via the entry of peripheral, operating system, and software choices that have been made for a given system. After this information is provided through a series of expert system menus, the system generates configuration load manager (CLM) files that the minicomputer uses in the management of its resources.

The second expert system, Page-1, aids the customer engineer in trouble-shooting of the Honeywell nonimpact Page Processing System (PPS) high-speed printers. Page-1 incorporates a knowledge base possessing PPS fault information that allows the customer engineer to determine probable trouble causes through interactive sessions with the remote expert system in dial-up mode.

While other similar customer engineering expert systems are said to be under development, little comment was forthcoming from Honeywell regarding other internal expert system development.

Digital Equipment Corporation (DEC)

XCON, the expert system originally used by DEC to configure its VAX-11/780 computers is equally as widely discussed as Cooker although it is considerably more sophisticated. Today XCON is used in the configuration of DEC's entire family of VAX systems. Because the VAX system is capable of being configured using an extremely broad selection of board components, customers' orders formerly required the attention of technical editors to assure the final delivery of an operational system.

Today XCON configures VAX systems complete to the specification of the required cables. Highlighting flexibility, XCON has required not only the incremental improvement that is characteristic of expert systems, but it has grown in capability as successive members of the VAX family have been brought to market over the years since its original introduction. DEC's involvement in expert systems must be considered as a major effort in the application of this technology if for no other reason than that the VAX itself is a popular development and delivery vehicle for expert systems.

The International Business Machines Corporation (IBM)

Often portrayed in the trade press as the sleeping giant, IBM rarely plays the role of pioneer. Nonetheless, once a novel development in the computer arena prompts a response from Armonk, New York, IBM's command post, the entire industry respects the novelty as a staple. Until recently, IBM's use of expert systems has been a rather silent affair.

During a 1986 seminar, IBM personnel divulged the existence of over 170 internal expert systems hard at work making money for the corporation. Among them is an expert system addressing disk-storage diagnostics that required an 8-month development effort. The system is now paying IBM back at the rate of $5 million per year in savings.

As we shall see in later chapters, IBM is quickly establishing itself as a major force in the expert systems development market.

Foreign expert systems

That expert systems extend beyond national borders is demonstrated at Austria's Vienna General Hospital where Cadiag-2's knowledge base includes over 260 profiles of diseases (rheumatic, pancreatic, gall bladder, bile duct, and colon). An integrated expert system, Cadiag-2 runs on an IBM 4381 under DOS/VSE as a guest under VM. Five hundred cases tested on Cadiag-2 involving information on patient symptoms, family history, and laboratory test results produced diagnoses yielding an accuracy of up to 93 percent when compared with clinical and pathological diagnoses. Cadiag-2 is considered a computer-based diagnostic system.

Over 10 provinces in China are using an IBM PC-based expert system in their central hospitals for the diagnosis and treatment of liver disorders. In Xinjiang Province alone, over 800 patients have been treated in the 2 years of this expert system's existence. A modified version of this expert system has been attracting over 200 people per day at the Nanjing College where it is used for the treatment of obesity via acupuncture.

Miscellaneous expert systems efforts

Cigna Corporation of Philadelphia, a major insurance company, supports two expert systems development teams. Hughes Aircraft Company of El Segundo, California, has been involved in expert systems development since 1981. General Motors Corporation has purchased an interest in Teknowledge, Incorporated, an expert system development company. American Express Company plans to benefit from an IBM mainframe-resident expert system that will advise credit authorizers regarding borderline credit card purchases.

IBM has joined with Pillsbury Company, Campbell Soup Company, and Sara Lee Corporation in the support of a 5-year project at Duke University. The objective of the program is the development of a marketing-oriented expert system in support of the packaged food industry.

In a separate effort IBM has undertaken a joint 3-year AI study in conjunction with Carnegie-Mellon University. IBM announced its gift of 225 RT personal computers to the university. The gift is valued in excess of $5 million.

Teknowledge, Incorporated, of Palo Alto, California, has been granted software patents for a manufacturing design expert system. The company has a number of additional patents pending.

Applications in development

If we turn our attention to expert systems under current development, we discover that the National Archives is working on an expert system soon to be commissioned to handle the routine queries of public researchers, thus relieving its archivists for more creative tasks. In a similar effort the Manhattan law firm of Davis, Polk & Wardwell is developing an expert system to facilitate the retrieval of legal briefs and other text material through apprehension of concepts contained in those documents

The United States Navy is developing BANS to support the decision-making activity of a limited number of budget analysts. The objective of this expert system is to enhance productivity in this area by capturing expertise lost through retirement. Analogous to the SEC financial expert system described earlier, budget requests are the input documents in this instance. Initial tests indicate that with expert system support, 2- to 3-hour analyses will require as little as 15 minutes of the analyst's time.

In the interests of protecting combat pilots the Defense Advanced Research Projects Agency (DARPA) has joined with the Air Force Avionics Laboratory in evaluating the use of an expert system to pilot combat aircraft. For use in particularly dangerous missions, the completed expert system would be able to autonomously control the aircraft throughout the entire combat engagement.

That expert systems have captured the imaginations and budgets of government and corporations both major and minor cannot be denied—the evidence is overwhelming. The resultant systems are both mundane and exotic. Their applications extend from the oil-soaked Indianapolis Speedway to the antiseptically clean examining rooms of hospitals. We have reviewed only a very few of these systems. Indeed, directories are currently being published that detail the known expert systems and proceed to speculate upon expert system development being kept under wraps.

How Does an Expert System Differ from a Data Processing System?

It is natural for the professional data processor to view expert system technology as a variation of the same technology with which he or she is already well acquainted. While the decision-support qualities of expert systems do lend them an air of familiarity, the techniques employed and the objectives sought differ from those in data systems. The fact is that expert systems depend upon a totally different technology from that found in routine data processing applications. The difference is so great that, in AI quarters, programming for data processing applications is said to be algorithmic while expert system programming is referred to as symbolic.

Data processing algorithms embody knowledge

By way of illustration we see, in Figure 1.1, the familiar decision table that gives rise to a number of rules determined by the number of conditions. In this case, eight rule columns result from three conditions.

Figure 1.2 displays the decision paths associated with the resultant rules. We are familiar with the algorithm governing the creation of such a decision table, and it is no surprise to find that we are faced

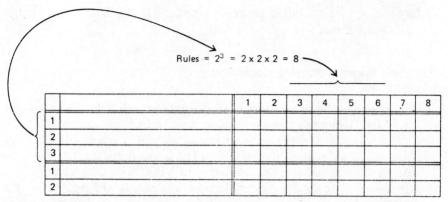

Figure 1.1   The number of rules in a decision table is determined by the number of conditions.

with an exponential increase in the number of rules as the number of conditions increase.

Few data processors would deny that the If-Then ingredients of the decision table constitute knowledge. It is, after all, this knowledge that we seek in the development of the many data systems with which we work each day. This knowledge actually defines the algorithms that we code into programs that process data. We take for granted the

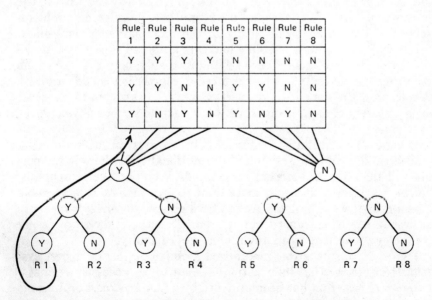

Figure 1.2   Each rule in the decision table gives rise to a decision path.

fact that traditional data processing technology embodies knowledge in its algorithms.

Knowledge separate from processing algorithms

It is precisely here, in their basic approaches, that traditional data processing technology and expert system technology radically differ. Expert system technology separates the knowledge—the If-Then rules—into a database distinct from the algorithms that do the processing. The database thus created is called a "knowledge base." The algorithms that do the processing are collectively referred to as the "inference engine."

The reason for this separation of knowledge from algorithms lies in the expert system's objectives. Traditional data processing technology seeks to create information from data while expert system technology seeks to solve specific problems using knowledge. An oversimplification leads us to the conclusion that traditional technology enables the processing of data while expert system technology enables the processing of information.

Were we to attempt the creation of an expert system using traditional data processing technology, the resultant program would be prohibitively large even if only 50 to 100 If-Then statements were elicited from an expert explaining a problem-solving method in a particular area of concern. Moreover, the task of frequently retrofitting the program to include the expert's continuously developing problem-solving skills would be defeating to the most skilled programmer. While it is, nonetheless, possible to create a limited expert system using the traditional techniques of data processing, both the size of the resulting system and the time required to completion would seriously detract from the system's benefits. Certainly, any attempt to create an expert system of significant scope would lead to serious development problems.

Beyond the limitations immediately obvious in a knowledge-embodied algorithmic system of the traditional type, there is the permanent inability to represent uncertainty. When an expert explains, "If the machine is off center more than 10 centimeters, it is probable that a gear tooth is broken," we are hard pressed to convey a measure of probability in an algorithmic system. Traditional data processing technology functions in an environment of certainty.

Figure 1.3 displays the generalized architecture of the expert system. Here we see that information is input to be processed against a knowledge base that has been provided by a human expert or, in some

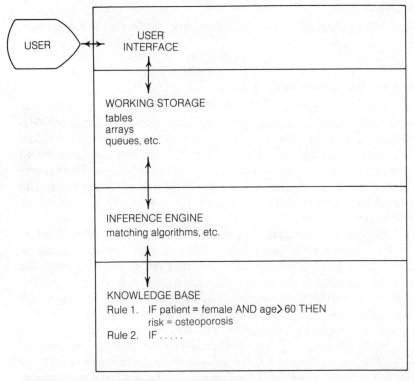

Figure 1.3   The generalized architecture of an expert system.

cases, by a book or manual. The processing algorithms are isolated to the inference engine. Working storage is a familiar buffer.

Typically, in a stand-alone system, the user interface is interactive. The user may not initially supply adequate problem-defining information and the success of the inference engine in finding a solution will determine how often the user is asked for additional input by the interface.

The symbolic processing carried on by the inference engine is an artifact of the strategy that defines the particular inference engine's design. The design strategy of the inference engine also determines, to a large extent, the method used in representing the knowledge in the knowledge base.

Not all expert systems are identical in their designs just as not all data processing systems are alike in their algorithmic development. The strategy employed in traditional data processing algorithms may require linked-list data structures, relational databases, hierarchical organization, VSAM clusters, or ISAM file structures. In a similar fashion, the method of knowledge representation varies in expert systems.

What is symbolic processing?

Symbolic processing involves the manipulation of forms or symbols as opposed to the strict adherence to mathematical calculations and boolean operations so familiar in traditional data processing algorithms. Expert systems accept, as input, problem information that is matched against the knowledge base to produce problem solutions. The matching procedure is determined by the algorithms that characterize the particular inference engine being used by the expert system under consideration.

Because the problem information is treated as a symbol or set of symbols to be matched against knowledge represented in the knowledge base, we may conclude that the method of representing the knowledge in the knowledge base is heavily dependent upon the design of the algorithms that constitute the inference engine. Any of a number of designs may be chosen depending upon the nature of the problems for which the knowledge base will be developed.

A significant feature of most expert systems is that the knowledge base may be modified, augmented, or reduced with relative ease. Coupling this with the fact that the inference engine is a fixed component, we see that ease of maintenance is a hallmark of expert systems.

The expert system development environment

No review of the differences between expert systems and data systems can be complete, however superficial, without giving consideration to the development environment. Data system development is characterized by top-down design, structured walk-throughs, chief programmer teams, and standards. Expert system development differs considerably.

Because of the malleability of the knowledge base, the expert system development environment is characterized by prototyping. The expert system is not designed exhaustively prior to an attempt to create computer-resident code. The emphasis in expert system development is upon obtaining expert knowledge, establishing a knowledge base, and working with the system and the expert to further the effort.

As we shall see in later chapters, even the algorithms of the inference engine may become a negligible issue in the development of a practical expert system. Expert system development procedures constitute a set of protocols that do not conform to the traditional methods of data system development. These changes in practice offer to some a radical departure from traditional development habits. It is probable that this less-structured approach will cause some seasoned data processors difficulty in adopting expert system technology.

There is, after all, some security in having a soundly thought out system design represented by a set of HIPO charts or even a complex collection of flowcharts. We know where we are going and we will know when we get there—we work in an atmosphere of certainty. In opposition to all of this, expert system development is a constant adventure in discovery. We do not know what the expert knows and we do not know that we have accurately understood what he or she has said. The effect of presenting a prototyped session as soon as possible is that we are able objectively to demonstrate a quite subjective entity—human knowledge.

The Journey Ahead

We have reviewed a number of expert systems in current use. They vary in size and complexity. AI researchers as well as senior management are prone to encourage major systems development, yet the practical applications often seem less ambitious. This big system-little system conflict can often be crippling to data processors hoping to initiate expert system efforts in their organizations. All too often senior management frowns upon any system development effort whose benefit objectives are of less than major significance. Professional data processors must be prepared to effectively address these and other issues if their efforts are to be established on a firm foundation.

The chapters ahead will introduce the reader to the psychological as well as the detailed technological components of expert system development. This chapter has established an awareness of the acceptance that has greeted the new technology. Also, we now have some understanding of the differences between expert systems and data systems.

2

Picking a
Profitable Problem

Now that we have observed the expert system activities of some of our colleagues, let us take a closer look at our possibilities. This chapter will take us on a tour of the data processing environment as a potential beneficiary of expert systems. After we have reviewed the many opportunities here in our own department, we will pay visits to other areas of the company looking for . . . problems? Not really! What we are seeking is expert system profit potential—tangible benefits.

The opportunities we uncover will become technical problems only later when we begin to create an expert system that yields a payback. We may feel that our present knowledge of the details of expert system technology is inadequate to permit this undertaking. The strange truth is that the more we know about a particular technology, the fewer seem to be its applications. Novices see application possibilities everywhere—experts are more conservative. We will consider the technical details that will make us expert system experts later, but for now let us just brainstorm.

So that our brainstorming will be productive we should have a rule of thumb to guide us. Let us agree that we will withhold our judgement of the big system-little system philosophies we encountered in Chapter 1. We are in search of cost savings and benefits. We will not be fettered by knowledge of technological constraints; thus we really cannot distinguish a major undertaking from a minor one at this point.

Since we are really not sufficiently conversant with the details of expert systems development to know what we can and cannot do, what it might cost or how long it might take, we are in a position to consider only the benefits just now. This does not prohibit us from determining the size of the budget or investment we will be permitted to expend given the required payback period. To shape our thinking early in our encounters with candidate expert systems let us review the payback concept.

Return on Investment

We will define payback as:

$$R = C/I$$

R is the rate of annual return determined by dividing the annualized cash benefit C by the amount of the total investment (budget) I.

An example will help. Suppose we determine that our $6-an-hour tape librarian is being paid time and one-half for working Saturday [($6 × 1.5) × 8 = $72 per week or $3744 per year] for staging the tapes for processing over the weekend. Because the weekend processing requirements vary from time to time, her knowledge of the tapes required versus the published weekend run schedule makes her presence necessary.

If her knowledge could be employed on Saturday without her presence being required, this cost would be avoided. The assistant operator could simply retrieve the tapes using a list provided by her substitute knowledge base. The $3744 annual cash benefit constitutes the value of C in our equation. This renders:

$$R = 3744/I$$

Now let us suppose that we encounter the following expenses in creating her substitute knowledge base (an expert system):

Software	$ 1,000
Programming	8,000
Hardware	1,500
Total investment	$10,500

Our payback equation now shows us:

$$R = 3744/10,500 = 0.3566 \text{ or } 35.66\%$$

Each year we receive a payback of 35.66 percent of our investment. Using the following equation where Y is the number of years to complete payback:

$$Y = 100/R$$

we will find the number of years required to recoup our entire investment by substituting the value we found for R:

$$Y = 100/35.66 = 2.8 \text{ years}$$

Now let us see how these formulas may be used to calculate the budget permitted for the development of an expert system whose required payback period is known. We simply calculate in reverse order and solve for unknowns. An example helps once more.

Let us say that we have decided not to become involved in the development of a given expert system if it will not pay back within 4 years. We may start by substituting 4 for Y and solving for R:

$$4 = 100/R$$

multiplying by R: $$4R = 100$$

dividing by 4: $$R = 100/4 = 25$$

We see that our return must be 25 percent per year for a 4-year payback.

Returning to our initial formula, $R = C/I$, we substitute 0.25 for R:

$$0.25 = C/I$$

multiplying by $4(I)$: $$4(I) \times 0.25 = 4(I) \times C/I = 4\,C$$

Our investment may be 4 times the calculated annualized cash benefit. Thus we have established a budget for our intended expert system development effort.

This simple procedure for calculating payback is not without its shortcomings. The question arises: If we invested the money in our customary vehicle, at the end of 4 years we would have more than the original investment. How can we compensate for the gain? In response, we might reply that the benefits will probably increase over the period of time because of the tendency for business costs such as salaries and so on to rise.

There are a number of more precise measures of return on investment. However, it is safe to say that if the payback period is reasonably short, discounted cash flow and present value calculations will most likely produce optimistic results also. We are ultimately bound by our company's preferred method of calculating return on investment. Payback is employed here for its simplicity and ease of application. More important is that we become accustomed to thinking in terms of opportunities for improvement and the consequent benefits as they relate to permissible budgets.

Welcome to the Data Processing Department

In the Preface we encountered an expert system designed to help manage emergency conditions associated with UPS support of computing equipment. The payback of that application was determined by an analysis of costs associated with system crashes caused by public service company quality control failures.

Data processing operations

Continuing our investigation of the operations area we find, aside from IBM's YES/MVS (Yorktown Expert System for MVS), few if any commercially available expert systems. This should not dull our interest.

The computer run scheduling expert system.   The creation and updating of computer run schedules has been a vexing nuisance at best and the cause of massive rerun costs at worst. In the whirlwind created by program modifications, the introduction of newly developed application software, and personnel turnover, operations errors abound. Notwithstanding the availability of traditional commercial scheduling systems, errors persist largely through the absence of expert system technology in their design. If the availability of an expert computer run scheduling system could reduce operations error costs by as little as 10 percent, payback combined with a reduction in stress level would interest most data processing professionals.

Recalling from Chapter 1 that the expert system may be classified as a decision support aid, we see that the actual scheduling is still the product of trained personnel. The expert system's knowledge base simply brings in-depth experience to bear on a task that may be the responsibility of relatively new staff members. We might note that even with extensive experience, conflicting file dependencies often elude the most diligent schedulers.

Potential benefits of this expert system may be quickly and easily assessed by consulting system run logs for time and material expenditures associated with file restoration and rerun. The intangible benefits of reductions in risk to database integrity, stress upon personnel, and user anxiety must be considered even though they are not easy to quantify.

The file backup expert system.   Linked to computer run scheduling is the need to assure that necessary file backups occur. It is not unusual to find a file update translated to a later time slot because of a software or hardware failure. All too often the scheduled backup then takes place before the update. Consequently, we are exposed to the risk of data loss or the need to engage in forward recovery should that backup copy be restored to remedy a subsequent failure. When such multiple disasters are avoided, it is usually because a truly alert operations expert has intervened to set things right.

An expert file backup system whose knowledge base contains program file update knowledge reduces this risk. It reads the job logs before backup execution and advises us of such anomalies.

As we extend the scope of the expert systems we seek to employ, our search for benefits begins to encompass personnel acquisition cost avoidance. By producing an expert system capable of freeing or replacing the expert, we are able to maintain the same level of service with less-experienced personnel. Alternatively, we are able to extend the scope of influence of our available experts. An assessment of the benefits requires attention to such details as fringe benefits, bonuses, profit sharing, travel, training, facilities, and administrative support.

The network management expert system. The design of an information network with a high availability requirement must include fail soft and backup capabilities. Usually, because of a failure, the ability to reconfigure the network using the remaining operational hardware is preferred to employing a more costly fully redundant configuration. Network operations requires expert skill. The more infrequent the failures, the more necessary becomes the availability of an expert system to diagnose and respond to the emergency.

Expert systems in this area function to minimize losses caused by network outages. Even more beneficial is the expert system created concurrently with the design of the network. Costs are reduced initially in the ability to avoid redundancy and again later in the efficiency of support provided in day-to-day operations.

The benefits associated with the implementation of an expert network management system are not difficult to identify. The costs of delayed financial transactions, lost reservation opportunities, and so on reveal only the obvious potential savings. When we include personnel acquisition costs the total can become impressive.

Systems and programming

Rare is the systems and programming group that is without its experts. By virtue of necessity, systems and programming personnel become associated with one or another system or program group for purposes of maintenance. The rationale for this lies in the fact that familiarity with an application and its attendant programming code assures maximum productivity.

The software support expert system. The scene is repeated across the country hundreds of times every night: A batch program crashes late on the second shift and the call goes out for the programmer in charge of the application. Expertise is necessary to assess and correct the error. Before staging the rerun he or she must identify the affected files and restore them. The following day the expert is exhausted and of little value or remains home for the entire day to recuperate.

The development of an expert software support system permits the cloning of the programming specialist's knowledge, thus raising the call-out threshold. The second shift operations personnel may interrogate the expert system and recover from many of the relatively minor difficulties without calling out the programmer. In those cases requiring the expert, the expert system provides an excellent memory jogger for diagnosing the more infrequently encountered causes of failure.

A compilation of the benefits of such an expert system most often begins with an interview of the expert responsible for the application. We usually learn that the application is too large and complex to attempt rewriting given the current backlog of requests for higher-priority applications. It is not unusual that such an expert will move to another company purely to escape the rigors of being constantly on call. The alert investigator assesses the contingent benefits of personnel acquisition cost avoidance in these cases. Replacing the expert here could be quite costly given the general shortage of skilled personnel. The data processing department teems with potential for expert system development largely because it is a center for experts.

The software package modification expert system. The purchase of major software packages is becoming more and more the option of choice for data processing departments. Purchased software packages are almost never without the need for modifications to match the company's unique requirements. Modifications are expensive and time consuming.

Given the software vendors' frequent upgrades and new version releases, there is an ever-present need to migrate the modifications to the new modules. New releases rarely are created with an eye to easing the current users' need to migrate modifications—no vendor could anticipate the multiple possibilities. Consequently, software package users are faced with these often unanticipated problems for years after implementation.

The knowledge that husbanded the original modifications may be captured in an expert system. Quantification of the benefits becomes a straightforward matter of summing up the costs of migration. We might also consider the costs of not upgrading purchased software.

One company in our acquaintance waived the implementation of new releases to its purchased package and, through necessity, was ultimately faced with a $250,000 retrofit to stay competitive in its industry. There is little wonder why expert system technology is taken so seriously by some cost conscious data processing organizations.

The personal computer configurator expert system.   The scope of responsibility of the data processing group has been extended by the personal computer (PC). Few tasks can be more time consuming than advising a user department on the acquisition of a PC. Not only must the computer be configured, but the necessary application dependent software must be specified.

First-time users often prepare by reading numerous personal computer magazines. They are frequently presold on one or another software or hardware item that is not within the scope of the department's support capability. If the configuration is created by way of an interview with the prospective user, the computer professional is often faced with the need to defend the choice of each individual item. Yielding to exceptions leads to an intolerable situation: support of a PC software-hardware menagerie.

There is also the possibility that the harried data processor acting in the role of advisor might make a costly mistake. The development of an expert configurator system places the entire matter on an objective footing. The expert system permits the users privately and independently to configure their own PCs. The expert system defends its specifications and certainly will not yield to exceptions. The final output is a priced order for the configuration. The user department is able to preview the budget implications and valuable time is saved by all parties.

The direct benefits are simply a result of man hours saved. The indirect benefits of avoiding costly errors, the need to support competing word processors, spreadsheet programs, project management and database packages are difficult to quantify. The indirect benefits are certainly not difficult to appreciate, however.

Welcome to the Company

We could linger much longer in the data processing department to review the benefits of creating expert systems for project management, system design, and quality assurance procedures. A close review of our own department will turn up a number of applications beyond those indicated here. Having become acquainted with the availability of benefits, it is time to turn our attention to the company at large.

Training

Probably one of the most vexing problems facing the company is the need to create training facilities and maintain them in a state of constant update. The computer was long ago perceived as the delivery device of choice. Computer-assisted instruction (CAI) and computer-based training (CBT) have been alive and well in the hands of users for some time. The advent of expert system technology has materially influenced both the quality and effectiveness of these approaches to knowledge transfer.

Typically, the expert training system differs from the traditional CBT in that the expert system determines course content based upon the student's past performance. The traditional CBT requires that the author program for every possible performance and provide branches and loops for each. The expert system is capable of factoring into its judgement the amount of time taken by the student to respond to questions. The traditional CBT usually reacts to the student in the same fashion regardless of the time required for his or her response.

Recalling the features of expert systems that were presented in Chapter 1, we noted there that ease of modification is a primary benefit. Thus, keeping the expert training system updated is relatively much less complex than maintaining the traditional CBT. The benefits are quantified by simple summing of cost savings in man hours combined with the measured differences in time to complete student training when using the expert training system.

Given current and anticipated dependence upon online data processing systems, user departments' training requirements are expected to grow. Expert training systems will become increasingly visible.

Insurance underwriting

If a company markets insurance or is self-insuring in any area, underwriting is required. The expert underwriting system captures the knowledge of the experienced underwriter in assessing the level of risk presented by the candidate for coverage. If the risk falls outside of the range considered normal, the applicant's premiums are rated up or the coverage is refused altogether. The expert system provides an excellent vehicle in support of underwriting and permits the productive employment of less experienced underwriters. In the case of the self-insuring company, expert systems can identify risks that are more profitably transferred to commercial carriers.

Once more, the benefits are quickly measurable in terms of reduced personnel costs, improved loss experience, and time savings in the decision process.

Insurance claim processing

Insurance claim processing, like underwriting, is a decision-making activity based upon an examination of submitted facts according to a set of rules. While, because of faulty judgment, it is possible to insure a bad risk, and few would believe the frequency with which insurance claims are paid in error.

The expert claim processing system that has access to the database is able to verify the status of the risk at the point of claim submission, the age of the policy, facts relative to the original application, and so on. Only the individual carrying company knows the frequency and cost associated with its erroneous claim payments. Any system that offers to minimize or eliminate this source of loss is enthusiastically welcomed largely because the benefits are clearly measurable.

A number of major insurance companies are actively developing expert systems in both the underwriting and claims areas. Any organization whose activities involve either of these functions should take advantage of an immediate expert system benefit analysis. Even if the decision goes against the development of such an expert system, it is wise to know what the implications may be.

Cost estimating

Any company involved in construction, printing, custom manufacturing, or contract services estimates costs. The skill of the estimator is often the difference between the success and failure of the venture. This is an area well suited to the development of an expert system.

While an expert system will not replace the expert, it will function as a multiplier for his or her productivity. A number of traditionally programmed cost estimating systems are available for one or another industry group. They more often than not require the intervention of the estimator if the final estimate is to reflect his or her knowledge and current market conditions.

The expert system embodies the knowledge of the estimator and its ease of modification permits quick updating to reflect changing conditions. Beyond all of this is the ease with which the company's proprietary manufacturing techniques may be incorporated to provide a true marketing edge not obtainable using traditional programming technology.

An assessment of the benefits of such an expert system usually begins with a quantification of the cost per estimate contrasted with estimating methods currently in place. Add to this the potential for equipping the sales force with portable computing equipment that allows the system to be accessed remotely. The benefits of fast response function to increase sales by bringing a virtual expert estimator to each sales interview.

Shop floor scheduling

The entire area of manufacturing scheduling and shop floor control has been the preserve of many software development efforts. Central to the design of these systems has been the incorporation of various algorithms—calculation routines—whose execution requires specific parameters. These systems have functioned to aid the scheduling expert in his attempt to bring order to an environment that might otherwise become chaotic.

As we shall see in the next chapter, the expert functions using a nonalgorithmic rationale. The expert shop floor scheduling system allows the combining of expertise with algorithmic execution to produce a result not available in the traditional scheduling system. Unexpected equipment failure, the need to control backlog development and maintain material availability all militate to require continual rescheduling. Expert systems in this area permit the instantaneous assessment of alternatives not possible in the purely algorithmic system.

Benefits are found in reduced downtime, greater throughput and a reduction of work in process inventory. This enumeration of benefits is familiar as it relates to the traditional scheduling approaches. Expert system involvement introduces a major difference in the degree of benefits that may be expected. The proof of value is in the large number of major corporations and software vendors currently creating such expert systems.

Financial applications

All business organizations require financial applications to the extent that they participate in commercial activity. Those companies lending funds are well situated to take advantage of expert systems in the area of loan application analysis. Similar to insurance underwriting, the analysis of a loan application requires the assessment of risk and the decision to accept or reject it.

Loan officers are experts. Presumably the larger the loans they make, the greater is their expertise. This follows from the fact that poor judgment leads to defaulted loans and losses that either result in the removal of the loan officer or the dissolution of the company. In this respect it may be observed that it is a jungle out there and only the fittest survive.

Again, it is the expert system that allows the capture of the loan expert's skill thus freeing him of many of the preliminary activities. Through the use of such an approach, the loan expert's scope of control is extended so that both the quantity and quality of loans improve.

During periods of either ascending or declining interest rates the mortgage market often accelerates to the point that lending activity falters under the sheer volume of applications in need of analysis. Customer satisfaction wanes considerably if closings are delayed with real estate transactions jeopardized. Poor loan performance either at the application or experience level impacts the organization's entire family of financial services. The benefits of expert systems in this environment are obvious.

Financial planning whether at the individual or corporate level requires an assessment of the relative benefits of one or a group of investment vehicles from among the available universe of possibilities. Example applications of the financial planner's skill are buy recommendations for bonds under one set of circumstances, stocks under another, and consolidation in cash under others. The specific choices within each of these categories are made from a huge field of possibilities.

We conclude that all financial planners are not equally expert from a review of portfolio performance. Several financial institutions employ econometric models in their research facilities. Because final decisions are dependent upon the individual planner's skill, expert systems have gained a wide audience in this area. Evidence that such expert systems have become marketable properties during the past few years has been enough proof of their value to encourage many organizations to undertake in-house development.

Are Expert Systems an Unqualified Success?

Clearly not all expert systems survive. Neither are all traditional computer systems successful. The reasons for failure are somewhat similar and at the same time startlingly different for both groups. We will be dwelling on the issues of success and failure throughout the coming chapters. As we might expect, it is not the technology that fails in the case of the expert system any more than it is the technology that is responsible for the failed inventory control, payroll or order entry system.

Because we are experienced data processing professionals we already have the seeds of successful systems development—our experience and knowledge already qualify us as experts in this area. Extending that expertise to the development of expert systems is a simple but necessary task. It is the currently practicing data processors who will give birth to the unlimited potential expert system applications awaiting development.

Choose wisely

One of the axioms of expert system development is that while many are called, few are chosen. This is not true of traditional data processing applications—we are rarely free to decide not to implement a traditional data processing application such as payroll or general ledger. Since we are free to choose here we must ask "Just what are the task characteristics of a well-chosen candidate expert system?"

The task should be a product of intelligent behavior. Similar to an expert system for personal computer configuration, the excellent candidate expert system should address a task currently being performed successfully by knowledgeable individuals—experts.

The experts should generally agree upon the methods required. Similar to an expert system for computer run scheduling, the excellent candidate expert system should address a task having generally accepted requirements for successful completion.

The task should have a beginning, middle, and end. Similar to the expert system in support of batch program failure, the excellent candidate expert system should address a clearly defined domain or problem area. The failing batch program problem is solved by fact assessment, solution of the main difficulty, and finally, reestablishing the environment. By contrast, an expert system to solve the problem of world hunger would address a number of global domains and could have no clear beginning point.

The task's duration should be limited. Similar to the expert system in support of network management, the excellent candidate expert system should address a task that the expert is capable of performing in a time frame of minutes or hours. If duration is not considered, the expert system may suffer from performance and memory management degradation. Let us not confuse this with limits upon iterations—the expert system may continually execute its task.

In general the excellent candidate expert system is crisply targeted at a specific area or domain of understood and describable expert activity. Ruthlessly avoid pseudo-expert domains requiring fundamental knowledge—those requiring common sense or basic job skills. These ingredients reduce payback and they are extremely difficult if not impossible to incorporate in an expert system.

Our chosen expert system must have a sponsor

It is said that nothing happens until someone sells something. Only then do the wheels of progress begin to turn. This is as true for expert systems as we know it is for traditional data processing applications. If nobody in authority really wants it, the best system will never succeed—it will collect dust, complaints and grief. This is why payback is so important. Nothing gets attention faster than a system that adds to the bottom line.

Clerks, production workers, and tradesmen are not profit oriented. Their interests frequently center upon personal and life-style issues. Experts care about their standing in their professions or the fulfillment their unique skills offer. Truly forward looking management realizes this and contrives methods for involving their personnel in the quest for profits through participation in the material benefits.

The sponsor we seek must have concern that comes from a genuine vested interest in company profitability. When we have chosen the excellent candidate expert system, our final task is to locate this sponsor.

We may well benefit by taking a page from the IBM sales manual. It apparently has succeeded well over the years. The technique is elegant in its simplicity: present the features and benefits of our candidate system and then elicit a response from our intended sponsor (Features, Benefits, Response—FBR). The responses we elicit will alert us to unanswered questions or objections.

Like many other leading edge technologies, expert systems must be sold in those environments unaccustomed to promoting research and development efforts. Later chapters will delve further into the issues that impinge upon successfully establishing expert system sponsorship.

The next chapter discusses the environment and motivation of the experts. There are some surprises lurking there. The expert plays a major role in the success of our expert system. He or she must also be convinced of its value and benefit.

Enter: The Experts

We recently witnessed an event at a place we will call Fred's Tap. It deals directly with the subject at hand and highlights features of the expert system environment that might otherwise be overlooked. A man at the bar having an animated discussion with a friend suddenly climbed up and stood precariously upon his stool. "I need an expert," he yelled. "I don't care what the field is, but if you can prove you're an expert in anything, I'll buy you a drink."

No one moved a muscle. Finally Fred appeared to quell the disturbance after determining that the extra sale would not develop. The rebuked stool orator got down, finished his libation, and wobbled out the door.

We then observed a systems programmer recently trained in the development of expert systems—now a knowledge engineer (KE)— sitting with a group in one of the back booths. He turned to an inordinately attractive young lady at a nearby table and said: "Are you an expert? You could have volunteered." "What does a packaging estimator know?" she replied.

We do not know how the systems programmer/knowledge engineer and the packaging estimator concluded their quest for understanding. The instance did demonstrate that even a newly trained KE cannot recognize an expert although other attributes are usually obvious. Similarly, experts may not always see themselves as such—the packaging estimator obviously did not. Just what does qualify a person to be called an expert?

What Is a Domain Expert?

Without the further clarification needed in a consideration of expert systems, dictionary definitions state that a person may be considered an expert if that person is able to solve problems in a specific field better than his or her contemporaries. The field is called a "domain" in the expert system environment. The mathematical notion of a domain limits the area of expertise in that it is less extensive than might be implied by the word "field."

For the purposes of expert system development, an expert is normally described as one who has had formal education or training in the domain. Added to the education or training must be some considerable exposure to the practical application of skills in the domain—experience. The requirement that the domain expert have considerable experience is to be expected since an expert establishes his or her preeminence only through repeated performances that exceed those of contemporary practitioners.

Notwithstanding the abundance of descriptive material, we may still be unable to identify a true expert in real life. We have frequent daily encounters with experts, but we tend to recognize them only when they have a dramatic and meaningful impact on us. Consider the auto mechanic who installs a new set of brakes on our automobile. The task was performed according to the manual, yet, driving home we hear a faint squeal that grows louder. Several days later, unable to put up with the strange sound, we return to the auto agency with a complaint. The original installer is absent for the day and old Ben gets the job of investigating our problem.

Ben works on the wheels for about 15 minutes and then says: "Let's go for a ride." The squeal is gone! We look at Ben in amazement and ask: "Did the other mechanic make a mistake?" "No," says Ben, "he did it according to the book, but when he's been around as long as I have, he'll realize that in the summer those pads swell up from the heat and humidity. You have to back off on the adjustment just a turn or a turn and a half."

The expert characteristic

We might simply agree that Ben is an expert in the brake domain but in so doing we would overlook the most salient feature of his expertise. This underlying element of expertise that Ben possesses may be identified. This element is what the KE seeks out when attempting to capture the expert's true skill in an expert system under construction.

This element is called the "heuristic." AI developers quickly explain that heuristics are rules of thumb that seasoned experts employ to solve problems rapidly, thus circumventing more lengthy efforts. While the words "rule of thumb" provide a succinct explanation, they do not carry the full flavor of the expert's achievement. It is important to the success of an expert system that we understand the genesis of heuristics.

We observe that Ben did not quickly calculate a formula, and so we know that his rationale is not algorithmic. Even if the expert does employ an algorithm, it is not the algorithm that is the heuristic. The heuristic is the discovery that this algorithm or that procedure will solve a specific problem. Ben discovered, somehow and at some time, that those brake pads swell up on a hot, humid summer day. Ben then devised a rule upon which he could rely to solve this problem.

Pursue the heuristic

Ben was able to explain his heuristic simply and so it appears to be no more than a superficial rule of thumb. If we are interested in Ben and his discovery only out of passing curiosity, we may cease our investigation here. Knowledge engineers, because they are responsible for the creation of expert systems, do continue to explore the mind of the expert. They must think in terms of consequences. For the sake of further illustration we shall too.

Ben's discovery is actually a solution procedure that depends as heavily upon the composition of the brake pads as it does upon climatic conditions. When we delve deeper into Ben's knowledge, we find that both the problem of squealing brakes and Ben's heuristic date back only to the advent of asbestos-free brake pads.

If we are going to incorporate this knowledge in an expert system, we must consider the consequences of purposely misadjusting brake pads during hot, humid weather. Aren't the brake pads already reacting to the weather before they are installed? Will the onset of cold weather constitute a severe risk to brake function in view of the misadjustment? When the weather cools in the fall, will the customer have to return to have the brakes readjusted? Won't a change in the manufacturer's brake pad formula render the heuristic worthless?

When we attempt to play the role of KE, we often find that we are brought face to face with truly creative activity. We must be prepared to pursue complete understanding lest the simple rule of thumb we incorporate in our expert system serves only to dissatisfy or endanger users. We cannot allow ourselves to be awed by the expert's ingenuity. We cannot assume that a heuristic is both valid and safe under all of the circumstances in which it might be used.

In pursuing the matter with Ben, we might ask the open-ended question: "Ben, how did you ever discover that?" Ben proceeds to explain: "Well you know they put the brake pads in those plastic bags and then they evacuate the air before they seal them. That keeps the fittings from rusting. Well, one day I was pulling and tugging to get the plastic open when suddenly it went to pieces and one of the pads popped right into my coffee. That pad puffed up like cotton candy."

We learn how Ben made the connection between heat, humidity, and the swelling of the brake pads. We also learn why the brake pads are not affected by the weather in storage—vacuum packaging.

Our next objective is to determine the validity of the heuristic. Will it always work or is there a criterion for applying it? We might ask: "Do all brake pads swell up in the heat like this?" "Actually, no," says Ben. "I put a drop of hot water on the edge of each pad and if that raises a welt in a minute or so, I know how they have to be adjusted in the summer."

We have determined that Ben does not blindly apply his heuristic since there is, indeed, a criterion for its use. He performs a simple test upon each brake pad to determine the applicability of his rule of thumb. Now we must verify the safety of this heuristic. Many heuristics handed down from worker to worker are like folk remedies in that their consequences must be investigated before they are given the support of an expert system. Similarly, sophisticated engineering heuristics, because of their empirical nature, must also be evaluated relative to their ultimate effects.

We might continue our discussion with Ben: "That is really thorough. I suppose that when the weather becomes cold and dry, you just have to press a little harder on the brake since the pad will shrink back to original size?" "Not at all," Ben replies. "You see, all the models that require this type of brake pad have self-adjusting brakes. The brakes will automatically adjust for pad wear and so when the pad shrinks, the brakes adjust—you never experience a difference in pedal pressure required to stop the car." We drive home not only satisfied that our automobile is safe and silent but that we have acquired a thorough understanding of Ben's expertise.

In retrospect we might make a number of observations. The expert has made some practical discoveries and has formulated some rules for their application: heuristics. As KEs we must pursue the heuristic and learn its genesis—how the discovery was made. We must then validate the heuristic—is it always blindly applicable or are there criteria for its use? Finally, we must verify its safety. If it develops that the heuristic is not always safe, we must determine the conditions under which the potential expert system must issue warnings. Because there is no guarantee that the warnings will be heeded, there may be the final need to determine the risk that misuse of the expert system will pose.

It must be noted that lack of total safety is not sufficient reason to abandon an expert system. Many nonprescription drugs would not be on store shelves if their manufacturers insisted upon total safety.

Psychology and the Domain Expert

If domain experts differ from their contemporaries, they must have some personal attributes that are responsible for the distinction. Being expert in a domain is not just the result of experience or training. How many times have we seen the programmer with 10 years of experience who performs as though he or she is a programmer with 1 year of experience that has been repeated 10 times? No one is more aware of individual differences than the professional data processor.

For most practitioners achievement of expert rank requires aspiring, striving, and, finally, vaulting oneself into a position of preeminence. For some this is the result of insecurity. For others this is a compensation for feelings of inferiority. For still others expert status is the result of extreme brilliance—their basic ability produces far-above-average performance. Without knowing the specific underlying causal factors that have produced expert stature for any given practitioner, we must recognize that when approached regarding an expert system, the expert becomes aware of this unique status.

For the KE faced with the need to capture these achievements in an expert system there exist a number of objectives. The engineer must win over the expert in such a way that the expert is not only cooperative but an enthusiastic participant in the development of the system. The system must become another achievement of the expert.

Engineer, know thy expert

The KE can only benefit from as thorough a knowledge of the expert's background as can be obtained through the resources of the company. Knowledge of the expert's education or training background, achievements both within and outside of the area of expertise, and personal interests serve to acquaint the engineer with the subject's system of values. Is the expert a hard-driving aggressive achiever? Is he or she a shy and retiring meditative person who lives largely an interior life? Is the expert a restless researcher constantly looking for that next discovery? Are we dealing with a ruthless pragmatist interested only in ideas that produce expedient results? Is our expert one who seeks shortcuts to quality results, taking pride in good work?

While we were able to sell our sponsor on the profit potential of our excellent candidate expert system, our expert will most likely purchase only those ideas that fit personal values. It can be a tragic mistake to believe that an expert will be cooperative just because the company has decided to "soak up" accumulated years of expertise in a computer.

If the undertaking can be presented to the expert in terms of personal values, the KE's system goals are more certainly within reach. Recalling our conversation with Ben, we saw an expert who takes pride in his craftsmanship. In fact, our whole conversation dealt with craftsmanship. Had we commented on the number of returning dissatisfied customers his expertise could eliminate, thus increasing company profits, the chances are great that Ben would have become much less forthcoming.

Reduce the intensity

Even though the system-building effort is a company sanctioned activity, it is often stressful to the expert if he or she feels alone in the spotlight. If at all possible, it is better to select more than one expert. This must be done so that neither expert will feel that he or she is a runner-up. Rather, each should be made aware that a particular skill constitutes a unique contribution.

Working with more than one input source is common in the development of data systems. This is no more complicated in the knowledge engineering environment. The multiple expert approach is particularly valuable in addressing complex domains such as scheduling or process control. The company that has more than one such expert is fortunate. More likely is the availability of a single expert.

The goal of stress reduction is important regardless of the number of participants. The expert is busy. A value set determines performance, and the development of an expert system is an intrusion at best. A schedule must be developed for knowledge engineering sessions, and it must be meticulously observed by the engineer who must expect that the expert will sometimes be unable to conform. These disappointments must be constructively managed by the KE lest they become accumulating evidence that the effort "just will not work out."

Under stress, tempers flare if personalities are sanguine. If we are dealing with a more introverted person, stress tends to lead to withdrawal. At the base of the matter is the individual's mechanism for dealing with a sense that control has been lost—that things are closing in. We have seen this in data system development. There the system often becomes a juggernaut largely because management has decreed that implementation will take place and on such and such a date. When data systems fail, it is usually only because no one in authority cared enough to bite the bullet and get tough.

Expert system development is a radically different matter. Traditional management pressure, decreed performance, schedules etched in stone, and other tactics that have proven popular in data system development are almost guaranteed to destroy an expert system effort. This inventory of facts must be sold to your sponsor along with the payback benefits. Clearly, the low-pressure development environment should be presented as a feature whose major benefit is the cooperative participation of the expert. In a later chapter, when we build our expert system, we will witness a typical FBR (features, benefits, response) presentation to the sponsor.

Your immediate response to this new element may be that your company is not ready for so radical a departure. You may still recall the last system that was installed, problems and all but on time—you are still fighting the consequences. Your own stress level may currently be near the edge as a result. Let us recall Chapter 1 and the many tough companies that have implemented successful and profitable expert systems. It is not surprising to note that an expert system effort often has quite a civilizing effect on the whole data processing environment. This is a goal well worth achieving. As we go forward, we will see that success is not elusive.

The Quiet Expert

The quiet expert is the knowledge engineer—a title given to the data processing professional who is trained in the art and science of expert system development. This may simultaneously be a programmer, systems analyst, or even the director of MIS. We saw examples of the KE's skill at work in our discussions with Ben.

In those organizations in which expert system development is a well-established function, the KE usually ceases other activities and concentrates on AI applications. Generally, if the director of MIS undertakes the development of expert systems to establish the function, he or she relinquishes the title of KE as soon as the knowledge engineering team has been developed. We will look in on team building later in this chapter. Right now we want to concentrate on the KE's role.

The potential knowledge engineer

You are a potential KE because you have the primary prerequisite—interest in furthering computer technology. If this were not true, you would be reading *Sports Illustrated,* the financial pages or *Cosmopolitan.* None of this implies that you do not read those publications, but right now you are reading this book and thereby sacrificing time you could be devoting to something else. You are fascinated by technology.

You firmly believe that the whole of computer science has not developed to its current level solely to facilitate traditional applications. Faster CPUs with greater memory capacity, coupled with miniaturization of physical size has placed expert systems within reach—you want to be part of this achievement. Your intuition is without flaw. Let us talk about you and the role you must play as a KE.

Curiosity is the key. The potential KE has to have a high curiosity quotient (CQ). We know of no test that produces this as a measure. IQ is defined as mental age divided by physical age (MA/PA) and there are many tests for this. Probably the best measure of one's curiosity quotient is personal knowledge attainment divided by physical age (CQ = KA/PA). Only the curious go on learning independent of age. Because of this, their knowledge attainment exceeds the norm for their age manyfold. For now, this is a measure only you can make. For a start, how many programming languages do you know?

The KE will have to become acquainted with new languages such as Prolog and LISP. Add to this familiarity with several expert system shells (for now we can look upon these as application generators). Then there are a number of radically different programming techniques that must be understood—we will become acquainted with them in the chapters ahead. Clearly, the KE is not a one-programming-language specialist. He or she must have the sustaining force of curiosity as a personality ingredient.

Everyone has a personality. When we describe people who are curious or people who are hard driving or people who are laid back, we are describing personality types. We have all read about A-type personalities and B-types and so on. In discussions of nearly every walk of life the question arises: What type of personality is most likely to succeed? The KE's profession is no exception. Since everyone has a personality, whose is best constructed for the KE's endeavors?

At some time in the future questions of this sort may be answerable with unerring accuracy. For the present we know that, like the systems analyst, the KE must collect information from a human informant while constructing a system. The major difference between the two is that most often the systems analyst interviews a user who seriously wants the system implemented while the KE must interview an expert to whom the system may appear as an intrusion. Beyond this the expert may become recalcitrant if made to feel that his or her skill is being misemployed.

Clearly, the task of the KE requires some learned skills that may be easier to acquire for some personality types than others. Having experience as a successful systems analyst is an excellent qualification in that it verifies the existence of a personality compatible with knowledge engineering. Add to this the skills of a salesperson, and the KE's required interpersonal skills are defined.

Here are the selling skills

We encountered the need for sales skills in relation to obtaining a sponsor in Chapter 2. There we became familiar with the FBR pattern that characterizes the sales presentation. In this chapter we encountered the experts and recognized the need to persuade them to join us in our effort through a presentation of our goals as they relate to their systems of values. We noted that learning of their interests and educational or training backgrounds could help to prepare the KE for encounters with these experts.

There remains the task of effectively determining the expert's system of values—those things and ideas that are most prized. Aware of the interests and values of the expert, the KE is able to uncover needs that relate to the proposed expert system development effort. When the expert's perspective is given full consideration, the portrayal of features and benefits and the solicitation of responses may be placed in the expert's gestalt or frame of reference. Again, an example may be of help.

A KE approaching Ben might say, "Ben, you are the best brake man in the company. Wouldn't we have a great group if all the other mechanics were as skilled as you are with brakes?" Pausing at this point to listen to Ben's comments, we might hear, "Well, it would certainly give me an opportunity to get more transmission work done. Besides, with the factory incorporating more and more electronic sensors, it takes a lot more concentration to keep the power train in top shape. Brakes aren't really a challenge to a master mechanic, you know."

Obviously Ben has a need that the development of an expert brake system would satisfy. This is an opportune point to present Ben with a feature of a vehicle that will satisfy that need. The KE describes a system that could free Ben for more advanced work. Ben's response is then solicited. Ben may question the possibility that such a system would work. In responding, the KE's familiarity with similar system developments is called upon—not to overpower Ben with statistics but to illustrate workability.

We frequently hear the seasoned salesperson respond to an outright objection by saying, "I'm glad you asked that question." The KE too turns the expert's objections into questions. Suppose Ben says, "If these young mechanics can't get the feel of a good brake job, I don't think they will be able to work a computer." The KE might reply, "I'm glad you brought that up, Ben. The people at the factory thought the same thing when they created the system they use in the installation of new car brake systems." The KE then goes on to defuse Ben's objection by citing a solid success story.

The chief objective to be reached in a benefit presentation to the expert is the development of his or her proprietary involvement. Introducing the fact that a powerful sponsor has decreed that the expert system be created is a positive aid in lending the effort importance, but it will not supplant the need to persuade and involve the expert. The sponsor's power is a feature that may be flattering to the expert, or it may become an element of unwanted intimidation, depending upon the manner of its presentation.

The true power of the FBR sales technique lies in its ability to draw out questions and objections. Its effectiveness is forfeited if the presentation is not personalized. Personalization requires well-phrased and sincere questioning of the expert in order to uncover latent needs that the proposed expert system will satisfy.

The importance of turning objections into questions is that head-on disagreement is avoided. Further, in citing the success story the KE seeks agreement from the expert. " . . . that's the way they found the system would work best. Top mechanics like yourself would agree with that approach wouldn't they, Ben?" When Ben responds, "Yes that probably would do the trick," it's time for another step up the FBR progression.

How is success measured? When Ben sends out his first buying signal, an indication of interest in the program, we have aroused his enthusiasm. The KE must become an expert listener. The data systems analyst listens for facts and conditions. The KE is sensitive to the nuances of an expert's words throughout the system-building effort but especially during this phase of their relationship. Suppose Ben remarks, "How do you get a thing like this started?" That is an excellent time to make the first interview appointment. Responding to a clear signal of interest with another system success story could dull the expert's enthusiasm. A fault of otherwise excellent sales personnel is their reluctance to close the sale.

If the KE responds to Ben's buying signal with, "Let's get together Wednesday at three o'clock and we can get started," a yes or no response is being solicited. The chances are great that Ben will have a conflicting appointment and the KE will be derailed by a refusal. When the KE sets up the close of this sale, Ben must be offered a choice of positives, "We can get together and work that out Wednesday, or would you prefer Thursday?" When Ben makes his choice, the KE firms up with a positive time a place.

Let us quickly review the steps to the sale:

1. Determine what is important to the expert.

2. Uncover a latent need the system will satisfy.

3. Explain a feature and its associated need benefit.

4. Solicit a response from the expert.

5. Turn objections into questions.

6. Answer the question with a success story.

7. Seek agreement from the expert.

8. Be alert for buying signals—indications of interest.

9. Do not ask questions that invite yes or no answers.

A natural question that arises is: What happens if you cannot detect a buying signal? You have been getting agreement as you move through several of the FBRs. You have thoroughly covered the features and benefits of the system and no detectable interest signal has developed.

There are differences in response patterns. It is wise to assume a buying signal if none is obvious. In this case it is necessary to present the options for the interview appointment as a beneficial feature and proceed to seek agreement on place and time. Again, sensitivity is of paramount importance. Be ever ready to recognize that the absence of a signal of interest may be a product of incomplete agreement on the benefits offered by the prospective system. Persuasion is an art guided by sound principles. Unfortunately, the principles are not infallible success formulas. Becoming an expert in any domain requires experience.

The Expert System Team

There is a strong tendency to discount the need to be persuasive in the data processing environment. New versions of the operating system are implemented because the hardware vendor withdraws support for the earlier ones. The steering committee, a vice president, or the owner decides to buy a new inventory system praised in a leading magazine article and so be it. Very little persuasion is involved. Data processing professionals perform their technical magic and are seldom praised for their achievements. If the environment becomes too callous, professionals move on to other pastures unless they have made a serious career commitment. We need not go into a great deal of detail about the effects of turnover upon expert system development; we are already familiar with this phenomenon's effect when it occurs during the development of a data system.

The expert system development program must become an effort within an effort as it relates to the data processing department's structure. The expert system environment, by its nature and certainly by its charter, must be characterized by a team atmosphere. The team members (and this includes the domain expert) have a single goal: the successful creation and implementation of an expert system. This requires a degree of separation from the rest of the data processing staff at least psychologically. Membership in the team must satisfy a need for each of the participants. Their involvement in the creation of expert systems cannot be arbitrarily decreed. Each data processor who will become a team member is, in his or her own right, an expert. As we have seen, experts must be persuaded.

How does the team develop?

An expert system development team could very well begin with you. We have considered the quantity of new knowledge to be acquired by the KE, e.g., sales skills, languages, shells, programming techniques, and so on. One's skill develops in stages. Many first expert systems are of the nature of the UPS system described in the Preface.

In building a first expert system from a manual, the budding KE becomes acquainted with the methods of representing knowledge and the programming requirements. Any complexities the domain expert's involvement might introduce are eliminated by depending upon the manual for input. The result is a workable, useful expert system that supports the functioning or maintenance of one or another piece of equipment. Lest we are inclined to discount the importance of such expert systems, recall Chapter 1 and the Ford Motor Company's success in expert robot maintenance system development.

A further benefit associated with the manual as domain expert is the realization that the resultant system may need revision whenever the manual is updated by the vendor. In a similar fashion, the domain expert's knowledge also grows. The expert system, like a data system, is never really complete. Constant updating is a fact of computer life. The major difference, as we shall see, is that the expert system allows greater ease of modification than does the data system.

While creating an expert system from a manual provides an excellent preliminary effort, eventually a budget and management support must be obtained. This step must not be confused with obtaining a sponsor for a specific expert system.

Management's involvement may be cultivated in a number of ways. Interest may be generated by a formal presentation to the data processing steering committee, a demonstration of a working expert system—perhaps one developed by the data processing department—or by a cooperative seminar venture between data processing and one or another of the AI expert system vendors. As we have seen in Chapter

1, IBM, DEC, and Texas Instruments are all heavily involved in the marketing and promotion of expert system development.

Education becomes the key to success once expert system development has been accepted by management. Depending upon the computer configuration supporting your company and the expert system software chosen, the candidate KE(s) are off to class. It is neither wise nor practical to end educational efforts with this initial training. The ultimate needs of your company may not be met by one vendor or its software. It is incumbent upon the data processing department that expert system personnel be capable of supplying solutions regardless of the limitations of one or another vendor. Later chapters will highlight further educational opportunities.

Depending upon the budget authorized by management, the expert system development team may consist of one KE or a number of KEs and one or two expert system programmers for each. Because the KE is the analog of the systems analyst in the data systems environment, the expert system programmer's role is not hard to identify. In any event, the team is incomplete until a domain expert is integrated into its ranks with a defined expert system development goal.

The domain expert must be made to feel his or her importance as a team member despite protestations of unfamiliarity with computers. Again, sensitivity is all important. It is not unusual to find that the domain expert feels much more comfortable in the maintenance department, for example. Thus, even the required presence in an office setting may be an added difficulty to be overcome with the team's help and understanding.

Our odyssey has thus far introduced us to expert systems being used and under development. We have observed expert system opportunities available both in the data processing department and in the company at large. We have discovered the heuristic and its implications for expert system development. We have become more fully acquainted with both the domain expert and the requirements of data processing's resident expert, the KE. We have reviewed the avenues available for obtaining management's advice and consent. It is now time to confront the new technology: the techniques of AI as they relate to the development of expert systems.

The Expert System
Knowledge Base

In our introduction to expert system design in Chapter 1, we saw that an expert system consists of an inference engine, a knowledge base, an area of working storage, and an interface. We noted that problem information presented as input to the interface is matched against elements in the knowledge base, by the inference engine, to produce the problem solution for which the system was designed. We will now consider the three popularly employed methods of representing knowledge in the knowledge base. As we describe each of the three schemes, we will consider the respective inference engines and their functions in as much detail as practical.

As data processors, we are already familiar with application-specific database organization. Most of us have designed or programmed in the environment of relational databases, hierarchical databases, or monolithic structures such as VSAM clusters, SAM, ISAM, or DIRECT files. In a somewhat similar fashion, the knowledge base of an expert system may be organized as production rules, structured objects, or as elements of predicate logic. Expert systems implemented using these knowledge bases are frequently called pattern-directed inference systems—we shall see why shortly.

Production Systems

A production system's knowledge base contains production rules or condition-action rules in the form of "If (condition), Then (action)" statements. The production rule's parts are referred to as the left-hand side (condition side) and the right-hand side (action side). The rules contain variables.

As an example, the knowledge base of a production system for configuring the first generation of PCs was populated by rules such as:

1. IF application = word processing, THEN memory = 512K

2. IF application = spreadsheet, THEN memory = 640K

3. IF application = games, THEN memory = 128K

4. IF memory = 512K, THEN option = expansion board

5. IF communication = yes AND application = spreadsheet, THEN memory = 640K

The rules above contain the variables *application, memory, option,* and *communication*. These rules are actually patterns that will be matched against information from working storage by the inference engine. As in rule 5's left-hand side, logical operators may be used to connect multiple variables. Each variable expression, e.g., application = games, in the condition, or left-hand, side is said to be a condition clause. This nomenclature is important in that it will be used frequently in what follows.

The inference engine

We might visualize the CRT screen that confronts the user of this production system upon entering the sign-on. A menu might appear that directs the user to choose from among a group of itemized screen options. The user interface supports the menu and makes the selected screen options available to the inference engine by placing them in the working storage area. Let us suppose that the screen options include intended applications for which the PC is being configured. The issue under consideration is memory size. The screen options would include:

    A) Word Processing
    B) Spreadsheets
    C) Games
    D) Why?

The user chooses D to learn the reason for being required to specify the intended applications. The enter key is pressed. The interface presents this input to the working storage area. The inference engine returns "I must determine the memory capacity required by your intended use." The inference engine then seeks more input from the working storage area and, not finding it, returns control to the interface. The message is displayed at the bottom of the screen by the interface.

We see that the control features of the interface allow the user to interrogate the inference engine at each stage of the configuration process so that the user is not forced to blindly cooperate or to accept the results of this consultation or session without an understanding of why and how the input information is being requested and used. Explanations of why input is requested, what the current conclusions are, and how the final conclusions were reached are all available from the inference engine through its ability to keep track of the input variable values and the matching results—conclusions. We will see how this proceeds.

Let us assume that the user, with this explanation, enters A, indicating that the intended application is word processing. The interface presents "word processing" to the working storage area, whereupon the inference engine is in possession of the information "application = word processing." The variable *application* is said to be instantiated or given a value. The inference engine matches this information against the left-hand side of the knowledge base rules and finds that because of the instantiation of *application,* Rule 1 is true. Because every occurrence of *application* in the rule set is instantiated to the value *word processor,* only Rule 1 is true. Rule 1 is said to *fire.*

The inference engine updates the working storage area with the newly derived information from the right-hand side of Rule 1: memory = 512K. As in the previous iteration, the inference engine seeks additional input from the working storage area and finds "memory = 512K" now available. The process of matching repeats and this time Rule 4 is found to be true and it fires, resulting in the inference engine's updating of the working storage area with that rule's right-hand side: option = expansion board.

At this point the user has chosen word processing as the application, but the expert system possesses a data structure in the working storage area that "knows" that among the options to be defined in this session, an expansion board is needed as well as 512K of RAM memory. Terminating our example here, we are able to observe a number of the features of our production system.

Forward chaining. The processing goes on in a cyclical fashion. The strategy used by the inference engine is forward chaining—it is said to be data driven in that the user knows the conditions and is seeking consequences. Thus it is the conditions (left-hand sides) that are being matched to determine what the consequences or actions must be. This strategy is opposed to backward chaining wherein the user knows the consequences and is interested in determining the causes. Forward chaining is well employed in those systems in which a bill of requirements is input to determine the implied consequences such as in the configuration of equipment. Backward chaining, which we shall soon investigate, is well employed in situations in which the user possesses a symptom list and wishes to arrive at a diagnosis.

We will dwell briefly here on the distinction between these two strategies only because it is important that the data processor firmly grasp it. For example, forward chaining applies when we know our income requirements and are seeking a job that will meet those requirements—backward chaining applies when we know our skills and wish to know the job for which we are best suited. When we know the conditions, we use forward chaining to learn the consequences. When we have symptoms, results, or consequences and wish to learn the causes or conditions, we use backward chaining.

In this brief rule example we also see that the expert's knowledge regarding the requirement of an expansion board for the 512K of RAM memory will be reflected in the configuration—the kind of requirement that was often overlooked in configuring the first generation of PCs. Finally, we might observe that should the sponsoring company's choice of supported word processor later require a different minimum memory capacity, it is relatively simple to modify the knowledge base. The same ease of modification greets the possibility that the PC manufacturer may incorporate current options as standard features at some later time—rules related to those options are then simply deleted from the knowledge base.

Backward chaining.   If we were interested in creating a production system to be used in the identification of biological samples, the debugging of a malfunctioning program, or the determination of cause for an item of industrial equipment that has failed, we would create a knowledge base containing production rules that would be processed by an inference engine whose strategy is backward chaining—such a system is said to be goal driven in that the symptoms or consequences are known. We will illustrate backward chaining strategy using a subset of the production rules that could be found in the knowledge base of an expert system designed to solve the brake problem that was introduced in Chapter 3:

1. IF pad = disc contact AND installation = new, THEN procedure = hydrotest

2. IF brake = noise, THEN pad = disc contact

3. IF brake = locked, THEN pad = disc contact

4. IF age < 1 week, THEN installation = new

Here the variables are *pad, installation, procedure, brake,* and *age.* Now we may visualize the busy mechanic signing on to the system in order to make use of Ben's knowledge. Upon the sign-on, the interface presents a screen that poses conclusions that the system is being requested to verify—among other more drastic measures, should the moisture test be performed?

A) Verify the hydrotest procedure?

```
B) Verify an overhaul of the entire brake system?
C) Why?
```

The mechanic enters A. *Procedure* is placed in working storage whereupon the inference engine determines that it is the conclusion variable of Rule 1. The first condition variable of Rule 1, *pad*, is returned to working storage.

The inference engine now determines that *pad* is a conclusion variable of Rule 2. Attempting to instantiate *pad*, the inference engine finds that *brake* is a condition variable of Rule 2 that must be instantiated and since *brake* is not a conclusion variable of any rule, a screen is displayed requesting that the mechanic instantiate *brake*:

```
A) Brake is noisy
B) Brake is locked
C) Why?
```

The mechanic chooses A, indicating that the brake is noisy. Thus *brake* is instantiated to noise and Rule 2 fires, instantiating *pad* to disc contact. The inference engine now accesses condition variable 2 of Rule 1 in an attempt to continue its effort at instantiating the condition variables of this rule. *Installation* is returned to working storage and a subsequent matching effort determines that *installation* is a conclusion variable of Rule 4. Rule 4's condition variable, *age,* must be instantiated and because it is not a conclusion variable of any rule, another screen is displayed requesting the mechanic's input for instantiation:

```
A) Brake was installed < 1 week ago
B) Brake was installed > 1 week ago
C) Why?
```

The mechanic chooses A, instantiating *age* to < 1 week. Thus, Rule 4 now fires, instantiating *installation* to new. Hence, all of the required conditions of Rule 1 have been met and Rule 1 now fires, resulting in the display of a screen directing the mechanic to perform the hydrotest to determine the moisture absorption tendency of the brake pads.

We have given an example of backward chaining, but we have not presented an expert system. Many additional rules would be required to complete an expert system that would be capable of addressing the full spectrum of possible causes of wheel noise such as scarred wheel bearings and so on.

At this point the professional data processor should appreciate the difference between forward and backward chaining in the production system and the nature of production rules. The data processor should have some idea of how the inference engine functions using working storage and executing pattern matching to arrive at conclusions.

Further inference engine considerations

The example rules presented above conveniently avoid the need for conflict resolution capability in the inference engine that is a required feature when two or more rules are eligible to fire during the same cycle. Production systems whose rules are designed so that no two will be able to fire in the same cycle are said to be deterministic. As more production rules are required for a problem's solution, the ability to produce a deterministic system diminishes, and conflict resolution is required to stabilize performance.

The techniques involved in conflict resolution include prohibiting a rule from firing more than once, using a last-in, first-out (LIFO) approach to the application of working storage elements in the matching process, and giving firing preference to rules having the greatest number of condition clauses. There may also be coded into the knowledge base rules that serve to direct the inference engine's activity. These rules are referred to as "meta" rules in that they are rules about rules in the knowledge base.

Finally, we have not addressed the incorporation of facts in the creation of the knowledge base nor have we discussed the conditions of uncertainty alluded to earlier in Chapter 1. Many experts work in an area of uncertainty and are able only to state their conclusions about the diagnosis of an equipment problem, for example, in terms of some confidence value or rating. The incorporation of factual knowledge and confidence factors and how the inference engine treats these will be addressed in later chapters in which we will extend our view of expert system technology.

An implementation of forward and backward chaining

Although the broad scope of this book does not allow detailed examples of techniques at the implementation level for every mode of knowledge representation, we will illustrate forward chaining and backward chaining in production systems because they are probably the most popular of expert systems in current use.

Forward chaining. The data processor will be aware that a number of data structures must exist in working storage to facilitate the activities of the inference engine. Among those actively involved in the matching process is an array that contains the condition clause variables. This array is initially built allowing the maximum number of condition clause variables in any rule to determine the number of elements that will be dedicated for each rule. Hence, given our PC configuration example, two condition clause entries will be allowed for each rule—Rule 5 contains the largest number of clause variables, two:

5. IF communication = yes AND application = spreadsheet, THEN memory = 640K

The condition clause variable array appears as follows:

01. application
02.
03. application
04.
05. application
06.
07. memory
08.
09. communication
10. application

In this instance the rule number relates to its corresponding first array element's index, E, through the simple algorithm:

$$\text{rule number} = (E - 1)/2 + 1$$

For array element 1 we have rule number $(0) / 2 + 1 = 1$ and for array element 9 we have $(8)/2 + 1 = 5$. Clearly, we may locate a rule number (rule's address) from the index value of its first array element.

We next create a variable instantiation table that will contain a single instance of each condition variable along with its status, instantiated or not instantiated, and the value to which it has been instantiated if instantiation has occurred. Our table will consist of three entries representing the variables *application, memory,* and *communication.*

We now require two final elements, a pointer to keep track of the rule with the associated condition clause we are addressing and a conclusion queue to allow us to control the variable involved in the current matching effort. Our assembled environment appears as shown in Figure 4.1

Returning to our PC configuration session at the point of the user's first information input, we find that A was entered, indicating that the intended application is word processing. The interface deciphers the value of A and places *word processing* in the working storage area whereupon the inference engine updates the variable instantiation table, changing the status of the variable *application* to instantiated by marking it with an X and recording its value: word processing. The inference engine then places the variable *application* in the next

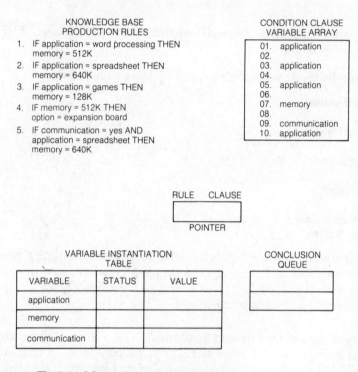

Figure 4.1   The initial forward chaining environment.

available place in the conclusion queue. The condition clause variable array is then searched to find the first occurrence of the variable *application*. This is found in the first element, allowing the earlier described algorithm to be executed and producing the variable's rule number: 1. The pointer is then updated to address Rule 1, clause 1. Figure 4.2 illustrates the conditions in memory at the termination of this activity.

The inference engine now matches the input information against the production rule addressed by the pointer and finds that the entire left-hand side matches. Hence, Rule 1 may fire—there are no additional condition clause variables to satisfy for this rule. This instantiates the variable *memory* to 512K. The variable *memory* is placed in the next available place in the queue and the variable instantiation table is updated to reflect the status and value of *memory*. The inference engine continues its search of the condition clause variable array, seeking further instances of the variable *application*. For each in-

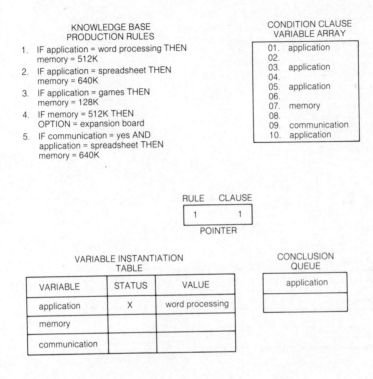

KNOWLEDGE BASE
PRODUCTION RULES

1. IF application = word processing THEN
   memory = 512K
2. IF application = spreadsheet THEN
   memory = 640K
3. IF application = games THEN
   memory = 128K
4. IF memory = 512K THEN
   OPTION = expansion board
5. IF communication = yes AND
   application = spreadsheet THEN
   memory = 640K

CONDITION CLAUSE
VARIABLE ARRAY

01.	application
02.	
03.	application
04.	
05.	application
06.	
07.	memory
08.	
09.	communication
10.	application

RULE   CLAUSE

1	1

POINTER

VARIABLE INSTANTIATION
TABLE

VARIABLE	STATUS	VALUE
application	X	word processing
memory		
communication		

CONCLUSION
QUEUE

application

Figure 4.2 The variable *application* is instantiated and located in clause 1 of Rule 1.

stance that is located, the pointer is updated to address the respective rule and the rule is tested to determine if it will fire.

As we know, *application* has been instantiated to word processing and consequently will not produce a match that allows any other rule to fire. Upon exhausting the condition clause variable array, the variable *application* is removed from the top of the queue. *Memory* is now at the top of the queue and so the inference engine searches the condition clause variable array, seeking the first instance of the variable *memory*. This is located in element 7 of the array. Algorithm execution produces the address of Rule 4, thus updating the pointer to Rule 4, clause 1. Figure 4.3 displays the condition of the table, pointer, array, and queue at this instant.

Rule 4 is found to fire, thus instantiating *option* to expansion board. At this point we have exhausted our example. Once more, this time in closer detail, we see that the expert system has inferred a number of the PC configuration requirements from a minimum of user involve-

KNOWLEDGE BASE
PRODUCTION RULES

1. IF application = word processing THEN
   memory = 512K
2. IF application = spreadsheet THEN
   memory = 640K
3. IF application = games THEN
   memory = 128K
4. IF memory = 512K THEN
   OPTION = expansion board
5. IF communication = yes AND
   application = spreadsheet THEN
   memory = 640K

CONDITION CLAUSE
VARIABLE ARRAY

01.	application
02.	
03.	application
04.	
05.	application
06.	
07.	memory
08.	
09.	communication
10.	application

RULE	CLAUSE
4	1

POINTER

VARIABLE INSTANTIATION
TABLE

VARIABLE	STATUS	VALUE
application	X	word processing
memory	X	512K
communication		

CONCLUSION
QUEUE

memory

Figure 4.3 Rule 4 now fires, instantiating the variable *option* to expansion board.

ment. A more interesting observation is that the implied programming requirements could be satisfied by any of a number of high-level languages. We shall look into such possibilities in later chapters.

Backward chaining. Similar to the forward chaining implementation just reviewed, backward chaining makes use of a condition clause variable array whose index may be algorithmically related to the knowledge base's rule address. The algorithm here is a modification of the earlier algorithm in that its objective is the location of the array index related to R, a given rule number (rule address):

$$\text{array index} = 2(R - 1) + 1$$

A condition clause variable instantiation table is also employed. Note that only two variables are truly condition clause variables, *brake* and *age*. Other condition clause variables that also appear as conclusion variables will be instantiated by the firing of those rules. At this point the similarities end because we are chaining backward.

Facilitating our backward chaining activity we will employ a conclusion table containing an entry for each rule in the knowledge base. Each entry consists of the rule number and the conclusion variable associated with that rule's right-hand side. Finally, we will use a push-down stack rule-clause pointer. Figure 4.4 displays the assembled structures in memory using the brake problem's production rules.

Returning now to the mechanic's sign-on, we recall that a screen appears that permits the user to ask the system if the moisture test should be performed on the brake pads. The selection of A from the screen option results in the number of the first rule containing *procedure* as a conclusion variable being placed upon the push-down stack: Rule 1. This is accomplished by a top-down search of the conclusion table. The clause portion of the push-down stack entry is set to 1 with the array index initialized to 1 as the result of the earlier described

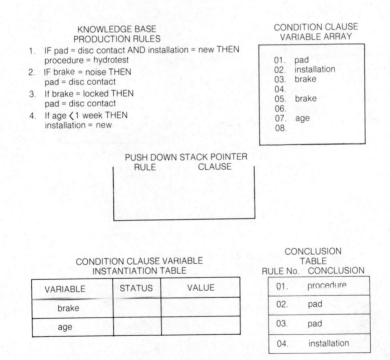

Figure 4.4 The initial backward chaining environment.

algorithm's execution, thus pointing to the condition variable *pad* in condition clause variable array entry 1.

A scan of the variable instantiation table determines that *pad* is not present there. Following this, a scan of the conclusion table indicates that *pad* is a conclusion variable of Rule 2. Rule 2 is now placed upon the push-down stack with the algorithm's result indicating clause 1 and initializing the condition clause variable array index to 3, thus pointing to the variable *brake* in the third element of the array.

As before, the variable instantiation table is scanned to determine that *brake* is present but not instantiated. Because no variable in the variable instantiation table appears in the conclusion table, the search ends. Consequently, the mechanic must supply the information necessary to instantiate this variable. The screen now asks the user to identify the brake condition as noise or locked. The status of memory at this point is illustrated in Figure 4.5, in which we see that the push-down stack now contains two entries.

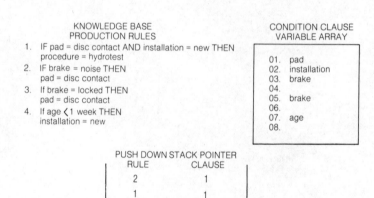

KNOWLEDGE BASE
PRODUCTION RULES

1. IF pad = disc contact AND installation = new THEN
   procedure = hydrotest
2. IF brake = noise THEN
   pad = disc contact
3. If brake = locked THEN
   pad = disc contact
4. If age ⟨ 1 week THEN
   installation = new

CONDITION CLAUSE
VARIABLE ARRAY

01.	pad
02.	installation
03.	brake
04.	
05.	brake
06.	
07.	age
08.	

PUSH DOWN STACK POINTER

RULE	CLAUSE
2	1
1	1

CONDITION CLAUSE VARIABLE
INSTANTIATION TABLE

VARIABLE	STATUS	VALUE
brake		
age		

CONCLUSION
TABLE

RULE No.	CONCLUSION
01.	procedure
02.	pad
03.	pad
04.	installation

Figure 4.5 The push-down stack pointer identifies the variable *brake*.

Upon the mechanic's choosing noise as the brake condition, the variable instantiation table is updated to indicate that *brake* is now instantiated to noise. This allows Rule 2 to fire since its left-hand side is now true. Rule 2, having fired, is now removed from the push-down stack, bringing Rule 1 back to the top. The inference engine has instantiated the first condition clause variable of Rule 1, *pad,* via the firing of Rule 2. The attempt is now to instantiate condition clause 2 of Rule 1. Hence, the clause in the push-down stack and the array index are incremented by 1. Thus, the array index addresses element 2, *installation,* in the condition clause variable array.

The variable instantiation table is now scanned to determine if *installation* has been instantiated. Finding it not present, the conclusion table is again searched in top-down fashion with the result that *installation* is found to be a conclusion variable of Rule 4. Rule 4 is placed upon the push-down stack, the algorithm executes, and the index points to entry 7, the variable *age.* A subsequent search of the variable instantiation table determines that *age* is present but has not been instantiated. Again the mechanic is called upon to supply the instantiating information. Figure 4.6 displays the current status of memory.

When the mechanic chooses less than 1 week as the time since the brake installation, *age* is instantiated to \ 1 week, allowing Rule 4 to fire. Rule 4 is then removed from the push-down stack, again bringing Rule 1 to the top. Because the firing of Rule 4 instantiated *installation* to new, Rule 1's left-hand side became true, allowing it to fire and produce the conclusion of the backward chaining sequence in that no uninstantiated variables remain.

Structured Objects

A discussion of structured objects is facilitated by an understanding of object-oriented programming in the current expert system environment. Although object-oriented programming departs considerably from the procedural (subroutine-oriented) programming common in the data processing environment, its development may be viewed as having its roots in an area familiar to the data processor—record design.

The representation of knowledge as structured objects developed in AI as an outgrowth of attempts to organize knowledge in a fashion that would allow natural language to be interpreted. Efforts in the development of natural language systems in AI gave rise to the development of networks of associated language concepts called semantic

KNOWLEDGE BASE
PRODUCTION RULES

1. IF pad = disc contact AND installation = new THEN
   procedure = hydrotest
2. IF brake = noise THEN
   pad = disc contact
3. If brake = locked THEN
   pad = disc contact
4. If age < 1 week THEN
   installation = new

CONDITION CLAUSE
VARIABLE ARRAY

01.	pad
02.	installation
03.	brake
04.	
05.	brake
06.	
07.	age
08.	

PUSH DOWN STACK POINTER

RULE	CLAUSE
4	1
1	2

CONDITION CLAUSE VARIABLE
INSTANTIATION TABLE

VARIABLE	STATUS	VALUE
brake	X	noise
age		

CONCLUSION
TABLE

RULE No.	CONCLUSION
01.	procedure
02.	pad
03.	pad
04.	installation

Figure 4.6 The push-down stack pointer identifies the variable *age*.

nets. The semantic net later became an artifact in the development of expert systems.

Semantic nets

The net or network consists of concepts that are related by links. The links are also called arcs in the AI environment. The type of link or arc specifies the relationship between the concepts or nodes. For example, the isa arc establishes a transitive relationship along the path it creates, linking the nodes in Figure 4.7.

Although nowhere in the knowledge base of Figure 4.7 are the facts that John Smith and Mary Roe are physicians, both conclusions may be inferred from the transitivity of the isa relationship. Thus, the semantic net allows the inheritance of properties through the relationships represented by its arcs. A number of relationships may be defined to facilitate the passing of one-time coded characteristics down through the hierarchy to nodes beneath. Hence, not only does the se-

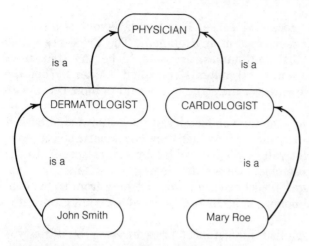

Figure 4.7 Both Mary and John inherit the characteristics of physician.

mantic net realize the objectives of economy of storage and effort, but an inference technique is facilitated as well.

Frame-based systems

An introspective examination of the manner in which we mentally store knowledge divulges that we deal with wholistic concepts that may be more complex than those allowed by a simple node. A concept such as "motor vehicle" illustrates this.

Our generic concept of motor vehicle includes engine, wheels, doors, body finish, and so on. These features are inherited by the classes of motor vehicle that we add to our knowledge as learning takes place. Ultimately, associated with "motor vehicle" in our mind set is a collection of classes such as truck, automobile, motorcycle, and so on. Each feature, such as wheels, has associated with it a value: 2, 3, or 4. When we discuss motor vehicles with our friends, we draw on this classification system by asking, "What kind of motor vehicle?" The response, "Automobile," results in our attempting to fill in the details by inquiring about the body finish and the number of doors, and so on. This more complex node is called a frame.

The frame differs from the node in the semantic net in that each frame is further defined by an assembly of additional notes that provide for the multiple notions we associate with a given concept.

Object-oriented programming

Relating these knowledge sets to the programming environment, we find that our generic concept of "motor vehicle" is analogous to a record in the data processing sense. This record layout is termed a "structure" in the expert system environment. The fields are called "slots." The field labels, or names, are said to be the structure's "attributes" and the slot (field) contents are called "values." When the knowledge items are entered, the structure is said to have become an "object."

As we add each new motor vehicle class to our knowledge base it "inherits" its attributes and their values from our generic object; however, some of the slot values are overridden by values specific to the particular class whose object we are developing. Inheritance is a feature that distinguishes object-oriented programming from traditional data processing technology as is the technique of overriding inherited values.

In order to accomplish inheritance, procedures (subroutine-type blocks of code) must be implemented as must hierarchical relationships that allow the procedures to operate upon the objects (knowledge base). Procedures must be implemented to allow actions to be taken when values are added, changed, or needed for critical slots. At the implementation level this is achieved through the use of flags or other indicators associated with various slots. Finally, procedures must be implemented to allow the sending of messages between objects and to the users of the expert system.

In the mind's eye of the data processor the development of such a system is within the realm of possibility, but the attendant complications are ominous.

We have entered the environment of specialized expert system tools, a topic that will be addressed in a later chapter. For now it is important that the data processor appreciate that unlike production systems, the implementation of structured objects requires an order of magnitude increase in sophistication that can be gained in a practical way only through the application of a specialized tool. To realize the economies of allocating memory storage for inherited information from hierarchical objects in the knowledge base, thus avoiding redundant storage, requires a specialized programming vehicle.

In comparison, where production systems we have viewed store their knowledge as rules, the frame-based system stores its knowledge as slot-bearing nodes. In the production system the user presents symptomatic information from the real world and it is applied to the rules by the inference engine to determine the conclusions that may be derived. In the frame-based system the user presents information that the inference engine attempts to incorporate in a solution by invoking procedures to process knowledge-laden objects (frames) stored in the knowledge base.

Again, an illustration will help. Figure 4.8 displays a designer's conception of a make of vehicle frame as it relates to a specific vehicle frame. We might imagine that the user has just signed on to a vehicle identification expert system at a local law enforcement agency to attempt the identification of a hit-and-run vehicle. The next available make of vehicle frame is made accessible to the user, and the witness-provided slot values are entered. The inference engine locates a matching DeLorean vehicle frame from the hierarchy of frames in the knowledge base. Unknown witness slot values will now be inherited to complete the description of the vehicle sought. The DeLorean vehicle

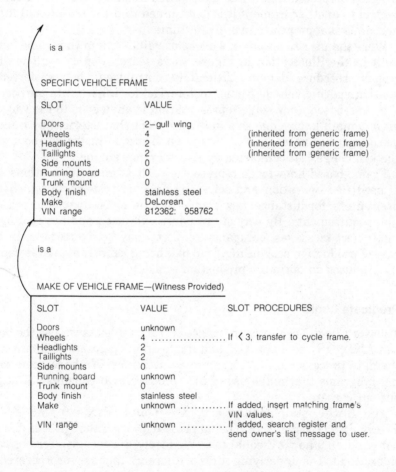

Figure 4.8 A frame-based expert vehicle identification system completes an identification from available witness observations.

frame has, in turn, inherited some of its values from a generic vehicle frame higher in the hierarchy and not shown here. Witness-entered slot values override inherited values. A key slot value such as "stainless steel" has determined the match in this case.

The make of vehicle frame's procedures execute if a value is added to a slot via inheritance or as the result of a witness-supplied value. In this case, inheritance adds the make and causes the message to issue when the Vehicle Identification Number (VIN) range is inherited. If the user supplied the make of vehicle, the owner's list message would result when the search located the specific vehicle frame, resulting in the inheritance of the VIN range. Critical slots may be provided with triggers or procedures (sometimes called demons) that will transfer control to another frame if it is determined that the situational information is inappropriate to a given frame.

Were the user to specify a wheel slot value of 2, in the frame being built in the illustration in Figure 4.8, a search would result via the trigger procedure (demon). Ultimately control would be transferred to another specific vehicle frame (motorcycle) for inheritance purposes.

Frame-based knowledge representation is analogous to the way we view domain knowledge as a unified concept characterized by numerous descriptive notes. The particular application illustrated above sees the vehicle gestalt completed by the inference engine.

Frame-based knowledge representation has broad applications and is used in reservation and scheduling expert systems in which the user enters, for instance, new frames describing occupancy or production requirements. By way of procedure execution and the issuing of interobject messages, occupancy conflicts may be averted, or, in the case of production scheduling, load balancing against available capacity produces an optimum production schedule.

Predicate Logic

The word "logic" conjures up images of truth tables as well as the boolean AND, OR, exclusive OR, and implication operators so familiar to the data processor from programming activities. We have been writing programs that make use of the "propositional calculus" throughout our careers.

The BASIC statements $Z = 0$, $X = 6$ and IF $X = 9$ IMP $Z = 5$, THEN PRINT Z result in Z being printed (0) even though X is clearly not equal to 9 nor is Z equal to 5. We rarely, if ever, give serious consideration to the underlying rules of inference that are incorporated in the compiler's design, thus allowing us to make use of these constructs without fear of error. (In this case, the rule is *modus ponens*.)

While the propositional calculus is useful in processing data, a more extensive set of logical tools is necessary in the processing environment of the expert system. In creating a knowledge base we are interested in making statements about specific things. Rather than being content with simple truth values which suffice in the data processing environment, we seek to predicate or assert the presence of relationships among the things of our knowledge.

We would like to express, for example, that the pad touches the disc in reference to our previously described brake problem. Here "touches" is a predicate that we might represent by T. Allowing pad to be represented by p and disc by d, we have $T(p,d)$, representing our expression in symbolic predicate logic. We say that "touches" is a two-place predicate.

Of necessity we introduce the one-place predicate, is, that establishes the existence of a set. For example, allowing A to represent the one-place predicate "is an animal" we have $A(x)$, meaning "x is an animal." Associated with our assertions is the need to be able to quantify the extension of an assertion—"Some animals are carnivores," or "All animals die." We further need to express functional relationships in our knowledge base such as "X is the generator of Y." The function, unlike the predicate, returns a value.

Having accomplished the creation of these additional logical implements, we have to reassess the way in which we use the concept "equals." Finally, we need to develop an extended set of inference rules that allow us to draw conclusions from these expressions.

Fortunately, all of these extensions to the propositional calculus with which we are familiar have already been created by logicians, thus producing the first-order predicate logic. The vehicle for the representation of expert knowledge in logic is available. The remaining intellectual challenge for the data processor is the expansion of personal knowledge to grasp these extensions to a logic with which a good deal of familiarity already exists. Beyond this, there is the emotional challenge of programming in a language that demands symbolic problem definition as a prerequisite to its effective performance as opposed to data processing languages that require procedural specifications detailing a problem's specific solution steps.

In the next chapter we will give more detailed consideration to Programming in Logic (Prolog). There we will become more familiar with the inference engine in the logic programming environment as well as the modes of expressing domain knowledge.

In Retrospect

The professional data processor may be inclined to believe that there are little more than three modes of knowledge representation now that they have been briefly reviewed. The fact is that there are a number of modes of knowledge representation—we have seen but three.

Perhaps because of the activity of the trade press, the impression has been left that rather like the Cobol compiler, both knowledge representation and the design of inference engines is an accomplished fact left only to suffer later minor improvements at the hands of interested users. Nothing could be further from the truth.

The frame concept was first introduced in 1975. Logic programming has been practiced only since the early 1970s although the underlying logical equipment was available earlier. Many AI researchers are currently working on further development of the very techniques we have reviewed—these techniques are far from being considered exhausted areas of research. Expert system technology is a new element in computer usage, and it must be assumed that many of the systems currently under development will be rebuilt again and again as the environment evolves.

The conservative professional data processor interested in becoming involved only with technology that is tried, tested, and proven has, nonetheless, no reason to hesitate in the face of the ongoing development of expert systems. As we have seen and as we shall see, the competitive advantage offered by expert systems is such that the benefits are far from being simply speculative. Although this technology is still in development, it is capable of highly productive application now.

Expert System
Programming Languages

If we were to trace the generations of software technology, we would find that the first generation saw the development of assemblers for use where formerly only machine language (often called "actual" in the early days) had existed. The second generation saw the development of compilers which freed the data processor from the requirement of an intimate knowledge of the CPU's design. The third generation ushered in database technology which was closely followed by the fourth-generation languages—the application generators. The publicity agents who glamorize all of this often refer to the emergence of expert system technology as the fifth generation. Unfortunately the real world, with its backlogs and crises, often manages to remain a generation or two behind technology's leading edge. The competitive environment of international business has, of late, demonstrated that this is not a profitable strategy despite the problems associated with remaining current.

Conservatively, 95 percent of commercial data processing involves the use of six programming languages: Cobol, PL/I, RPG (II & III), APL, ALC (Assembly Language Coding—formerly BAL), and Fortran. With the qualified exception of RPG, all of these languages are procedural in their orientation. That is, the programmer must specify the step-by-step solution of the problem being addressed by the intended program. RPG is quasi-procedural in that the file opening, I/O, and file closing may be delegated to the compiler. The RPG compiler generates a cyclic program whose logical structure facilitates report writing, file updating, and the like through the manipulation of indicators that condition instruction execution.

On the whole, professional data processors' thought processes have come to reflect this procedural need to explicitly specify problem-solving strategies. The data processor's predilection with this step-by-step problem-solving approach led to what has come to be termed "bottom-up" system development: initially specifying the minutiae and hoping the result will be a workable system. The latter-day development of structured system design and structured programming techniques immediately fell upon hard times in that they challenged the data processors' long entrenched habits of thought.

Evidence that these habits of thought are economically counterproductive is manifest in the often heard comments of corporate management: "These computer types are in a world of their own." Such complaints simply reflect the fact that the professional data processor's creative abilities are being constrained by programming language limitations.

There is, indeed, a dichotomy that separates entrepreneurial management from the rigorously technical data processor. The two were brought together out of mutual need, but a tug of war developed that continues to this day with the management faction believing that data processors should do more and the data processing faction believing that management has no appreciation for the complexities of the problem-solving environment.

Expert systems may well end the hostilities and usher us into a new era of international leadership through increased profitability. The key to such a result is not totally independent of the data processor's need to overcome his or her submission to habits of thought that run counter to this new technology. The programming languages of expert systems are, by and large, nonprocedural.

It can be disorienting to attempt programming in an environment so radically different from one's habitual mind set. The challenge of this chapter and the ones that lie ahead simply involves the data processor's willingness to surrender the almost innate need to control every aspect of the processing sequence and thus depend upon the built-in features of the programming vehicle.

The Prolog Personality and Behavior

A programming language based upon a subset of predicate logic known as the "Horn clause subset" was implemented at the University of Aix-Marseille in France during 1972. The French Programmation Logique quickly became known as Prolog.

Just as the RPG compiler generates a characteristic cyclic program, Prolog's personality presents a behavior best described as backward chaining with backtracking (a new feature which will be explained shortly). We use the word "personality" here because the programmer's first encounter with Prolog will probably be with the Prolog interpreter which, like a PC's BASIC interpreter, is interactive and will allow immediate execution of programmer-supplied input. Prolog compilers are also readily available, and so it is quite probable that the programmer's final Prolog program version will be compiled to execute as does any other compiled program.

Our introduction to backward chaining in Chapter 4 exposed us to a purely rule-oriented production system. Indeed, our exposure to production systems there saw the user interactively providing the facts, thus informing the system that the brakes were noisy and so on. Prolog provides a means of incorporating facts in the knowledge base as well as rules, and so our exposure to Prolog will round out our view of the expert system knowledge base in that it introduces the need for the inclusion of facts. Clearly, the expert's knowledge does include a great amount of factual information as well as the rules for applying those facts.

Another feature of our introduction to the inference engine in Chapter 4 saw us asking the user to supply facts whenever the inference engine found that it could not instantiate a particular variable in order to prove a rule so that it would fire. We saw there that the inference engine would instantiate variables, request the user's input as needed, and continue its activity, driving toward a conclusion. In no example presented there did the inference engine ever become stymied, reset the instantiated variables, and start anew with another rule. Prolog not only functions in a backward chaining mode, but it will abandon its direction when it finds that a rule cannot be proved. Prolog will reset the instantiated variables to an uninstantiated state and begin again, attempting to work with other elements in the knowledge base. This behavior is called "backtracking."

Because Prolog allows the inclusion of facts in the knowledge base along with rules and performs the services of backward chaining and backtracking, the programmer (knowledge engineer) is required only to define the problem environment. Prolog is a nonprocedural language in that the program's behavior is a product of the interpreter or compiler—the programmer cannot determine the performance of a Prolog expert system, but the programmer may control performance through his or her phrasing of the problem and specification of the knowledge base.

The Prolog Language

Unlike the procedural programs with which we work daily, Prolog is free of data types, numeric and so on. Prolog is also free of reserved words although it does possess a number of "evaluable" predicates, such as is, >, <, and others. We shall soon see how these are used. Further, facts and rules that constitute a Prolog knowledge base are stored in what is best described as being analogous to a relational database.

Recalling that a relational database stores data in tables (analogous to files) having rows (analogous to records) and columns (analogous to fields), each row is called an "instance" of the relation represented by the table. Each column contains an attribute of the instance.

One might imagine a weight table whose rows each contain attributes that store the weight and name of a kitchen appliance. If we wished to introduce such a structure into a conventional program, we would first reserve memory (Data Division in Cobol, E specification in RPG, or DS in ALC) and having done so, the die would be cast in that the table could not be expanded after program creation without considerable modification.

The unit clause

Prolog permits us to represent factual information as "predicate clauses" in which each clause of a given predicate has the same number of arguments. The predicate name is rather like the table relation name with the clausal arguments analogous to the table arguments or attributes in the relational database environment. Thus, we represent our appliance weight information in Prolog unit clauses as follows (note the necessary period (.) after each clause):

```
weight(mixer,2).
weight(toaster,1).
weight(coffee_maker,2).
weight(can_opener,1).
weight(disposall,5).
weight(dish_washer,180).
weight(stove,210).
weight(refrigerator,319).
weight(microwave_oven,110).
weight(water_filter,35).
```

Each unit clause represents an instance of the relation. The appliance names are atoms and, because spaces may not appear in an atom that is not surrounded by quotes, the underscore is used in place of a space. The weights are integers. Although we have not as yet encountered variables, they are like unquoted atoms whose first (or only) letter is capitalized: stove is an atom, Stove is a variable as are X and Y while x and y are atoms. A variable may assume any value as we shall see.

There is no need to become involved with memory management in Prolog. We may add unit clauses for this relation without concern over the fact that the atoms (appliance names) are of widely varying sizes in bytes. Even after the program has been completed, new unit clauses may be added as additional kitchen appliances are selected for the knowledge base. Because these clauses are stored in the Prolog database in arrival order, program behavior may be influenced by our choice of sequence as the number of clauses grows, but beyond that consideration, we are not constrained.

Let us demonstrate by developing a "toy" minisystem, written in Prolog, that will allow a purchasing agent to distinguish between what are called "traffic appliances" in the retail industry and "major appliances." The need for such a system is not totally fictional. The agent must send RFPs (requests for proposals) to different vendors who supply one or the other but not both classes of appliances. Since the agent is also purchasing numerous other materials, help is always welcome, and therefore an appliance minisystem will enhance productivity.

The unit clauses have been entered to the interpreter as shown above. Clearly, we now need to incorporate some rules in our knowledge base in order to permit the purchasing agent to quickly distinguish the traffic appliances from the major appliances. We have determined (our heuristic) that the weight of the appliance is the chief distinguishing factor in that an appliance over 100 pounds is considered to be a major appliance while the lighter appliances are traffic appliances.

Prolog rules

We will need at least two sets of rules, one for traffic appliances and one for major appliances. Our objective is to allow the purchasing agent to simply type one word such as "major" or "traffic" followed by a period. We want Prolog then to list the appliances belonging to the group of major or traffic appliances. Prolog will accomplish this through matching and unification, which we will explain shortly.

Rules in Prolog are constructed of statements of the form "predicate(argument1,argument2,...,argumentn):-goal." where the predicate and its arguments are referred to as the head while :- is interpreted "if." The goal consists of that which Prolog must prove using the facts in the knowledge base. We might broadly interpret the Prolog rule B IF A. Our earlier encounters with rules saw the equivalent form: IF A THEN B.

A rule is invoked in Prolog by stating a rule's head whereupon Prolog proceeds to search the knowledge base, seeking the first rule whose head matches. Prolog then attempts to match the arguments in the located rule's goal with elements in the knowledge base. Upon finding a match, unification takes place—the variables are instantiated. Each argument, left to right, is subjected in turn to matching and unification. Successful matching and unification is said to prove the argument. When all of a rule's arguments have been proved, Prolog has proved the goal, and the matching activity ceases unless the user requests that Prolog continue searching the knowledge base.

When any argument's proof fails because matching or unification cannot occur, Prolog backtracks by uninstantiating the arguments' variables, in reverse order, moving right to left through the rule's goal. When backtracking through the goal has finished, Prolog goes on to the next successive knowledge base element that matches the goal's first argument and again tries to establish a proof. If the first rule cannot be proved, Prolog moves on to the next successive rule whose head matches the input.

Prolog in action

We do not want our purchasing agent to have to request additional effort of Prolog since this will require that we expand the agent's training. We must create rules that will search the entire knowledge base of appliance weight facts without ceasing when the first goal is proved.

Our first two rules dealing with major appliances are as follows:

```
major:-weight(App,Weight),check(App,Weight),fail.
major.
```

The first rule's head is "major" as we had planned. This rule will be invoked when the purchasing agent enters major. Prolog will begin its search of the knowledge base, matching the first argument of the goal, weight(App,Weight), with knowledge base fact: weight(mixer,2). The match succeeds because both predicates match and the number of arguments, or "arity," is the same. App and Weight are variables and variables unify with atoms—instantiation takes place giving all occurrences in the knowledge base of the variables App and Weight the same values, mixer and 2, respectively.

In order to test the weight, check(App,Weight) is specified as an additional argument of the goal to be proved. We have not yet entered the check(App,Weight) rule, but regardless of the outcome of the weight check, we are finally specifying fail. The predicate, fail, essentially tells Prolog that whether the goal has been proved or not, Prolog is to assume that the proof failed. Hence backtracking begins with Prolog working its way, right to left, back through major's goal toward the rule's head. As Prolog works its way back, the arguments' variables are uninstantiated. Prolog then seeks to prove major's arguments by attempting to match its first argument with the next weight clause in the knowledge base. In turn, each weight clause is matched until all of the weight clauses have been processed.

Since major always fails because of the fail predicate in its last argument, Prolog would publish a "no proof" message at the completion of its processing of the weight predicate facts if it were not for the second major clause. At the completion of Prolog's processing of the facts in the weight predicate, the second major clause is successfully matched and, because it has no arguments, a successful proof occurs immediately. Prolog then publishes a "proved" message. We see that the fail predicate forces Prolog to continue working with the initial major rule until the knowledge base of facts has been processed from top to bottom. Prolog then moves on to the next rule whose head matches major and since it offers no arguments, the final status is that major has been proved.

We now enter check:

```
check(App,Weight):-weight(App,X),Weight is X,Weight < 100,!,fail.
```

Let us return to Prolog's activity in the first major rule now that we have an overview of the processing. We have seen that Prolog has successfully matched and unified the weight(mixer,2) fact with major's first argument. The next argument that Prolog must prove is the check argument. To accomplish this proof Prolog searches for a match with the check predicate and finds a match with the head of the check rule that we have just entered. (Again, the predicates match and the arity is the same. Moreover, the variable values are identical since the earlier unification has instantiated every occurrence of App and Weight to the same value.) In order to prove the check argument in the major rule, Prolog must prove the goal of the check rule.

The check goal to be proved is weight (App,X) but we know that App is instantiated to mixer and so X will take on the value 2—X is a new variable not yet instantiated. The evaluable predicate, is, effects a computation, setting Weight to 2. Thus, the final evaluable predicate, <, proves that Weight is, indeed, less than 100.

For the next argument in the check rule, we have used ! which is "cut," a predicate that, like fail, always succeeds; ! effectively interrupts backtracking when a goal is not proved. To ensure that backtracking is under control we finally specify fail.

Let us now take a look at how this proof proceeds. As we have noted, check's goal is proved, the cut succeeds, and then fail tells Prolog that the whole matter was not proved. Backtracking begins with Prolog working its way left through the check rule from the predicate, fail. The cut informs Prolog that backtracking must cease. If backtracking ceases with the check rule unproved, "control" returns to the first major rule, and it has failed in its proof of the check argument without ever encountering its fail predicate—backtracking starts in the first major rule and proceeds as described during our introduction of that rule. That is, the arguments' variables are uninstantiated and the next weight predicate is processed in the knowledge base—this time addressing the second knowledge base fact, weight (toaster,1).

It is important to note that when a goal failure occurs, the remainder of the goal is ignored and backtracking begins. Thus, if check had failed prior to encountering !, backtracking would, indeed, begin immediately. Further, the arguments' variables are uninstantiated only for the rule in which backtracking is taking place. This leads us to a final consideration of how we will ultimately arrange to have our major appliances appear on the screen.

If we take a closer look at the check rule, we see that if Weight < 100, the proof succeeds; Prolog encounters the ! argument, which succeeds; and then fail is encountered with the result that the rule fails and backtracking is prohibited when Prolog encounters ! in its return, right to left, through the goal. If the first check rule is followed by another check rule which will print the appliance's description, it would only be sought if the first check rule failed prior to encountering !, thus allowing backtracking to start. Recall that when a rule fails, Prolog goes on to find another matching predicate when backtracking has completed. Consequently, we wish check to prove until it encounters ! and to fail only for traffic appliances. For major appliances, we wish check to fail prior to encountering ! so that backtracking will allow a second check rule to publish the appliance's description on the screen.

Hence we enter the second check rule:

```
check(App,Weight):-write('Major Appliance : '(App,Weight)),nl.
```

Here we have the predicate, write, which, like fail, always succeeds. The arguments of write are an atom in quotes, because we will have spaces embedded and the variables App and Weight, which are still instantiated to the appliance's name and weight. Finally we have specified another predicate that always proves, nl, to provide a new line for output on the screen each time the goal is proved.

Let us retrace the Prolog activity with all of our rules in place. The rules are:

```
major:-weight(App,Weight),check(App,Weight),fail.
major.
check(App,Weight):-weight(App,X),Weight is X,Weight < 100,!,fail.
check(App,Weight):-write('Major Appliance : '(App,Weight)),nl.
```

The user enters major. Prolog matches major with the head of the first rule and proceeds to attempt proof of the first argument: weight (App,Weight). Prolog matches weight with the first fact: weight

(mixer,2), unifying mixer and 2 with App and Weight, thus instantiating these variables to those values for every occurrence of the variables in the knowledge base—a successful proof. Prolog then goes on
to match the check argument with the first check rule—Prolog must
now prove the arguments of the check rule.

The first check rule argument, weight(App,X), matches with the
first fact in that the value of App matches and X, being a variable,
will unify with its value—a successful proof. The evaluable predicates
succeed and the goal is proved. The ! is now encountered and proves,
having no effect (until backtracking is attempted). Finally, fail causes
the goal's proof to fail. Backtracking begins but is terminated by !, and
the goal fails, returning control to the first major rule, which has now
failed without encountering its fail predicate.

Prolog now backtracks through the first major rule and goes on to
find a match with another weight predicate, prompting a proof of major's arguments once more but now addressing the second knowledge
base fact.

Let us assume that a heavy major appliance is finally encountered.
The proof steps would proceed as above with the exception that the
evaluable predicate clause containing \ in the first check rule would
fail because Weight would be > 100 for a major appliance. Backtracking would start immediately since ! would not yet have been encountered. The second check rule would match the check predicate, and its
arguments are all going to succeed because their predicates, like fail,
always succeed. The result is the appearance on the screen of Major
Appliance : with the major appliance's name followed by its weight.
The check rule is proved. Again "control" returns to the first major
rule, all of whose arguments are thus far proved. Now the fail predicate is encountered and backtracking follows. The next weight predicate is matched, which reinstitutes the proof of arguments that terminates with the exhaustion of knowledge base facts. Finally, the second
major rule is matched, but because it has no arguments, the proof is
successful and the proved or yes message terminates the session.

We may now present the set of rules necessary to identify the traffic
appliances. They are identical in form to the major appliances with
the exception that the weight test is just the opposite of that used for
major appliances and, of course, the rule heads' predicates are different in that traffic and check1 are used:

```
traffic:-weight(App,Weight),check1(App,Weight),fail.
traffic.
check1(App,Weight):-weight(App,X),Weight is X,Weight > 100,!,fail.
check1(App,Weight):-write('Major Appliance : '(App,Weight)),nl.
```

The entire program appears as follows:

```
weight(mixer,2).
weight(toaster,1).
weight(coffee__maker,2).
weight(can__opener,1).
weight(disposall,5).
weight(dish__washer,180).
weight(stove,210).
weight(refrigerator,319).
weight(microwave__oven,110).
weight(water__filter,35).
major:-weight(App,Weight),check(App,Weight),fail.
major.
check(App,Weight):-weight(App,X),Weight is X,Weight < 100,!,fail.
check(App,Weight):-write('Major Appliance : '(App,Weight)),nl.
traffic:-weight(App,Weight),check1(App,Weight),fail.
traffic.
check1(App,Weight):-weight(App,X),Weight is X,Weight )100,!,fail.
check1(App,Weight):-write('Traffic Appliance : '(App,Weight)),nl.
```

Upon entering major, the following appears on the screen:

```
Major Appliance : (dish__washer, 180)
Major Appliance : (stove, 210)
Major Appliance : (refrigerator, 319)
Major Appliance : (microwave__oven, 110)
```

followed by a proved or yes message indicating that the proof is complete. Upon entering traffic, the following appears on the screen:

```
Traffic Appliance : (mixer, 2)
Traffic Appliance : (toaster, 1)
Traffic Appliance : (coffee__maker, 2)
Traffic Appliance : (can__opener, 1)
Traffic Appliance : (disposall, 5)
Traffic Appliance : (water__filter, 35)
```

again, followed by a proved or yes message.

Prolog in summary

We can see clearly why Prolog has built-in backward chaining. Given the B IF A design of its rules, we see that the equivalent, IF A THEN B, finds that backward chaining always proves B—a feature of Prolog's method of proof. We have introduced backtracking and the use of ! (cut) as well as a number of the evaluable and "never fail" predicates in the development of a minisystem. We also have seen that new facts may be added to the knowledge base with ease, and we are aware that Prolog carries on its activity in a top-down, left-to-right fashion.

While we have made no attempt to teach Prolog, the reader has been exposed to some of the most difficult aspects of this language—backtracking and the use of !. The professional data processor may be inclined to believe that the whole matter could have been more easily programmed in his or her favorite procedural language, but we must agree that "more easily" has meaning only in relation to the learning process—it is easier not to have to learn a new language. Prolog's built-in backward chaining and backtracking abilities solve knowledge processing problems that would prove quite difficult, if not impossible, if attempted using conventional data processing languages in the development of expert systems that deal with more complex domains that require sophisticated search techniques. Later chapters will reference educational materials that deal at length with the full capabilities of Prolog.

The LISP Personality and Behavior

LISP (an acronym for LISt Processor) is an old language predating most of today's popular computer languages—Fortran is the only language in popular use that is older then LISP. Based upon the lambda calculus which was developed in the 1930s as a mathematical system, LISP's creation was begun during 1958, at MIT. Because this language is under constant development due to its popularity in AI circles, numerous dialects have resulted, as has the outcry for standardization, and for good cause.

While Prolog is the choice for Japan's Fifth Generation Project, LISP is the programming vehicle most widely used in the United States. There are indications that standardization may soon result although we still hear that this or that LISP is the de facto standard. Unfortunately, the dialect of LISP often cited in these comments is determined by the area or organization affiliation of the speaker. Because standardization is more important to software portability than to an understanding of the language, we will proceed, ignoring LISP's multiple dialects.

The entity upon which LISP operates is the "symbolic expression," or "S-expression" as it is often called. An S-expression is an atom or a list. A list is simply a parenthesized succession of items such that each item is an atom or a list enclosed in parentheses.

An atom, as we saw in our encounter with Prolog, is a single element; however, capital and lowercase distinctions do not apply in LISP: BOY is an atom as is boy as is BoY. This kind of atom is called an "identifier," and its sole restriction is that it must begin with an alpha character and may not contain embedded spaces. When quotes are used to enclose the atom such as "Press the button", the contents may be any characters. This atom is called a "string." Atoms may also be numbers such as 25 or 10 or +25 or −25 if the number is an integer or 25.2 and so on, with + or − if the number is a floating-point number. A list might appear as follows:

```
(people 2 (male (boys men) female (girls women)))
```

This list contains two atoms, people and 2, and a list that contains two atoms and two other lists, each of which contains two atoms. It is clear to the data processor that the parentheses must be paired properly or trouble may develop. Further, it is plain that the delimiter is the space rather than the comma needed in Prolog. The period (.) plays no role in LISP other than in the representation of a floating-point number such as 2.66.

The LISP interpreter has a number of built-in precoded procedures which may be used by the programmer in processing a list just as data processing languages, such as Cobol, contain precoded elements that are available for inclusion in a program. These built-in procedures in LISP are called primitives. We shall discuss primitives a bit later. For now, it is important to point out that in LISP a procedure may also be a function; that is, it may produce a value when evaluated by the interpreter. Some procedures are not functions in that they produce side effects rather than values when evaluated. We will encounter these shortly.

LISP's behavior capabilities are quite different from those of most data processing languages. Where data processing programs make use of iterative routines, LISP programs, more often than not, will employ recursion. Because recursion is foreign to much of the data processor's daily experience, contrasting examples may be helpful. Given:

```
          A = 100
   START
          A = A - 1
          IF A < 0, GOTO EXIT
          GOTO START
              .
```

we have an iterative routine that will terminate as soon as A is decremented below 0. Given:

```
          A = 100
          PERFORM SUBR1
              .
              .
   SUBR1
          A = A - 1
          IF A < -1 PERFORM SUBR1
          EXIT
```

we see that SUBR1 has been defined in terms of itself, or recursively—it calls itself until the conditional test requirements are met.

The data processor will observe that any language that allows recursion must make use of a stack. While a programmer may explicitly code stack handling, languages such as LISP that provide this service lessen the programming task, thereby allowing the opportunity to concentrate on problem definition.

The LISP Language

Because a LISP program consists of lists, the LISP program is itself a list. Hence, LISP programs may be self-altering and self-augmenting, or a LISP program may generate a new LISP program. All of this is related to the manner in which LISP evaluates S-expressions. When LISP is given a symbol, it searches its memory space, seeking the value that has been assigned to the identifier unless the symbol is a number, whereupon LISP simply returns the number since a number is its own value. When LISP is given a list, it expects that the first element of the list is the name of a procedure to be evaluated. LISP simply wants to evaluate S-expressions.

LISP primitives

Two built-in procedures (primitives) that we will review now are CAR and CDR (although we have explained that caps and lowercase have no significance in LISP, we will use caps to represent procedures for the benefit of the reader). It should be noted that while most procedures have names that to some extent relate to their actual performance, CAR and CDR (pronounced coo-der) have been retained from LISP's early days when CAR represented Current Address Register and CDR represented Current Decrement Register on the IBM 704. Both CAR and CDR are procedures that are also functions in that they produce a value when evaluated.

CAR returns the first element of a list while CDR returns all the elements of a list with the exception of the first element. Clearly, these primitives are used in taking lists apart. When a function is used in a list, as we noted earlier, it must be the first element of the list and it must be delimited by a space. A single quote may then be posted to notify LISP that the remaining elements are list contents upon which the function will operate—the single quote tells LISP to stop evaluation. For example:

```
(CAR ' (boy (rags tags tails)))
```

returns boy.

```
(CDR ' (boy (rags tags tails)))
```

returns

```
((rags tags tails))
```

If we wish to nest procedures in our list, we do not introduce the single quote until the nesting encounters the list elements:

```
(CAR (CAR '((boy girl) (rags tags))))
```

returns boy.

The innermost primitive, CAR, returns the first element of the list, itself a list, (boy girl), which is passed to the outer CAR that returns the first element of that list, the atom, boy. Hence, we see that the functions are executed beginning with the innermost and working to the outermost function.

We have already noted that the lists above are called S-expressions. Because these S-expressions are discussed here as evaluable rather than being viewed as simple lists, they are called "forms." LISP evaluates forms, returning values dictated by the procedure specified as the first item in the form—in the examples above, CAR and CDR.

Let us now consider another primitive, SETQ, which may be used in a form in order to assign a value to an atom that is an identifier. SETQ is not a function since it has a side effect—a result that persists after the evaluation takes place. The persisting result is the assignment of value:

```
(SETQ seat '(rocker stool bench))
```

SETQ is a special form in that it is not required that seat be preceded by a single quote in order to keep seat from being evaluated. After LISP has evaluated this form, seat becomes the identifier for the list:

```
(rocker stool bench)
```

Now if we specify the form (CAR seat) without the single quote, we are telling LISP that seat is an identifier for a list whose first element we wish to have returned:

```
(CAR seat)
```

returns rocker.

Recall that the single quote tells LISP to stop evaluation. Its absence here results in LISP evaluating seat, thus producing the list upon which the function, CAR, will operate. If we specify the form (CAR 'seat), LISP returns an error message because the single quote signals that we are treating seat as an atom and the procedure CAR requires a list in order to execute. The conclusion is that if the single quote is specified, a list must follow for procedures requiring lists. If the list is represented by an identifier, the single quote must be left out so that LISP will evaluate the identifier, thus producing the list to be presented to the procedure, in this case, CAR.

Defining functions

We now know enough about LISP to define our own function, FIRSTSEAT. We specify the following:

```
(DEFUN FIRSTSEAT (lst) (CAR lst))
```

The function definition is a list whose first element is DEFUN, a primitive that is followed by the name of the function we are defining, FIRSTSEAT. The list following FIRSTSEAT constitutes the defined function's parameter list. In this case there is only one parameter, lst, and it appears elsewhere in the definition. Later when the defined procedure is specified for evaluation by LISP, an argument will be provided that will determine the value of the respective parameters that appeared in the definition. The list (CAR lst) specifies the body of the procedure—what is to be performed. The primitive, DEFUN, is not a function since it has the side effect of producing a function definition that will persist after LISP has processed the list containing it.

Because of our earlier SETQ the LISP interpreter knows that seat is an identifier that represents the list (rocker stool bench). Consequently, when we specify:

```
(FIRSTSEAT seat)
```

rocker will be returned.

Effectively, we have defined a function that renames the primitive, CAR, with a more meaningful name. The importance of this exercise is that we see that we may define functions in LISP that incorporate primitives or other defined procedures in their definitions. This ability to build functions using already defined procedures is called procedure abstraction. It allows the programmer to rise above the detail level, thus enabling programming at an extremely high level.

Building a list

Now that we have discovered how LISP takes lists apart using CAR and CDR and we have learned how to define our own functions, let us take a look at one primitive used by LISP to build a list, CONS (for construct). CONS places a new first element on a specified list:

```
(CONS 'a ' (b c d))
```

returns (a b c d).

Here we find the single quote being used twice in order to prohibit LISP from attempting to evaluate. The first quote establishes that a is an atom and not an identifier while the second quote specifies that (b c d) is a list, thus prohibiting LISP from attempting to evaluate b as a procedure (recall that LISP expects the first element of any list to be a proce-

dure name and that LISP evaluates from the innermost elements out).
Were we to specify:

```
(CONS 'chair seat)
```

we would receive (chair rocker stool bench). Why? Our earlier SETQ
made seat an identifier. LISP would evaluate seat and produce the list
(rocker stool bench) and, finding that chair is specified as an atom, it
would place chair as the first element of the list.

LISP predicates used with COND and AND

We will discuss three of LISP's predicates, ATOM, NUMBERP, and
GREATERP. A predicate in LISP is a primitive that returns true or
false. True is represented by T and false is represented by NIL. Were
we to specify:

```
(ATOM 6)
```

LISP would return T because 6 is a numeric atom. Similarly, if we
were to specify:

```
(ATOM go)
```

LISP would return NIL. Because go is not quoted, it is not an atom.
ATOM insists upon finding an atom as its argument. If we specify:

```
(ATOM 'go)
```

LISP would return T because, with the quote, go is an atom and LISP
returns true, T.
Finally, if we specify:

```
(ATOM 'go) 'ok
```

LISP will return ok because it has found go to be an atom because of
the occurrence of the quote and has thus returned T. The return of T
allows LISP to evaluate and return the value of 'ok which is the atom
ok. When ATOM produces a return of T, it is as if 'ok has simply been
specified to LISP—evaluation takes place immediately following the
return of T. It is almost as if we stated "If go is an atom, then evaluate
'ok."
In a similar fashion (NUMBERP 6) will return T because 6 is, indeed, a number. GREATERP requires two numbers. If the first is
greater than the second, T is returned; otherwise NIL is returned.
Hence (GREATERP 9 4) will return T.
When we use COND (the conditional form) with predicates as follows:

```
(COND ( (NUMBERP seat)  (SETQ x ' (seat is a number) ) )
      ( (GREATERP 6 4)  (SETQ y ' (6 is greater than 4) ) ) ) )
```

each predicate form is said to be part of a "conditional clause." Here there are two conditional clauses. Each clause's predicate form is evaluated until a nonNIL is returned; then that clause's remaining forms are evaluated to produce side effects, with the final form being returned as the value of the whole conditional form.

We might trace the action of LISP in evaluating the conditional clauses. First, (NUMBERP seat) is evaluated with NIL returned because our earlier SETQ established seat as a list. Consequently, that clause's SETQ will not execute. Next, (GREATERP 6 4) is evaluated with the return of T since 6 is truly greater than 4. Because a nonNIL has been returned, the side effect (SETQ y '(6 is greater than 4)) executes, assigning the value (6 is greater than 4) to the identifier atom, y. Because this is the final form, its value is returned as the value of the entire conditional and LISP returns:

```
(6 is greater than 4)
```

Here we see that COND's clause tests are evaluated by LISP, one after the other, until a T is returned, whereupon that clause's remaining forms are evaluated with the value of the final form of the successful clause returned as the value of the conditional.

Suppose we wished to have two or more tests for each clause. We would then use AND, a logical operator, as follows:

```
(COND ((AND (NUMBERP seat) (GREATERP 6 4)) 'ok)
      (T (SETQ x '(the first clause failed)) 'better))
```

and LISP would return (the placement of parentheses determines the forms):

```
better
```

because when AND is used in a conditional clause, all test forms in that clause must return nonNIL in order for the final form to be evaluated. By specifying T in the last conditional clause we have forced a nonNIL because T is, by definition, nonNIL. Hence the SETQ form assigns to x the value (the first clause failed), and the final form, 'better, is evaluated, thus producing the returned value shown above.

The appliance minisystem in LISP

We have reviewed CAR and CDR, the LISP primitives. We have seen that we may define our own functions using DEFUN, we have become acquainted with CONS for building lists, and we have seen some of LISP's predicates, ATOM, NUMBERP, and GREATERP. Finally, we have seen how COND is used with predicates and with AND, another special form used as a logical operator. Now we are ready to consider the development of an appliance minisystem in LISP similar to that presented in our review of Prolog.

We begin by establishing a value for the identifier, appliance:

```
(SETQ appliance '(stove 210 mixer 2 refrigerator 310))
```

We have used an abbreviated list in order to conserve space—not all of the appliances are being used here.

We now define our function to identify the major appliances:

```
(DEFUN major (list)
    (COND ((AND (NUMBERP list) (GREATERP list 100)) 'yes)
          ((ATOM list) list)
          (T (CONS (MAJOR (CAR list))
                   (MAJOR (CDR list)))))))
```

When this function is called using the argument, appliance:

```
(MAJOR appliance)
```

LISP returns:

```
(stove yes mixer 2 refrigerator yes)
```

indicating that stove and refrigerator are both major appliances.

Let us see how this happens. The defined function's condition clauses return NIL because appliance is a list and is established as the value of the defined function's parameter when it appears as an argument of MAJOR, when the function is called as it is in (MAJOR appliance). Neither of the first condition clause's number tests will succeed when a list or a nonnumber is presented. The ATOM predicate in the second condition clause also returns NIL because it expects an atom, not a list. However, the T form forces the construction of a new list by CONS. The new list's elements are supplied by recursive calls to MAJOR, first with a parameter value that is an atom, the CAR of the appliance list, stove, and then with a parameter value that is a list, the CDR of the appliance list.

Upon the first recursion, the number tests fail because stove is not a number, but the ATOM clause succeeds and returns the atom, stove, which is saved in memory as a first element of the new list. Because the ATOM clause returned nonNIL, the T form is prohibited from functioning—as soon as one condition clause succeeds, COND ceases.

The second recursion now calls MAJOR with the CDR of appliance as its parameter value. Again the number tests fail as does the ATOM clause, but the T form results in another CONS being executed, thus placing the result of the next CAR recursion at the front of the result of the following CDR recursion. Again and again, the list is reduced to an atom by the CAR recursion and to a remaining list by the CDR recursion with CONS building the new list.

When numbers are encountered during the recursions, the number tests will all succeed only when the number is greater than 100, indicating a major appliance. When yes is returned by the condition clause, it is placed in the new list. Because COND ceases, the number is omitted from the list.

Proof that a new list has been created and returned by this function is readily available when we enter:

```
appliance
```

LISP evaluates appliance and returns the original list displaying the weights. No yes atoms are in the list.

LISP in summary

We have made no attempt to teach LISP. We have introduced but a sampling of the primitives available in LISP. We have not touched upon the way in which lists are managed in memory nor have we discussed LISP's handling of files. Although LISP compilers are available, we have not introduced them because this would involve discussing the benefit of one LISP version or dialect versus another. In fact, many of the examples we have presented could have been handled differently had our ultimate goal not been to demonstrate our familiar minisystem using recursion.

LISP has developed into an extremely powerful language over the years of its use in AI. Numerous myths have developed regarding LISP's capabilities and memory requirements. Virtually nothing negative that has been said about LISP in the trade press or in critical articles can be truly verified because the language is a moving target. Development continues and there is little reason to believe that it will soon cease.

It is said that Japan's adoption of Prolog has resulted in numerous modifications that have produced a LISP-like Prolog in order to meet the requirements of that country's Fifth Generation Project. Whether this is fact or rumor is difficult to determine. The fact of major importance to the data processor is that both LISP and Prolog have areas of application for which each is best suited. Despite the advocacy of the partisans, the data processor is best served by an open mind and an attitude that seeks out profit. As we shall see, there is no universal tool that may be deemed best for all expert systems. The nature of the problem determines the tool.

Other Expert System Languages

Most, if not all, AI languages were developed for use in conjunction with dedicated hardware that could provide enormous amounts of memory and very fast processing. LIPS (logical inferences per second) became the measure of these environments just as MIPS (millions of instructions per second) became the measuring rod in data processing. AI languages were developed as tools to further AI research in the academic world. In the grand scheme of things there was no basic effort to develop AI results that could be later merged with the data processing effort.

With the advent of commercially useful expert systems numerous successful efforts have been launched to produce LISP and Prolog interpreters and compilers for use in the PC and major mainframe environments. As would be expected, other less widely used AI languages have also been ported to traditional data processing computers while simultaneously special purpose computing equipment is also available to the data processor interested in developing expert systems well suited to special stand-alone applications. We have, then, languages that are restricted to special computers and languages that may be used in expert system development on mainframes and PCs.

We may go a step further and mention that numerous expert systems have been written in one or another AI language in order to take advantage of the interactive capabilities of such a language and then translated to another language such as C or Pascal for the creation of a final delivery system. This has given rise to the often-heard distinction that is made between the development system and the delivery or run-time system.

As we have learned, the expert system development environment is characterized by prototyping. The main thrust is to create a system and work with it until it performs as the expert does. The final delivered system may be written in any of a number of languages, but it is the development environment that is important—without the flexibility that only AI languages provide, expert system development is extremely difficult if not impossible.

A rather large number of languages have been developed, each with its own strengths. Not surprisingly, most of these languages have been implemented in LISP or Prolog. A later chapter will identify resource material, permitting the interested data processor to inquire further.

6

Expert System Shells

We began our familiarization with expert systems by reviewing systems currently in use. We learned that an expert system consists of a knowledge base, an inference engine, and a user interface. We became familiar with the practicalities of the data processor's environment as it relates to finding suitable expert system applications. We saw how the quantified benefits might be made known to management in order to gain sponsorship.

Later, we discussed the expert's role and we examined the elements that characterize both the domain expert and the expert system expert (the knowledge engineer). We then reviewed some popular modes of knowledge representation. In the process, we became familiar with forward and backward chaining, property inheritance, frames, and predicate logic. Most recently we were introduced to the major languages employed in expert system development and there we encountered the incorporation of facts in the knowledge base.

The ability of expert systems to compute when confronted with uncertainty was alluded to in Chapter 1, in which uncertainty in expert knowledge was contrasted with the data processing requirement that only exact entities be addressed in data system design. There we noted that the expert system must be capable of computing with less than exact information.

Because this feature is a built-in capability of the expert system shells we shall review in this chapter, we will benefit from a further explanation of inexactness as it relates to the expert system.

Measures of Confidence

The kind of inexactness with which we are most familiar is that afforded by probability theory that we encounter each time we enter into a game of chance. We reason with probability according to some well-defined algorithms. The probability that a fair coin will land heads up upon being flipped is 0.50. Consequently, the probability that the coin will land tails up is also 0.50. The probability that one or the other event will occur is 1, the sum of the events' probabilities. Such is not always the case.

If we are dealing with facts and rules whose exactness lends them this kind of calculation potential, we might employ probability theory in order to determine the confidence we may associate with conclusions. Unfortunately, the preponderance of expert systems deal with rules that state that one thing will happen if some other thing occurs. The expert may not be totally confident of the rule's conclusion and there may be less than complete confidence in the available facts.

When standard probability theory will not satisfy the requirements of determining the degree of confidence we may place in an expert system's conclusions, bayesian (conditional) probability is often employed. Bayesian probability allows us to calculate the probability that may be associated with the occurrence of an event when a predecessor event's occurrence may be established. A conditional probability factor is assigned to each event, thus allowing the application of a bayesian algorithm in order to compute the probability of the conclusion.

More recently, there has developed a theory of "fuzzy logic" that addresses the concept of partial set membership—degrees of belongingness. The facts of a knowledge base may involve imprecise predicates such as heavy or rare or valuable, imputing membership in the set of heavy, rare, or valuable elements to an item. We then proceed to draw inferences about these items based upon the rules in the knowledge base. The rules themselves are usually not absolute and therefore may be associated with a degree of veracity. Fuzzy logic provides algorithms that allow us to compute a confidence value for the conclusions derived using these rules. A confidence factor (CF) is associated with the facts as well as the rules.

Let us suppose the following knowledge base facts with the expert's CFs:

(Kryptonite is rare) CF = 0.9
(Kryptonite is valuable) CF = 0.5

We also have a rule in our knowledge base that our expert has explained has a confidence factor of 0.6. Hence:

Rule 1: CF = 0.6
Z is a military resource
IF Z is rare
AND Z is valuable

We have two knowledge base facts that are less than certain and we have a rule which will obviously prove, but the rule is less than certain also. We are in need of a computation method that will allow us to determine the CF of the conclusion that will be drawn.

The method afforded by fuzzy logic in expert system design combines confidence factors. Because the premise of the knowledge base rule involves AND, a conjunction, the confidence value of the premises is the value of the lesser CF of the individual supporting facts, (kryptonite is valuable) CF = 0.5. The CF of the conclusion is the product of the rule's CF, (0.6), and the premises CF, (0.5), or 0.6(0.5) = 0.30. Thus, we have a CF of 0.30 that kryptonite is a military resource.

Now let us consider the rule whose premises are related by OR, a disjunction, rather than AND. If we replace AND in the rule above by OR, the computation method requires that we choose the greater of the CF values of the supporting facts, (kryptonite is rare) CF = 0.9, and multiply by the rule's CF, (0.6). This would result in 0.6(0.9) = 0.54 or a CF of 0.54 for the conclusion that kryptonite is a military resource.

Hence when premises are in conjunction (AND), the lesser of their CF values is the CF value of the premises. The CF value of the conclusion is the product of the CF value of the premises and the CF value of the rule. When supporting facts are in disjunction (OR), the greater of their CF values is the CF value of the premises. The CF value of the conclusion is the product of the CF value of the premises and the CF value of the rule. In this context AND and OR are called "Zadeh's fuzzy operators," after fuzzy logic's pioneer.

Clearly, in the trivial case of a single supporting fact in the premise, the CF value of the conclusion is simply the product of the two CF values—the CF value of the single fact and the CF of the rule.

Finally, let us consider the case of multiple rules supporting the same conclusion in order to see how confidence factors combine to establish the CF of that conclusion. Consider the following:

(Kryptonite is rare) CF = 0.9
(Kryptonite is valuable) CF = 0.5
(Kryptonite is ductile) CF = 0.4
(Kryptonite is light) CF = 0.7

Rule 1: CF = 0.6
Z is a military resource
IF Z is rare
AND Z is valuable

Rule 2: CF = 0.8
Z is a military resource
IF Z is ductile
OR Z is light

We begin by finding the CF of the conclusion in Rule 1, the product of the lesser CF of the supporting facts and the CF of the rule: 0.5(0.6), or 0.30, the computation method when AND appears in the premises. We then find the CF of the conclusion in Rule 2, the product of the greater CF of the supporting facts and that rule's CF: 0.7(0.8), or 0.56, the computation method when OR appears in the premises. Finally, we combine the confidence factors we have calculated for the conclusion by taking the difference of their sum and product as follows: 0.30 + 0.56 − (0.30(0.56)) = 0.86 − 0.17 = 0.69. If more than two rules are in support of the same conclusion, say, n, we simply compute the conclusion's CF for each of the n rules and then find the difference of their sum and product.

Generally, it must be expected that the expert is unaware of confidence factors as such. The expert often mentions that his or her methods are based upon experience and that experience has demonstrated that, say, 8 times out of 10 (0.8) such and such a conclusion may be drawn. It is the KE's task to determine the best method for dealing with this uncertainty. As we shall see, expert system shells often offer options that afford simple true-false or 1 to 10 or 1 to 100 or −100 to 100 scales of confidence as well as the more sophisticated bayesian and/or fuzzy logic algorithms. Undoubtedly, if the KE is building an expert system using a programming language such as LISP or Prolog, appropriate implementation techniques must be employed to facilitate the chosen confidence factor calculations.

While the foregoing is an explanation of the major methods of arriving at the measure of confidence we may assign to our conclusions, we have not addressed probability theory, bayesian conditional probability, or fuzzy logic per se. As the data processor has already recognized, expert system technology is the result of a multidisciplinary effort that presumes considerable depth in logic, mathematics, linguistics, and computer science. A truly adequate treatment of the many facets of expert system technology could well fill a small library. Our objective is the profitable application of this technology, and therefore the data processor is referred to the resources identified in later portions of this book to satisfy desires for more in-depth understanding of one or another topic.

What Is an Expert System Shell?

As we have seen, the prospect of creating a first expert system from scratch could be quite daunting, so much so that quite probably only those organizations capable of expending considerable sums would be eligible to reap the benefits. Artificial intelligence researchers were among the first to fully appreciate this fact, and so they developed systems (collections of programs) that bridge the educational and skill gap. Today, expert system development systems abound in the marketplace. These systems do not totally absolve the user of the need for an understanding of expert system concepts, but they reduce the depth of necessary AI knowledge and thus bring the application of expert system technology within the reach of the smallest data processing department.

Typically, an expert system shell consists of manuals and software. The manuals include a tutorial to be used in conjunction with tutorial programming—expert system development demonstrations which step the user through the development protocols that are available in the development modules of the shell. Depending upon the shell's capabilities, the user is introduced to backward and/or forward chaining, the use of confidence factors, and the format of the rules and facts as they are supported in the system. After completing the tutorial, the user is usually encouraged to experiment with any of a number of the sample expert systems that are included in the examples in order to become more confident of their application.

Ultimately, the user is faced with the challenge of creating a first expert system—a task that proves to be overpowering more often than not. Two factors contribute to failure: The user's acquisition of a first expert system shell without sufficient prior knowledge to determine whether or not the shell will satisfy a later need and the inability of the associated tutorial to comprehensively convey the necessary intuitive grasp of the radically new environment imposed upon the first-time expert system developer.

If the student manages to become sufficiently acquainted with the shell to mimic one or another of the supplied expert systems, he or she is usually at a loss to conceive of a possible application within the range of reason. Most programmers are accustomed to fabricating fairly substantial programs and their first attempts at an expert system are often too ambitious to permit a successful experience. Clearly, many expert system shells are purchased only to gather dust after initial demoralizing experiences result in fading interest.

Undoubtedly, such experiences have prompted articles in the trade press that have often relegated expert system shells to the role of "hackers' toys," claiming that expert system technology will flourish in data processing only when the proper mainframe software is available.

Much to the contrary, the necessary software is available. Many of the expert systems currently in use have been developed using shells in both PC and mainframe environments. The missing element, more often than not, is a comprehensive program to address the education problem. No one is more aware of the need for hands-on experience in acquiring skill and understanding than the data processor.

While a number of hands-on seminars are available to those able to sustain the required travel and associated expense, there are also a number of expert system shells whose goal is teaching in a hands-on mode using the PC. Their costs are much less than half those associated with the seminar approach, and their acquisition affords a training vehicle that may satisfy the needs of a number of students of expert system development.

Expert System Shells that Teach

The authors have had hands-on exposure to all of the materials reviewed in this chapter. The omission of one or another popular product does not imply its inferiority but rather our own inability to schedule additional reviews consistent with publishing deadlines. We have made every attempt to select leading products that are representative of the facilities available.

Experteach

Available from IntelligenceWare, Incorporated, of Los Angeles, California, Experteach consists of a 2-inch-thick manual along with six disks for use with IBM PCs or compatibles. All of this may seem overpowering, but the material is presented in a straightforward fashion that provides the user with a step-by-step introduction to expert systems beginning with general background information on AI and continuing through explanations of the knowledge base, methods of inference, logic, fuzzy logic, and the building of an expert system. Case studies introduce the user to a number of sample expert systems.

Associated with the tutorial segment of the manual is an on-line tutor that is referenced in a coordinated way to reinforce the material presented in the manual. As a final feature, the on-line tutor provides a visible inference engine, allowing the user to view the step-by-step action of an inference engine as it processes the knowledge base.

Following the tutorial portion of this package is an assortment of sample expert systems that may be executed using the PC. An editor is supplied that allows the user to print or view the fact base, rule base, and the hypotheses involved in these sample systems. A bibliography is provided for the user who is interested in further explanation of expert system development.

Further, expert system shells are provided in Pascal, LISP, and Prolog. For each language there are expert system shells for backward and forward chaining. The Pascal shells execute from compiled Pascal while the LISP and Prolog shells are supported by LISP and Prolog interpreters that are included with the package. Finally, each of the interpreters is accompanied by complete documentation enabling the student user to become acquainted with these languages. While Experteach is an educational tool, either of the language interpreters may be used in the development of serious applications. Thus, nearly the full gamut of expert system technology is made available within the confines of a single educational vehicle.

For the user seeking a thorough textbook approach to LISP that can be adapted to the LISP interpreter, *LISPcraft* by Robert Wilensky (W. W. Norton & Company, New York) and *LISP* by Patrick Henry Winston and Berthold Klaus Paul Horn (Addison-Wesley, Reading, Massachusetts) should both be obtained for a detailed treatment of the language.

Active Prolog Tutor (APT)

The user of Experteach who is interested in an inexpensive educational hand-holding experience while learning Prolog can benefit in a major way from using the Active Prolog Tutor supplied by Solution Systems of Norwell, Massachusetts. APT contains its own built-in Prolog interpreter that allows the student to toggle from the screen tutorial to the interpreter at will. The student is permitted visually to observe the activities involved in such Prolog behaviors as recursion through the use of a trace that is under the full control of the user when toggled to the interpreter. The tutor painstakingly covers Prolog features, including natural language concepts.

APT coaches the user through the building of a game in Prolog that sees the language exercised through repeated encounters with the interpreter. The user is coached through the building of two expert systems as well. On the whole, APT allows a level of hands-on educational development that the otherwise unassisted student of Prolog might not achieve without a considerable expenditure of time and effort.

APT employs a modified version of the Arity/Prolog interpreter. Perhaps surprising to the user will be the explanation that the entire tutor was programmed using Arity/Prolog. Further mention of Arity Corporation's offerings will be encountered later in this chapter.

The data processor interested in developing an in-house expert system capability or in preparing for an encounter with AI consultants will do well to consider the acquisition of educational materials such as those cited above. At this juncture in the development of expert system technology, the preponderance of commercial effort has been focused upon the development and sale of expert system shells themselves with the attendant need for education satisfied, it is hoped, by the shell-related tutorials provided by the vendor. In most cases shell-related tutorials are excellent vehicles for conveying the capabilities of the particular shell, but little effort in their design is dedicated to providing an appreciation of the general field of expert system development. Without this broader view, the data processor is often poorly equipped, in a hands-on way, to intelligently choose an appropriate shell for an intended application or to evaluate recommendations made by a consultant.

Expert System Shells that Generate Expert Systems

The expert system shells of only 2 or 3 years ago pale when compared with the current versions. Along with a continuing improvement in shell capability, numerous additional products have entered the marketplace so that the data processor is today faced with a bewildering assortment of types, prices, and claims. One might be inclined to believe that there is a panacea or best general solution to the problem of creating an expert system—the mastery of one or another AI language or the obtaining of that *key* expert system shell. Unfortunately such is not the case even though most shells are flexible and will address a subset of expert system problems. We defer tool selection to the following chapter.

Exsys

Provided by EXSYS, Incorporated of Albuquerque, New Mexico, Exsys is a rule-based product that includes a menu-driven editor for use in creating a knowledge base and two utility programs, Shrink and Faster, for optimizing finished systems. A run-time program is provided for execution of the completed expert system.

Exsys is written in C in order to provide both faster execution and a lower memory requirement than would be afforded in a PC-based expert system shell written in either LISP or Prolog. That Exsys is aimed at the data processing professional is clear—Exsys has been ported to the DEC VAX and a number of Japanese computers including the NEC-9801 and the Hitachi 2020 supporting kanji characters. An IBM mainframe version is underway.

Typically, the KE executes the editor program whereupon he or she is requested to enter the name of the expert system being created. Following this is an opportunity to provide the expert system's title and the author's name. These items will appear formatted as a title screen when the completed system is executed.

The next screen addresses the need to choose the type of certainty factor (CF) calculation to be used in the system. The user may choose any of three modes: 0, 1; a boolean yes-no mode, a standard probability mode using 0 to 10 with 0 locking a condition as completely without certainty and 10 locking it as completely certain with the intervening values treated as standard probabilities; or the third, a probabilistic calculation scheme that allows values between −100 and 100. Most beginning KE's will choose the 1 to 10 mode. Associated with the CF calculation is a request to provide a threshold for solution display that sees only solutions whose CFs exceed it being displayed to the user.

After choosing the CF mode, the KE is given the option of having all rules applied in deriving data or stopping after the first successful rule is encountered. It is wise to take the "all rules" option since this may be changed later after the system has been verified. The KE is then asked if an external program is to be executed at the start of the expert system's run—external programs may be invoked from numerous points within an Exsys expert system in order to read monitoring devices, consult a database, or interact with a user. The editor then presents the KE with a blank screen for describing the intent of the expert system to its run-time user. This is followed by another screen to present the user with a summary explanation immediately prior to displaying the expert system's findings. Finally, the KE is given the option of displaying the rules to the user as they are run. The user is free to override this option and therefore the KE will most often decline the rule display.

At this point the first knowledge base screen is presented, allowing the KE to enter the choices among which the expert system must decide. For instance, if a knowledge base is to be created to assist in the determination of an equipment malfunction, the solution choices might be:

1 Drive gear tooth broken
2 Housing bushing cracked

and so on.

Finally, the editor's main menu is presented to the KE, allowing the entry, editing, move, save, or running of the knowledge base rules. The KE will begin by entering a qualifier (continuing our equipment example):

The crank shaft is

Beneath the qualifier the KE then lists the trouble-related conditions:

1 noisy
2 vibrating
3 locked

The qualifier, with one of the trouble-related conditions, now becomes the first rule's If part (let us assume the KE chose condition 1, noisy):

IF the crank shaft is noisy
THEN

The KE may now recall the list of malfunction choices entered earlier and might now specify 1, indicating "gear tooth broken" as the Then part of the rule under construction. The editor now asks for the CF of this conclusion and the KE enters a value consistent with the calculation method chosen earlier. The KE may continue entering conclusions from the malfunction list, assigning each a CF so that when the rule fires and its conclusions are subsequently employed, the CFs will be considered. Because Exsys supports If/Then/Else rules, the KE is given the option of specifying an Else part.

The KE is now invited, by the editor, to provide an explanatory note for the user's perusal if "Why" is asked when the running system asks for the crank shaft symptom. The KE may include references to support this note.

Upon completion of each rule's entry, the completed rule with accompanying notes is displayed for the KE's review and acceptance into the knowledge base. And so the cycle repeats, thus populating the knowledge base with If-Then and If-Then-Else rules.

Exsys supports the arithmetic operations of multiplication, division, addition, subtraction, and the modulus operation as well as exp, log, abs, sqrt, and int—the log and exponential functions are in base e. The trigonometric functions sin, cos, tan, asin, acos, and atan are supported where the angles are stated in radians. Thus, the expert system may address engineering problems.

The features described above do not completely define this system's capabilities, but they do illustrate the manner in which an expert system may be generated using Exsys. Exsys interfaces with programs written in other languages and features file and report-generating capabilities. Both forward and backward chaining are supported, as is "blackboarding"—a feature of expert systems not mentioned thus far. Blackboarding allows more than one knowledge base to share a common set of information. Thus, extremely complex systems may be executed using a relatively small PC.

A number of successful commercial expert systems have been created using this shell such as the Canadian Pacific Diesel Lube Expert which is installed in the Canadian Pacific Rail laboratories at Montreal and Vancouver in preparation for distribution to other sites across Canada.

1st-Class

Programs in Motion, Incorporated, of Wayland, Massachussets, markets 1st-Class, an expert system shell that makes preponderant use of

Iterative Dichotomizer 3 (ID3), an induction algorithm introduced in 1979. This algorithm builds a decision tree from numerous solution examples provided by a human expert. By way of illustration, we might suppose that the domain expert is a quality control inspector examining manufactured subassemblies that may be forwarded to any of a number of final product assemblies or to rework centers, all depending upon the degree of departure each subassembly is found to display from standard specifications.

When interviewed, the expert would explain the professional decision-making process in terms of a given subassembly's variance from the standard specification, suitability for inclusion in a specific product, and the inventory urgencies at that product's point of final assembly—the location to which the subassembly may be sent. He or she would express all of these conditions by way of examples. After collecting a large number of examples, without 1st-Class, the KE's next task would be to place the examples in classifications, thus building a decision tree each of whose branches would terminate in a disposition for the described subassembly with its associated conditions.

1st-Class, using the ID3 algorithm, almost instantly processes the examples to effect the classification and produces an optimized decision tree with accuracy and speed beyond that of a KE. It is this rapid classification and decision-tree building from which 1st-Class (classify first) derives its name. Redundant examples are omitted and noncontributing factors are uncovered and ignored by the optimizing process. Thus, the most important questions will be asked of the expert system's user first, reducing to a minimum the number of questions that must be answered when the end user consults the system.

The entire process of entering examples and creating the decision tree is menu driven. In all, six menus guide the KE through the development of the expert system. Provided are a screen for creating a knowledge base file and a definitions screen for defining the knowledge base—here the possible results of the knowledge base's consultation are entered along with the factors that determine the decision process such as "variance" or "distance," and the associated values assigned to each factor. The definition screen provides entry to a text editor, allowing the KE to supply preface, advice, and question text, or this may be left to 1st-Class. The third, example screen, provides the KE with a spreadsheet format for entering the expert's examples which may be assigned a CF between 0 and 100 from which a number of CF statistics are provided. The fourth screen addresses the method to be used in creating the rule or decision tree.

1st-Class provides the KE with four tree-building method options: the ID3 algorithm described earlier, a left-right method that builds a tree but does not use the full capabilities of the ID3 algorithm in that the tree is built taking the examples as they are presented in the examples screen, a customize method that allows the KE to build a decision tree without examples as would be the case when a repair manual's provided decision tree is used, and a match method that simply matches the user's responses against the examples. This last method is useful when the resultant decision tree would be extremely large—the exponential explosion so familiar to the data processor who has experience with decision tables.

The fifth, a rule screen, allows the KE to inspect the rule that has been created in order to review the resultant logic structure. Finally, the advisor screen permits the KE to test the expert system by entering responses and, if desired, trace back through the system to determine precisely what example has sponsored the system's advice.

Each decision tree represents one rule and so 1st-Class is not a rule-based expert system generator in the classic sense although any number of decision trees (rules) may be chained together in order to create a multirule system. The methods of chaining rules together are referred to as backward chaining and forward chaining, but these terms are not to be taken in the classic sense in that each tree (rule) constitutes a separate knowledge base file.

1st-Class is a PC-based expert system generator that affords an interface to the PC's DOS operating system and may be employed in conjunction with external programs on the PC. Mathematical functions are not supported. Generally, 1st-Class is an ideal vehicle for dealing with small- to medium-size example-based expert system applications whose development would be more time consuming if attempted using a rule-based generator. That 1st-Class is a serious tool is demonstrated at E. I. DuPont Company, Incorporated, where a site license has been obtained for that company's unlimited use of this tool.

Arity/Expert Development Package (Arity/Expert)

Because Arity Corporation of Concord, Massachusetts, is a popular supplier of Prolog interpreters and compilers, it is not surprising to see an expert system shell bearing the Arity name. This development package is integrated with the Prolog language, thus offering the KE the option of relying entirely upon the shell's development facilities, or Prolog goals may be called from the expert system rule base. All of Prolog's mathematical predicates are built into Arity/Expert and so the resultant expert system may be compiled as a stand-alone system or integrated with another Prolog program. While a knowledge of

Prolog is not required, it provides a considerable benefit in the creation of an expert system using this package.

Arity/Expert's components may be viewed as five related entities: the knowledge base, the explanation facility, control information, expert system predicates, and the inference engine.

The knowledge base contains "concepts" that comprehend a class of objects taken as a whole and rules that describe the interrelationships of the knowledge contained in the system. For instance, "automobile" is a concept describing an object that travels from point to point on wheels, propelled by an engine, and carrying people. The knowledge base stores concepts using a taxonomy of frames for classifying the concepts. These reside in the taxonomy file which is created using a relatively simple taxonomy language. The taxonomy file's contents declare the "type" of a given "property" or "role" that appears in a concept's definition. The concept definition acts as a frame whose slots store the qualities of the concept. Thus, the definition of automobile may be rendered in terms of slot identifiers such as ignition system, distributor, problem source, and recommended repair. In turn, each of the concepts, such as distributor, is defined, thus introducing additional concepts that are further defined in other concept-specific definitions. The rule file is created using a rule language.

The explanation facility enables the KE to supply English-language explanations that the system's user will view upon asking such questions as "Why?" The third component, control information, permits the KE to control the many facets of the system's performance—disallowing user's questions or altering the order in which values are calculated. Through the use of control information the KE is able to customize questions that the expert system may ask upon not being able to determine the value of a property. The system would ask its question using the elements in the knowledge base such as "What is the voltage_level of line 1?" The KE may alter this question to a more understandable "What is the voltage of distributor cable no. 1?" Other control options address the method of CF calculation, allowing the use of fuzzy logic, probability, or a standard method somewhat similar to fuzzy logic's. Control information resides in the rule file.

Arity/Expert provides three predicate types: development for use during the development of the expert system, primary for use during the running and testing of the expert system, and secondary for special purposes such as the asking of particular questions of the user during execution. Because system development is carried on under an interpreter with the option that the completed system may be also executed under the interpreter or compiled to execute in stand-alone fashion, both the development and primary predicates are built-in features of the interpreter. The secondary predicates must be imported to the interpreter. Little needs to be said about the inference engine in that, because of its Prolog support, it features the backward chaining for which Prolog is so well known.

Arity/Expert is a serious tool for the development of Prolog-based expert systems for the PC. Because it offers considerable flexibility, its requirements in understanding are somewhat greater than those of other more specifically focused shells.

Intelligence compiler

A hybrid expert system shell provided by IntelligenceWare of Los Angeles, California, Intelligence Compiler affords the KE a multiple paradigm tool that features rule-based (forward and backward chaining), logic-based (backtracking), frame-based, and traditional programming capabilities. A tutorial is provided that takes the user through the fundamentals of expert systems as well as through the multiple features of the shell. All of this is done using animated graphics where applicable and concluding with interactive sessions involving visible inference engines that visually illustrate the proving of various sample goals.

Intelligence Compiler provides the KE with an edit screen that allows the building of a named expert system. Backward chaining rules are placed in files ending with .bwd extensions on the PC, and forward chaining rules are placed in files ending with .fwd extensions. Files having extensions .fbs contain the knowledge base's fact base. Frames reside in files ending with the .frm extension. A file bearing the expert system's name and ending in a .top extension contains the top level goals that initiate the inference process after compilation.

Rules may be stated as backward chaining, forward chaining, or inexact. Both the forward and backward chaining rules make use of two-valued logic (0 is false, 1 is true) while inexact rules are assigned a CF value between 0 and 100 and are calculated using fuzzy logic algorithms—inexact rules reside in files with .inx extensions. Through the use of "select-best-of," a built-in predicate, semiexact reasoning is supported when the inference engine finds an optimal CF.

An expert system's multiple files are stored in a dedicated subdirectory on the PC. During execution, the different rule files are processed by the appropriate but separate integrated inference engines that are provided for inference using the forward, backward, and inexact rules while allowing common access to the fact base and frame files. Using built-in predicates, forward chaining rules may be called from backward chaining rules and vice versa; in addition, PC files may be opened, read, written, and closed during expert system execution.

Typically, the KE creates an expert system by establishing a dedicated subdirectory, making it the current subdirectory, and then calling the Intelligence Compiler's editor. The editor, via pull-down menus, prompts the KE through the process of naming the knowledge base and identifying the files to be built. At the KE's option both syntax and spell checking facilities may be invoked during the entry of facts or rules. During the entry of frames, a frame template is presented by the editor. The KE may employ a facility called the Masterscope which maintains a cross-reference of predicate and frame names along with a pointer to the locations in which they are defined, thus allowing the KE to view, via windowing, rule and frame definitions in other files.

Upon the completion of file building, the KE may call the compiler directly from the editor in order to compile the newly created expert system. At the compiler's termination, among the options the KE is given are the options of running the expert system, with or without tracing the execution steps taken by the inference engine with optional modification of the speed with which the execution will proceed, returning to the editor or returning to DOS.

If the KE chooses, the expert system may be compiled as a stand-alone program by calling the compiler from DOS with the stand-alone specification while in the expert system's dedicated subdirectory. The KE is then given the opportunity to provide the name which, when entered later by the user, following the DOS prompt, will result in the execution of the compiled expert system. This name is actually the name of a .bat file that is created by the compiler when invoked to compile the stand-alone system.

Intelligence Compiler supports the four basic arithmetic operations as well as sqr, sqrt, and the trigonometric functions of sin, cos, and tan, whose arguments are expressed in radians.

An ample supply of sample expert systems is provided with the software, thus allowing the KE to become acquainted with Intelligence Compiler by reviewing, modifying, and compiling progressively more complex systems that incorporate the full range of the shell's capabilities.

That Intelligence Compiler is an expert system shell of considerable flexibility and power has been demonstrated in the creation of an expert system for automatic fault tree generation for the emergency feed-water system at the Seabrook nuclear power plant in Seabrook, New Hampshire.

Mainframe-Based Expert System Shells

Our review has thus far concentrated upon those shells that originated as PC-based expert system generators. Although some have been ported to larger environments, none of the shells we have reviewed involves an investment greater than $1,000.00 when undertaken as a PC-based effort. The additional complexity involved in producing a mainframe-based expert system shell results in a quantum leap in expense resulting from the additional costs associated with interface programming that allows the created expert system to communicate with CICS and the mainframe's operating system.

We have also avoided discussion of dedicated workstation LISP environments offered by a number of vendors in that experience has shown that the majority of data processing professionals prefer to gain a hands-on knowledge of expert system implementation prior to making a major expense commitment. Recall that our perspective is that there must be a return on investment if this technology is to be supported by management and accepted in the data processing department. Consistent with these realities, it is certain that many data processors will want the assurance that larger undertakings will be supportable once expert system technology has become a staple in their departments. Chapter 8 addresses mainframe-based expert system shells as well as the place of the dedicated workstation environment in data processing.

How the Knowledge Engineer
Chooses Tools

A sage once wrote, "If the only tool you have is a hammer, every problem you encounter will look like a nail." This bit of wisdom antedates the development of expert systems technology, but its applicability is, nonetheless, undiminished. Those of us who have been on the computing scene since the early days of the 1401 will recall that, by and large, in those days there existed only three elements in the environment: the computer, the programmer, and the user. It was hoped that the programmer knew the one tool available—a programming language. Then, every user request looked like the same kind of nail and the programmer often had the program written, at least mentally, by the time the user's voice had faded from the room.

As time passed we found that it was best if a "systems analyst" talked to the user and then took some time to design, perhaps, a couple of programs that could be orchestrated to solve the user's problem. Still, most data processing departments were one-language shops and, whether we want to admit it or not, we were really dealing with the same kind of one-tool limitation—that programming language and the constraints accompanying it. We did, however, get beyond the immediate impulse to begin by writing a program although the systems analyst still viewed system design through glasses that had the hue of Cobol, ALC, RPG, or Fortran, depending upon the specialty of the house.

We are now addressing an environment in expert systems development that is rich in tools, so much so that the knowledge engineer is best served if the tools are ignored during the early stages of analysis. Tool selection grows out of the KE's understanding of the expert's modus operandi (MO) within the domain. For that reason this chapter will deal largely with the KE's techniques as they are applied in uncovering the expert's MO. We have already discussed the KE-expert interface; therefore, we will ignore involvement with motivational psychology while we proceed to become pragmatic behaviorists. Our objective is the application of methods that will allow us to understand the behavior of the expert and in so doing, replicate that behavior in an expert system.

Behavior

Although we often associate the word "behavior" with overt physical performance, it is really a mental activity wherein we respond to perceived conditions in our environment in such a way that, subjectively at least, the environment improves. Because much of our behavior quickly becomes habitual, we often respond to our perceptions without consciously evaluating anew the numerous options available once a satisfactory response has been developed. This is truly beneficial in the development of skill in that many of the preliminaries may become automatic, thus allowing us to deal consciously with the larger problems in our immediate environment. The seasoned truck driver unconsciously down-shifts on inclines to gain greater power in ascent and to provide braking in descent, while the novice often stalls on the way up the mountain and then pumps the brakes in a dangerous attempt to curtail speed on the way down. Most of us have witnessed these obvious displays of expertise (or the lack of it) without seriously considering the underlying learned responses. Indeed, in more complex problem-solving behavior the whole procedure may defy any attempt at a preliminary step-by-step analysis.

It is the behavior of the expert—the MO—that the KE seeks to understand. Two avenues are available: observation and interrogation. Both require that the KE employs inductive reasoning as an expedient in quickly gaining the needed knowledge of the expert's behavior. Observation often is quite time consuming since over any reasonable span it is to be expected that a relatively few of the complete set of domain problems will be manifest. Direct interrogation may (and probably will) lead to the expert's inability to verbalize the full set of unconscious responses that contribute to the decision-making process that leads to the expert's behavior.

Examples

An alternative to direct interrogation is the compilation of a set of examples of problem-solving instances provided by the expert. As an initial step it also quickly provides the KE with an opportunity to gain insight to the expert's environmental constraints—no expert operates under optimum environmental conditions. As the examples are described, the KE must be noneditorial; that is, the KE must record the examples without agreeing or disagreeing with comments relative to environmental constraints. This is important because any violation of this posture places the KE in the role of a sounding board for complaints, thus giving rise to the possibility of behavior modification. Clearly, the KE's objective is the discovery of the expert's MO, not to alter, criticize, or improve performance. The presence of a tape recorder often serves the multiple purposes of keeping the interview on target as well as preventing the interview from becoming a company gripe session, not to mention its value in later reviewing example data that might otherwise be lost in the note-taking process.

The preliminary example set should include between 10 and 15 instances of expert behavior in problem solving. Fewer examples may well not provide a basis for the appearance of a pattern while more may tax the expert and result in skipped details or waning enthusiasm. The KE must judge, based upon the available time, when to pursue the next level of investigation.

During the note-taking process, the KE has determined that a pattern has emerged or that the expert is using several processes of elimination in isolating the solution set from which the final solution is selected. The expert may be referring to some resource, perhaps memory, perhaps learned fact, that this or that item of equipment or application for credit has further implications, or the expert's behavior may show no obvious pattern because of as yet undiscovered heuristics. In any event, the KE will benefit from a step to the next level of investigation that sees several of the examples treated in greater detail.

The case study

Only two or three or as many as several of the examples may be candidates for further development into case studies after determining that they are potential sources for further divulging the expert's method of problem solving. The case study expands the example into an in-depth study of the resources employed, the decisions taken, the assumptions made, the probabilities considered, and the heuristics involved.

The KE should not expect that the expert's heuristics will, in every case, be outstanding discoveries. More often than not the heuristic is quite straightforward albeit a product of the expert's training and experience. For example, during an interview with a cardiologist one of the authors uncovered the heuristic that a patient's gall bladder surgery could be predictive of heart disease. The cardiologist pointed to the evidence that the same high-fat diet that precipitated the gall bladder problem could be an operative factor in heart disease.

It is not axiomatic that every knowledge engineering effort will involve the development of case studies; however, it is well worth the effort to avoid later disappointment and misunderstanding. The case study provides the closer look that confirms or denies the KE's perception of a characteristic pattern. The KE must be ever alert not to allow an earlier perception to color the case study. For example, the expert may consult maintenance record books or other history data during the preliminary stages of the analysis of a problem. This may lead the KE to conclude that these are sources for the ultimate decision-making processes when in reality the expert is using these sources to obtain mundane information rather than signing on to execute a terminal inquiry that would provide the same or superior information. Recall that the expert system is to embody the expert's wisdom. The expert's idiosyncrasies should not be incorporated.

The prototype expert system

The examples and case studies provide the KE with the material from which the prototype will be produced. Much to the horror of the tradition-bound professional data processor, at this point we need to have something working much more than we need to have it 100 percent correct. If the case-study level is never attempted prior to the creation of the prototype, the KE must be aware that he or she is nonetheless squarely responsible for the production of an early working model of an expert system. Why?

Expert systems technology does not bring with it a set of deductive protocols that allow us to unerringly fabricate a working system. Rather, it provides a set of techniques that will allow us to capture, relatively quickly, human decision-making behavior with which we may continue to work, in conjunction with the expert, to more closely replicate the expert's performance.

During the early stages of the project the KE depends upon inductive reasoning for the most part, drawing conclusions from a rather large set of examples or sample observations rather than proceeding deductively from general rules to their logical conclusions. The existence of a prototype places the KE and the expert in the posture of co-creators. The objective reality of the prototype hastens the process of eliciting the expert's rule-oriented rationale and the expansion of the prototype to include the features of the full domain being addressed. The inexperienced KE is wise to take advantage of the case study, thus assuring the optimal opportunity for a successful, albeit probably not exact, expert system prototype.

Planning the Prototype

The factors that must be considered in building a prototype lend some greater significance to the KE's perspective of the objectives to be reached in gaining example information from the expert and pursuing a subset of those examples in greater detail to create the case studies. If we postulate that the domain expert's mind contains a gigantic decision tree, we come much closer to the reality with which we are confronted.

The expert's mental decision tree constitutes a search space that is traversed each time a problem is being solved in the domain. For example, let us consider the hypothetical decision tree of a construction engineer. The top-most node from which the engineer's lower nodes branch may simply be a "build a large building" node. We might visualize the next node as presenting the question "Have soil samples been analyzed?" Branching from this node are two arcs, one for no and one for yes. And so the engineer's huge mental decision tree expands in breadth as we observe the multiple nodes that are generated at each successively lower level of development.

Nearly everything that has been said about the ideal candidate expert system is dependent upon this view of the expert's mind set. The present state of our technology allows us to embody only a portion of this huge tree in any given expert system. If we have chosen more than a reasonable portion of this tree, it will be extremely unlikely that we will be able to digest it into the confines of a practical, functioning expert system that will offer a return on our investment. Our task is the pruning of this tree to enable the pruned portion to be replicated in the expert system. Within the expert system, we wish to further prune the search space into manageable categories of investigation so that the user is guided to as successful an outcome as is possible within the constraints of the system's uncertainty.

The KE's acquisition of the expert's examples might be viewed as snapshots of the expert's mental actions as the expert prunes and traverses through the nodes of the tree to reach a conclusion. Recalling our earlier descriptions of forward and backward chaining, we quickly see that while the distinctions apply (backward chaining seeks causes from symptoms while forward chaining seeks consequences from known specifications), the expert may employ both. Consequently, it is the KE's task to classify the expert's knowledge into categories given the examples and case studies.

Creating the taxonomy

Perhaps the most simple approach to beginning the building of a prototype is by way of the creation of a taxonomy. Let us assume that we have just interviewed the plant's expert on refrigeration repair and that we have a collection of examples. The refrigeration expert is about to be promoted to maintenance manager and will be replaced by a trainee who will be schooled in some basic refrigeration maintenance activities such as taking voltage and pressure readings, recharging freon supply, and replacing motors. The objective is the creation of an expert system that will give the new trainee some direction while the newly appointed maintenance manager (the former refrigeration repair expert) will be available for support in the more difficult tasks. Because refrigeration repair is only a subset of the necessary tasks of the position, the expert is quite interested in getting the system underway. The following is a subset of the examples collected.

1. The maintenance department received a call from the production floor that the temperature alarm of a primary chiller had begun to "tweet." This indicated that the temperature varied from the set level. I went down to the floor and found the chiller about 5 degrees above the set point. I turned off the alarm. The compressor wasn't operating and so the first thing I did was check the power line voltage. It was zero. A circuit breaker had jumped—nothing wrong with the chiller.

2. The plant just has chillers and freezers, but we have standard refrigerators in marketing and the executive areas—we received a call from the president's secretary. His private office refrigerator wasn't making ice cubes, and they were afraid that the product samples he keeps in the refrigerator would spoil. I got up there with my pressure gauge and all and checked the power, the temp setting, and the temperature. It was sure enough getting warm and the compressor wasn't running, so I turned the system off and back on again—sometimes it's the control—but everything was dead. I next checked the circuit from the control to the compressor and there was a definite open. The wire at the compressor motor had broken off from the spade plug—vibration, I guess. I resoldered it and turned on the system—all OK!

The examples above and several of the ones that followed, along with the case studies, indicated that the diagnostic process went forward with a more or less definite pattern. The complaint was verified, the thermostats were verified, the compressor motor was checked to determine that the thermal overload had not jumped, the power was verified, the circuit was verified, and finally the condenser and pressure readings were checked.

In some cases of chiller malfunctioning it was noted that the thermal overload's triggering was related to low freon pressure that resulted in prolonged compressor action that overheated the compressor motor. Strangely enough, the freezer complaint examples saw the expert going directly to the roof to check the condenser fans and housing. The expert griped that management should install more up-to-date freezer equipment since birds were building nests and clogging the condenser coils, and that the fan motors were old and were getting to the point where a lot of motor rebuilding was required, and so on—a heuristic based upon experience with the equipment.

The KE detected a heuristic in the freezer diagnosis that circumvented the longer process of following a straight investigatory path from complaint verification through to the basic equipment, and therefore it was decided to end the interview with a few questions. The KE ascertained that the classes of equipment, chillers, freezers, and standard refrigerators, were all similarly treated in the process of diagnosis. It was found that brand differences did not alter the process. The KE retired to the MIS department to create the taxonomy.

The taxonomy, in part, appeared as follows:

A. Chiller complaint.
    A-1 Verify complaint on-site.
    A-2 Reset alarms if needed.
    A-3 Check thermostatic control.
        A-3.1 If nonfunctional, replace.
    A-4 Check compressor motor—on or off.
        A-4.1 Off, then check thermal overload switch.
            A-4.1.1 Overload switch out, check freon.
            A-4.1.1.1 Freon low, recharge.
        A-4.2 Off, then check line voltage.
            A-4.2.1 Line voltage poor, check source.
            A-4.2.1.1 Source out, restore.
            A-4.2.2 Line voltage OK, replace motor.
        A-4.3 On, then check control circuit.
            A-4.3.1 Control circuit failure, repair.
    A-5 Check condenser fan.
        A-5.1 ...

The taxonomy went on to treat B, the freezer complaint and C, the standard refrigerator complaint. Essentially a comprehensive outline that classifies the major problem areas and then proceeds to present each major problem as a set of subproblems, the taxonomy provides the KE with a recapitulation of the examples and the case studies that may have been created. Note that each of the subproblems (e.g., A-3.1 and A-4.1.1.1) in our example result in a solution action to be taken for that subproblem. The taxonomy may suggest avenues of pursuit for further interviews with the expert, but the KE should resist the temptation to attempt the creation of the ultimate taxonomy. The immediate objective is the creation of a working prototype.

Creating the decision tree

After having created the taxonomy, the subsequent creation of a decision tree often provides a helpful device for visualizing the numerous paths that lead to the various solutions. A decision tree related to the partial taxonomy above is displayed in Figure 7.1.

Each node of the decision tree in Figure 7.1 is numbered so that the various paths through the tree may be identified. For instance, nodes 1, 2, and 3 constitute one path leading to a solution and hence, one If-Then rule:

IF the Chiller malfunctions
AND the thermostat has failed
THEN replace the thermostat.

In all, there are seven If-Then rules embodied in the decision tree of Figure 7.1. In Figure 7.1, the circles are nodes and the ovals are actions. Path 1 is nodes 1, 2, and 3. Path 2 is nodes 1, 2, 4, 5, 6, and 7. Path 3 is nodes 1, 2, 4, 5, 9, 6, and 7. Path 4 is nodes 1, 2, 4, 5, 6, and 10. Path 5 is nodes 1, 2, 4, 5, 9, 6, and 10. Path 6 is nodes 1, 2, 4, 5, 9, and 13. Path 7 is nodes 1, 2, 4, 8, and 11. However, if If-Then-Else rules are used, only six rules are required. The data processor will note that Path 2—1, 2, 4, 5, 6, 7—may be combined with Path 5—1, 2, 4, 5, 6, 10—by using Else since node 6 leads to node 7, Else node 10.

Based upon the partial decision tree of Figure 7.1, we might estimate that the complete prototype will consist of not more than 100 rules if a rule-based production system is developed. Confidence factors (CF) have not been included on this first effort in order not to involve the expert in fine distinctions during a first interview session. The KE has acquired an early appreciation for the degree to which uncertainty plays a part in the problem-solving activity, however. Each rule and each premise, therefore, may be assigned a value of 1 in a boolean or probability confidence rating scale or a value of 100 in any of the other possible scales. The KE's appraisal of the importance of

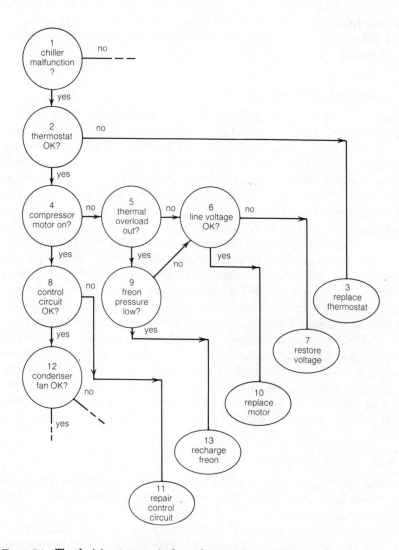

Figure 7.1   The decision tree equivalent of a partial taxonomy.

the more sophisticated CF calculations will serve as a guide in later choosing the appropriate tool.

Choosing the Tool

The selection of an adequate tool for the creation of our prototype, and quite possibly, the final delivery system, becomes a make-or-buy decision. We are realistically faced with the question of programming from scratch or using a shell. The experienced AI programmer would, most probably, opt for a LISP program or visualize the natural Prolog implementation dictated by the backward chaining activity that our problem implies. The professional data processor might see the situation in a quite different light.

The mainframe-based expert system

The professional data processor must give consideration to his or her total environment. Is the expert system to be used by personnel at numerous locations in the extended data processing network? Is the mainframe currently suffering response degradation because of loading and to what extent is this situation likely to continue? Is a mainframe conversion in the department's near-term future? To what extent has the return on investment been calculated using a mainframe-based expert system as a potential solution?

If the mainframe delivery of the expert system is the decision of choice, there are a number of advantages. Modifications to the system will be centrally controlled with no danger that the users at various locations will be exposed to the possibility that they are employing a down-level version of the system. The system's user activity may be monitored statistically on the mainframe in order to determine the frequency of utilization. Mainframe databases may be employed in the expert system to allow its extension to additional items of equipment and the possible establishment of maintenance schedules. The following chapter addresses the mainframe as a development and delivery vehicle. There, the make-or-buy decision as it relates to expert system development will be discussed from the perspective of the mainframe computer.

The PC-based expert system

If, on the other hand, this is a first or among the first attempts at expert system development and the company is small to medium in size, it is much wiser to employ a PC-based approach to expert system development and delivery. This is particularly true if one or only a few user locations are involved. A judgment based upon the probability of limited resource availability, this approach offers the optimum opportunity for a successful experience and minimizes the possibility of extensive involvement if the venture proves unsuccessful. Nonetheless, we are still faced with the make-or-buy decision.

The scope of involvement. Programming from scratch is dictated whenever the available talent resource is capable of producing a programmed product superior to that which could be created using existing expert system shells. Superior means lower in cost, more effective in performance, and less expensive in both time and money. Alternatively, programming from scratch is dictated whenever the scope of the problem exceeds the capability of shells available in the marketplace—quite unlikely in a first effort. The rationale for deciding the make-or-buy question should, like the physician's axiom, consider the least-extensive treatment first.

It is unwise to use any given expert system implementation as a boot strap for extending in-house programming capability or as an expedient for expanding the available inventory of expert system shells. In-house programming capability in the expert system area should be extended as an independent result of management's decision to pursue this technology. Similarly, the inventory of expert system shells should be expanded only if needed as determined through an assessment of required features in relation to the return on investment calculated for the specific project.

Knowledge representation. The creation of the taxonomy and decision tree and an assessment of the degree to which uncertainty will be involved in the expert system are all important elements in the selection of the prototype tool. More important is the way in which these elements support a decision regarding the method of knowledge representation that will be used in the expert system. The refrigeration repair example we have used clearly describes a rule-based production system or predicate logic representation. If we encountered sets of knowledge employed in distinguishing between vehicle types, structures, or schedules, in which inheritance of properties offers a decided advantage, the possible use of a frame-based knowledge representation scheme would offer itself as the option of choice.

In conjunction with the decision that we are dealing with a rule-based production system or predicate logic representation, there is the added question of the degree to which factual information must be stored in the knowledge base. As we have seen, not all systems are equal—some have an extensive factual knowledge component while others rely almost entirely upon the user's input to provide factual and status information to the system.

Because the example we have reviewed depends heavily upon user input to determine equipment status information and because the knowledge component is almost entirely rules, predicate logic may be ruled out in favor of a purely rule-based production system. This judgment could be strongly influenced in the opposite direction given a data processing department already in possession of Prolog programming expertise or a shell similar to the Arity/Expert development package reviewed in the last chapter.

Computation requirements.   The professional data processor is unaccustomed to evaluating the degree to which mathematical calculations are involved in a given system. Generally, the data processing programming languages provide ample mathematical support to handle the business or technical programming problems that are likely to be confronted. However, as we have seen, some expert system shells may not support extensive computational requirements in favor of other facilities as was demonstrated in our review of 1st-Class in the last chapter. If the KE's collected examples and case studies indicate that the expert calculates limiting voltage values, for instance, in determining power adequacy, it is clear that the vehicle chosen must provide that capability.

The KE must beware of excessive calibration. It is all too inviting to specify an expert system tool that provides an unneeded margin of capability, particularly when developing a first expert system. As capability in a tool grows, so too does the learning curve required for that tool's successful application. As time and experience accumulate, the KE's intuition will function to provide a sense of goodness of fit between the problem at hand and a given tool's true capabilities.

In the example presented above, the expert's knowledge pruning point is rather high in that the expert system's requirement is the guidance of the user in conducting a diagnostic investigation rather than providing the underlying protocols of voltage measurement and so on. The KE must be ever conscious of the scope of involvement lest unwarranted complexities enter the effort.

The budget consideration.   Having given consideration to the factors cited above, the KE's final decision is constrained by the budget and the associated calculation of return on investment. Keeping in mind the primary goal of delivering a working expert system within dollar and temporal limits, the KE should find, in the light of the foregoing, that the selection of the appropriate tool is all but complete. In the example presented above and in the absence of contraindications such as the availability of already acquired suitable expert system shells, 1st-Class or Exsys, each under $500.00, should adequately provide the necessary expert system shell for development and delivery on a conservatively configured PC. Let us review the factors that would lead us to this result.

Reaching the conclusion

Chief among the elements that constitute the KE's tool selection is the conservative axiom that the scope of involvement must be well circumscribed. Programming an expert system from scratch, like opting for the use of ALC in the creation of a data system, must be the course of last resort. Expert systems succeed because expert systems may be created relatively quickly, they function effectively and profitably, and they are easy to maintain. Any development decision that threatens to detract from any of these features is in need of close reappraisal.

The method of knowledge representation, until a relatively high level of AI expertise has been developed, should be a method that is clearly suggested by the examples, case studies, taxonomy, and decision tree. During the early stages of the development of expert system expertise, less than a clear indication of the form that knowledge representation should take may well be mute testimony to the fact that the scope of involvement is too wide or that the proposed expert system itself is inadequately defined.

Computation requirements should be carefully considered even if the probable candidate expert system development shell is already determined. A thorough analysis of the computation requirements acts as a reconfirmation of the scope of involvement. Unlike data system design, expert system design is rarely heavily mathematical in its orientation. The KE should be a devil's advocate where computation is involved.

Finally, because an expert system may, in its early stages of testing, evidence high potential profitability, management will elect to broaden its scope and, hence, its size, thereby redefining the system's goal. Alternatively, the initial challenge may be the creation of a PC-based expert system whose run-time version, because of its size, will execute in a reasonable fashion. Solutions prior to the announcement of PCs such as IBM's Personal System/2 family, often saw expert systems developed using shells with the resultant run-time expert system being reprogrammed in Pascal or C in order to accommodate PC memory and performance limitations. A number of expert system shells are now available that produce a high-level language source module that may subsequently be compiled to provide enhanced execution characteristics. The need for the re-creation of a completed expert system in a high-level language is minimized by the ever-expanding capabilities of reasonably priced personal computers.

In Retrospect

We see that the knowledge engineer finds the elements of the expert system solution embedded in the nature of the expert's method of operation. These elements are highlighted through the KE's collection of examples, the creation of case studies, and the final development of the taxonomy and decision tree. As the elements become visible, the appropriate tool is suggested by their interrelationship. Rewriting of the delivery expert system in a high-level language has all but been abandoned because of the availability of large-memory high-speed PCs.

In the next chapter we will address the issues to be confronted when the mainframe is to be the development and delivery vehicle. There we will meet the ubiquitous PC once more in its dual role as workstation and as an up-load/down-load agent. We may also see that the PC is not only the workstation of choice but the delivery vehicle of choice when configured as a terminal device for the mainframe.

Chapter

8

The IBM Expert System
Environment (ESE)

Some professional data processors even today are having a difficult
time accepting the PC as an important element in the computing environment. Perhaps a conflict is created when the data processor attempts to visualize serious computing being carried on using the same
device that is frequently advertised as ideal for playing games. Notwithstanding, PCs such as the IBM Personal System/2, Model 80, with
16 megabytes of memory offer a formidable challenge to such preju-
dices. The memory capacities and speed of today's PCs dwarf those of
some mainframes widely employed not long ago.

Nonetheless, numerous MIS directors have been quoted as firm be-
lievers that expert systems will not play an important role in data processing until mainframe expert system shells are available. While
this is not the authors' view, we will accept it for the purposes of this
chapter as we proceed to investigate the role of the IBM mainframe
expert system shell, past, present and future.

A Brief History of the IBM Expert System
Shell, ESE

The academic developers of expert system technology work largely if
not exclusively using dedicated workstations that have been designed
to support languages such as LISP. The focus of their attention is the
development of systems whose designs have been foreshadowed by rigorous theoretical investigations in any of a number of disciplines. The
considerations of researchers do not extend to the mundane realities of
operating systems, database interfacing, and teleprocessing monitors.
The result is the creation of new technology whose application problems are left to the vendor community for solution.

Because the PC is, by its nature, quite similar to the dedicated workstation, the vendors of PC software find little difficulty in porting the latest technological developments to their markets. The mainframe vendor, on the other hand, faces complex problems in accommodating new technology. An example of this complexity is seen in IBM's support of operating systems, SSP, CPF, DOS/VSE, VM, MVS, and MVS/XA as well as teleprocessing monitors CICS and IMS. Additional software such as TSO, ICCF, and CMS must be considered. We might add database management systems such as VSAM, DB2, SQL/DS, and DL/I. This reflects IBM's response to the diverse needs of a catholic market coupled with a desire for product excellence. Incorporation of an expert system shell in the resultant environment demands numerous software modifications, none of which are trivial.

There is little wonder why involvement of the mainframe in PC-based expert systems has been accomplished via emulation and upload-download of data and results. Rather than waiting for the vendor to provide the necessary interfaces, the savvy data processor has employed resourcefulness in dealing with the mainframe's expert system shell limitations. Additionally, many avant-garde data processors have turned to the use of specialized workstations and non-IBM vendors to simplify the implementation of expert system applications too extensive for PC-based support.

The atmosphere of impatience with hardware vendor development of mainframe resident expert system tools has been nowhere more manifest than at IBM. As early as 1984 a group of AI developers at IBM's Palo Alto, California, Scientific Center had completed the creation of an expert system tool called "Prism." Written in Pascal and designed to run on IBM mainframes under VM and MVS, its developers felt the product was ready for the marketplace. Frustration with the time-consuming processes of internal training, market planning, and readying the support environment for such a product resulted in the developers' departure from the company.

Convinced of the value of their creation, the developers founded Aion Corporation in Palo Alto and went on to create the Application Development System (ADS). ADS runs under VM and MVS on IBM mainframes, allowing the creation of expert systems that may be ported to the PC if desired. Aion has found its customers among software houses such as Boole & Babbage and Management Science America as well as organizations such as Arthur Andersen.

IBM ultimately modified Prism to produce its VM expert system shell, Expert System Environment (ESE), which became a "Program Offering" in 1985, and the equivalent system under MVS in 1986. IBM also announced a VM/CMS Prolog interpeter, VM/Programming in Logic, in 1985. The terms here are significant. A Program Offering affords the user "as is" program availability with limited vendor support while a "Program Product" is supported by the full power of IBM's cadre of software support personnel.

While the existence of a Program Offering from IBM often signifies that the company will accommodate but is less than convinced of the importance of the undertaking, ESE brought with it IBM's repeated assurances that it viewed AI as an important element in the future of data processing. IBM dispatched presentation teams to conduct day-long tuition-free ESE Concepts and Facilities seminars across the country featuring hands-on sessions with VM/ESE under CMS. Expert system educational facilities in support of ESE were established on both coasts. ESE became an offering complete with educational support.

IBM's Fortune 500 customers were listening and reacted in predictable fashion—they bought ESE. Among ESE users IBM counts companies such as Chase Manhattan Bank N.A., Citicorp, DuPont Company, McDonnell Douglas Corporation, Timeplex, Incorporated, and Travelers Insurance Company.

Consistent with its assurances, on June 30, 1987, IBM announced the upgrading of ESE to Program Product status and simultaneously announced, as a Program Product, Common LISP for MVS, making available both interpreter and compiler facilities. Because ESE is clearly here to stay, it is practical to review its capabilities.

IBM's ESE Program Product

The Expert System Environment consists of two products, one for VM and another for MVS. Each product consists of two subsystems, a consultation, or run-time, environment and a development environment. The consultation subsystem may be obtained additionally and separately for use on a CPU other than that used in developing the expert system. Provisions are made for those IBM customers currently using the earlier program offerings.

The development environment

The ESE development environment retains knowledge as "parameters" and "rules" while employing "Focus Control Blocks" (FCB) to control the later consultation by providing a structure for knowledge decomposition and control over inferencing techniques.

Parameters are the variables of the knowledge base. A parameter is given a name such as Loan_value or Pay_history. Each parameter is then provided a value range such as "taken from ('high', 'medium', 'low')" or "taken from ('good', 'fair', 'poor')." During the user's consultation, these parameters are resolved either through user interrogation or data derivation and thus acquire values such as 'high' or 'poor'.

Typically a parameter consists of a name, constraint, and prompt such as in the following example in which the prompt provides for a user response:

Parameter	pay_history
Constraint	taken from ('good', 'fair', 'poor')
Prompt	The applicant's payment performance is
	Good
	Fair
	Poor

A parameter sourcing sequence tells the system where the value for a parameter can be found and lists the allowable sources in the order to be tried. The default order is "R.U.D.E." where the sources are:

Rule, indicating that a rule will assign the value

User, indicating that the user is to be asked

Default, indicating that there is a default constraint

External, indicating that the value is to come from an external program

The rules express the relationship between the parameters:

If	loan value is 'high'
and	pay_history is 'poor'
then	recommendation is 'refuse'

A rule's premise (the If part of the rule) may compare two values as in the following example:

If	car_color is sample_color

or may use parentheses to set precedence for "and" and "or":

If	car_age is 'old'
and	(car_body is 'rust'
	or engine_condition is 'unreliable')
then	recommendation is 'trade'

Also, the action (the Then part of the rule) may assign a value to a parameter or provide for multiple actions:

If	car_age is 'old'
then	miles_driven is 'high'

If	hotel_days > 7
then	bill_discount = 0.1
and	show 'Give customer 10 percent discount'

An ESE development session. Before proceeding to a consideration of the use of Focus Control Blocks (FCB) and other advanced features, let us review a typical Knowledge Base Creation Laboratory session as conducted by IBM during a 1-day ESE Concepts and Facilities seminar.

The example frequently employed is the "Animal Problem" whose knowledge base provides the identification of an animal during a consultation with a user. The user provides information describing such observable aspects of animal behavior such as its eating habits or manner of locomotion. The system finally responds with an identification that is dictated by its limited knowledge base. Given but six rules, one to identify the class mammal, one to identify the class bird, and four to identify each of tiger, giraffe, penguin, and cardinal, the knowledge base is small but illustrative.

The Animal Problem's taxonomy appears as follows:

1. Animal_class is mammal.
    1.1 Animal_eats_meat is true.
        1.1.1. Animal is tiger.
    1.2 Animal_eats_meat is false.
        1.2.1 Animal is giraffe.
2. Animal_class is bird.
    2.1.Animal_locomotion is swims.
        2.1.1 Animal is penguin.
    2.2 Animal_locomotion is flies.
        2.2.1 Animal is cardinal.
3. Animal_appearance is fur.
    3.1 Animal_produces milk.
        3.1.1 Animal_class is mammal.
4. Animal_appearance is feathers.
    4.1 Animal_produces eggs.
        4.1.1 Animal_class is bird.

Quickly reviewing the taxonomy, we see that the qualifiers (parameters), animal_locomotion, animal_class, animal_appearance, and animal_produces may take values such as "fur" or "feathers," for animal_appearance, while animal_eats_meat is boolean, being either true or false.

The seminar attendee begins by signing on to CMS and invoking ESDX, ESE's development component. The ESDE screen illustrated in Figure 8.1 appears with the cursor positioned on the command line awaiting the name of the knowledge base to be edited or created. The attendee is instructed to type "animal" (without the quotes) and to press the Enter key.

The screen of Figure 8.2 now appears, displaying the name of the knowledge base, allowing a title but presenting zeros for all statistics since this is a new knowledge base. The legend at the bottom of the screen defines the function keys. The attendee types "edp animal" on the command line. The "edp" signifies that the editor (ed) is to accept a parameter (p) named "animal." The Enter key is then pressed.

The screen of Figure 8.3 appears, allowing the developer to assign a prompt to the parameter just supplied (upper screen portion) or to assign a "constraint" or set of values from which the parameter may be resolved, or both. The attendee is instructed to type "is a string" on line 1 of the constraint panel and then to press the Enter key. Having done this, the system verifies the text and returns the screen unchanged with the cursor positioned on the screen's command line. The attendee is then instructed to type "edp animal_ locomotion," thus providing the knowledge base with the next parameter. Upon pressing the Enter key, the screen displayed in Figure 8.4 is presented.

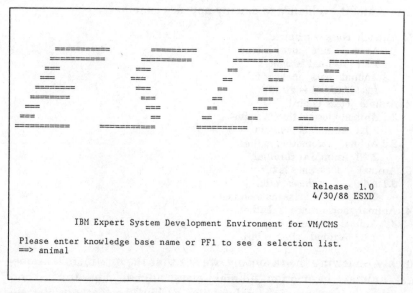

```
                                                      Release  1.0
                                                      4/30/88 ESXD

        IBM Expert System Development Environment for VM/CMS

   Please enter knowledge base name or PF1 to see a selection list.
   ==> animal
```

Figure 8.1   The knowledge base name is entered on the command line. (*International Business Machines Corporation*)

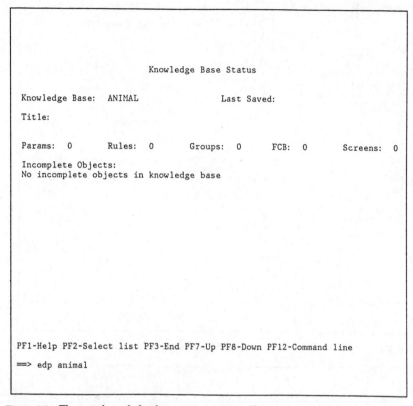

```
                        Knowledge Base Status

   Knowledge Base:   ANIMAL                   Last Saved:
   Title:


   Params:   0        Rules:   0       Groups:   0      FCB:   0      Screens:   0

   Incomplete Objects:
   No incomplete objects in knowledge base















   PF1-Help PF2-Select list PF3-End PF7-Up PF8-Down PF12-Command line

   ==> edp animal
```

Figure 8.2   The new knowledge base status screen allows entry of the first parameter.
(*International Business Machines Corporation*)

Addressing the screen shown in Figure 8.4, the attendee is instructed to type the constraint "taken from ('flies', 'swims')," thus providing the set from which the earlier entered "animal_locomotion" parameter's value may be chosen. (Note that the current parameter name in the screen's upper left corner identifies the parameter to which the value set applies.) Once more the Enter key is pressed and the system verifies the text, returning the screen to allow the attendee to supply the third parameter. The parameter "animal_class" is supplied by the attendee and the Enter key results in the appearance of the screen illustrated in Figure 8.5.

The screen of Figure 8.5 is provided with the value list "taken from ('mammal', 'bird')" which defines the values from which "animal_class" may be resolved. After verification by the system, the attendee enters the next parameter by typing "edp animal_eats_meat" and again pressing the Enter key.

```
Param:   ANIMAL                        Last Updated:   05/08/88  11:35:04

                                           For HELP Press PFKEY 1

Property:        |       Edit:      Prompt
Constraint       |   1
Sourcing seq.    |   2
Prompt           |   3
Long Prompt      |   4
Default constr.  |   5
Expect value     |   6
Owning FCBs      |   7
Screen           |   8
Procedure name   |   9
Procedure args   |  10
Val can chg flg  |  11
Comment          |------------------------------------------------------
Name             |       Edit:      Constraint
Print name       |   1 is a string
Author           |   2
I ref it list    |   3
It ref me list   |   4
Error Report     |   5
Current value    |   6
                 |   7
                 |   8
                 |   9
                 |  10
                 |  11


==> edp animal_locomotion
```

Figure 8.3 'ANIMAL' is a string. (*International Business Machines Corporation*)

```
Param:   ANIMAL_LOCOMOTION             Last Updated:   05/08/88  11:36:32

                                           For HELP Press PFKEY 1

Property:        |       Edit:      Prompt
Constraint       |   1
Sourcing seq.    |   2
Prompt           |   3
Long Prompt      |   4
Default constr.  |   5
Expect value     |   6
Owning FCBs      |   7
Screen           |   8
Procedure name   |   9
Procedure args   |  10
Val can chg flg  |  11
Comment          |------------------------------------------------------
Name             |       Edit:      Constraint
Print name       |   1 taken from ('flies','swims')
Author           |   2
I ref it list    |   3
It ref me list   |   4
Error Report     |   5
Current value    |   6
                 |   7
                 |   8
                 |   9
                 |  10
                 |  11

==> edp animal_class
```

Figure 8.4 The third parameter is entered. (*International Business Machines Corporation*)

Upon the appearance of the screen displayed in Figure 8.6, the attendee is instructed to type "is a boolean," thus restricting the values that may be assumed by the parameter "animal_eats_meat," to true or false. After system verification of the text, the next parameter, "animal_appearance," is typed on the command line and the Enter key is pressed.

The screen of Figure 8.7 allows the entry of "('fur', 'feathers')" as the value list for "animal_appearance," and finally the entry of the last parameter at which time "edp animal_produces" is supplied.

The screen displayed in Figure 8.8 sees the entry of the final value list "taken from ('milk', 'eggs')," thus completing the assignment of value sets to the parameters. Upon the system's verification of the entry, the attendee is instructed to enter the first rule by typing "edr tiger." Once more the character following "ed" defines the entry, now a rule (r).

The screen displayed in Figure 8.9 is designed especially for the entry of rules and so no longer provides an upper panel for prompts. The upper panel now addresses the FCB, which we will discuss later. The attendee is instructed to enter the "tiger" rule which, we observe, is taken directly from the taxonomy. The text is verified and the attendee is instructed to enter "edr giraffe" in order to invoke the rule screen for the "giraffe" rule.

The attendee is instructed to enter the subsequent rules on the screens displayed in Figures 8.10 through 8.14. Each rule is taken directly from the taxonomy. Upon reaching the screen of Figure 8.14, function key PF3 is pressed (see the function key legend at the bottom of the screen displayed in Figure 8.2) to signify the end of knowledge base creation.

Following the PF3 key, the Knowledge Base Status screen of Figure 8.15 appears, displaying the knowledge base statistics. The attendee is instructed to type "consult" on the command line. This allows the developer to invoke the consultation immediately following the creation of a knowledge base.

The screen shown in Figure 8.16 appears, whereupon the attendee is instructed to type an "x" next to the animal option, thereby directing the system to pursue a goal solution for the parameter "animal" which, as we have seen, is a string. The attendee then presses the Enter key.

The screen of Figure 8.17 appears allowing the entry of an "x" next to the parameter "animal," thus instructing the system to display the parameter "animal" with its value at the end of a consultation. The attendee is again instructed to press the Enter key.

The final screen, shown in Figure 8.18, allows the developer to enter the identification of those parameters the system should ask the value of at the start of each consultation. Because none are to be identified, the attendee is instructed to press the PF6 key. In accord with the PF key panel on the screen, PF6 represents "Unknown," meaning none in this case.

```
Param:   ANIMAL_CLASS                   Last Updated:   05/08/88 11:37:36

                                        For HELP Press PFKEY 1

Property:        |      Edit:      Prompt
Constraint       |   1
Sourcing seq.    |   2
Prompt           |   3
Long Prompt      |   4
Default constr.  |   5
Expect value     |   6
Owning FCBs      |   7
Screen           |   8
Procedure name   |   9
Procedure args   |  10
Val can chg flg  |  11
Comment          |------------------------------------------------------
Name             |      Edit:      Constraint
Print name       |   1 taken from ('mammal', 'bird')
Author           |   2
I ref it list    |   3
It ref me list   |   4
Error Report     |   5
Current value    |   6
                 |   7
                 |   8
                 |   9
                 |  10
                 |  11

==> edp animal_eats_meat
```

Figure 8.5 The expert system deals only with mammals and birds. (*International Business Machines Corporation*)

```
Param:   ANIMAL_EATS_MEAT              Last Updated:   05/08/88 11:38:35

                                        For HELP Press PFKEY 1

Property:        |      Edit:      Prompt
Constraint       |   1
Sourcing seq.    |   2
Prompt           |   3
Long Prompt      |   4
Default constr.  |   5
Expect value     |   6
Owning FCBs      |   7
Screen           |   8
Procedure name   |   9
Procedure args   |  10
Val can chg flg  |  11
Comment          |------------------------------------------------------
Name             |      Edit:      Constraint
Print name       |   1 is a boolean
Author           |   2
I ref it list    |   3
It ref me list   |   4
Error Report     |   5
Current value    |   6
                 |   7
                 |   8
                 |   9
                 |  10
                 |  11

==> edp animal_appearance
```

Figure 8.6 A constraint may be a list or a relation or a type, such as boolean. (*International Business Machines Corporation*)

```
Param:    ANIMAL_APPEARANCE          Last Updated:   05/08/88 11:39:45

                                        For HELP Press PFKEY 1

Property:          |   Edit:      Prompt
Constraint         |   1
Sourcing seq.      |   2
Prompt             |   3
Long Prompt        |   4
Default constr.    |   5
Expect value       |   6
Owning FCBs        |   7
Screen             |   8
Procedure name     |   9
Procedure args     |   10
Val can chg flg    |   11
Comment            |----------------------------------------------------
Name               |    Edit:      Constraint
Print name         |   1 Taken from ('fur','feathers')
Author             |   2
I ref it list      |   3
It ref me list     |   4
Error Report       |   5
Current value      |   6
                   |   7
                   |   8
                   |   9
                   |   10
                   |   11


==> edp animal_produces
```

Figure 8.7 A list is provided for the animal's appearance. (*International Business Machines Corporation*)

```
Param:    ANIMAL_PRODUCES            Last Updated:   05/08/88 11:41:08

                                        For HELP Press PFKEY 1

Property:          |   Edit:      Prompt
Constraint         |   1
Sourcing seq.      |   2
Prompt             |   3
Long Prompt        |   4
Default constr.    |   5
Expect value       |   6
Owning FCBs        |   7
Screen             |   8
Procedure name     |   9
Procedure args     |   10
Val can chg flg    |   11
Comment            |----------------------------------------------------
Name               |    Edit:      Constraint
Print name         |   1 taken from ('milk', 'eggs')
Author             |   2
I ref it list      |   3
It ref me list     |   4
Error Report       |   5
Current value      |   6
                   |   7
                   |   8
                   |   9
                   |   10
                   |   11


==> edr tiger
```

Figure 8.8 Mammals produce milk; birds produce eggs. (*International Business Machines Corporation*)

```
Rule:    TIGER                        Last Updated:    04/19/88 17:31:25

                                          For HELP press PF1

Properties      |     Edit:      Owning FCBs
Rule text       |  1
Owning FCBs     |  2
Rule type       |  3
Comment         |  4
Justification   |  5
Name            |  6
Print name      |  7
Author          |------------------------------------------------------
I ref it list   |     Edit:      Rule text
It ref me list  |  1 if animal_class is "mammal" and
                |  2     animal_eats_meat is true
                |  3 then
                |  4     animal is "tiger"
                |  5
                |  6
                |  7


==> edr giraffe
```

Figure 8.9 The tiger is a carnivore. (*International Business Machines Corporation*)

```
Rule:    GIRAFFE                      Last Updated:    04/19/88 17:31:43

                                          For HELP press PF1

Properties      |     Edit:      Owning FCBs
Rule text       |  1
Owning FCBs     |  2
Rule type       |  3
Comment         |  4
Justification   |  5
Name            |  6
Print name      |  7
Author          |------------------------------------------------------
I ref it list   |     Edit:      Rule text
It ref me list  |  1 if animal_class is "mammal" and
                |  2     animal_eats_meat  is false
                |  3 then
                |  4     animal is "giraffe"
                |  5
                |  6
                |  7


==> edr penguin
```

Figure 8.10 Giraffes do not eat meat. (*International Business Machines Corporation*)

```
Rule:     PENGUIN                    Last Updated:   04/19/88  17: 32: 00

                                          For HELP press PF1

Properties        |     Edit:      Owning FCBs
Rule text         |  1
Owning FCBs       |  2
Rule type         |  3
Comment           |  4
Justification     |  5
Name              |  6
Print name        |  7
Author            | ---------------------------------------------------
I ref it list     |     Edit:      Rule text
It ref me list    |  1 if animal_class is "bird" and
                  |  2    animal_locomotion is "swims"
                  |  3 then
                  |  4    animal is "penguin"
                  |  5
                  |  6
                  |  7

==> edr cardinal
```

Figure 8.11 The penguin rule identifies a flightless bird. (*International Business Machines Corporation*)

```
Rule:     CARDINAL                   Last Updated:   04/19/88  17: 32: 18

                                          For HELP press PF1

Properties        |     Edit:      Owning FCBs
Rule text         |  1
Owning FCBs       |  2
Rule type         |  3
Comment           |  4
Justification     |  5
Name              |  6
Print name        |  7
Author            | ---------------------------------------------------
I ref it list     |     Edit:      Rule text
It ref me list    |  1 if animal_class is "bird" and
                  |  2    animal_locomotion is "flies"
                  |  3 then
                  |  4    animal is "cardinal"
                  |  5
                  |  6
                  |  7

==> edr mammal
```

Figure 8.12 The cardinal rule fires if the bird flies. (*International Business Machines Corporation*)

```
Rule:     MAMMAL                        Last Updated:   04/19/88 17:32:37

                                            For HELP press PF1

Properties        |     Edit:      Owning FCBs
Rule text         |  1
Owning FCBs       |  2
Rule type         |  3
Comment           |  4
Justification     |  5
Name              |  6
Print name        |  7
Author            |------------------------------------------------------
I ref it list     |     Edit:      Rule text
It ref me list    |  1 if animal_appearance is "fur" and
                  |  2     animal_produces is "milk"
                  |  3 then
                  |  4     animal_class is "mammal"
                  |  5
                  |  6
                  |  7

==> edr bird
```

Figure 8.13 Class membership is determined by observable characteristics. (*International Business Machines Corporation*)

```
Rule:     BIRD                          Last Updated:   04/19/88 17:32:54

                                            For HELP press PF1

Properties        |     Edit:      Owning FCBs
Rule text         |  1
Owning FCBs       |  2
Rule type         |  3
Comment           |  4
Justification     |  5
Name              |  6
Print name        |  7
Author            |------------------------------------------------------
I ref it list     |     Edit:      Rule text
It ref me list    |  1 if animal_appearance is "feathers" and
                  |  2     animal_produces is "eggs"
                  |  3 then
                  |  4     animal_class is "bird"
                  |  5
                  |  6
                  |  7

==>
```

Figure 8.14 The bird rule completes the knowledge base. (*International Business Machines Corporation*)

```
                        Knowledge Base Status

Knowledge Base:   ANIMAL              Last Saved:   04/19/88 17:51:55

Title:   Animal Identification Knowledge Base

Params:  6        Rules:  6        Groups:  0        Control Blocks:  0

Incomplete Objects:
No incomplete objects in knowledge base




PF1-Help PF2-Select list PF3-End PF7-Up PF8-Down PF12-Command line

==> consult
```

Figure 8.15 The consultation is conditioned. (*International Business Machines Corporation*)

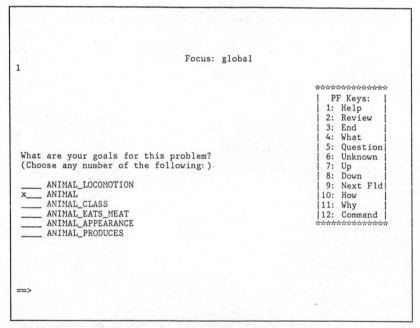

Figure 8.16 The parameter pursued is "ANIMAL." (*International Business Machines Corporation*)

```
                        Focus: global
1
                                                **********************
                                                |  PF Keys:      |
                                                |  1: Help       |
                                                |  2: Review     |
                                                |  3: End        |
                                                |  4: What       |
                                                |  5: Question|
  What are the results for this problem?        |  6: Unknown |
  (Choose any number of the following: )        |  7: Up         |
                                                |  8: Down       |
  ____ ANIMAL_LOCOMOTION                         |  9: Next Fld|
  x___ ANIMAL                                   |10: How         |
  ____ ANIMAL_CLASS                             |11: Why         |
  ____ ANIMAL_EATS_MEAT                         |12: Command |
  ____ ANIMAL_APPEARANCE                        **********************
  ____ ANIMAL_PRODUCES




  ==>
```

Figure 8.17 The parameter to be displayed at the consultation's end is "ANIMAL." (*International Business Machines Corporation*)

```
                        Focus: global
1
                                                **********************
                                                |  PF Keys:      |
                                                |  1: Help       |
                                                |  2: Review     |
                                                |  3: End        |
                                                |  4: What       |
  Do you have any initial data you wish to be   |  5: Question|
  considered?                                    |  6: Unknown |
  (Choose any number of the following: )        |  7: Up         |
                                                |  8: Down       |
  ____ ANIMAL_LOCOMOTION                         |  9: Next Fld|
  ____ ANIMAL                                   |10: How         |
  ____ ANIMAL_CLASS                             |11: Why         |
  ____ ANIMAL_EATS_MEAT                         |12: Command |
  ____ ANIMAL_APPEARANCE                        **********************
  ____ ANIMAL_PRODUCES




  ==>
```

Figure 8.18 There are no parameters the system is to seek values for at the start of a consultation. (*International Business Machines Corporation*)

An ESE consultation session. That the developer is immediately able to execute a consultation session is demonstrated to the attendee when the consultation environment is invoked. Questions are asked and the developer responds by identifying the subject animal's eating habits and so on. Within the confines of the knowledge base's limited scope, it is seen that, indeed, an expert system has been developed. It becomes equally clear that contradictions such as a "fur" response to "animal_appearance" combined with an "egg" response to "animal _produces," results in disastrous consequences. The seminar attendees are introduced to the need for rigorous analysis of the domain under consideration.

Advanced ESE capabilities. Although not demonstrated during a seminar, features such as the ability to incorporate certainty factors, the creation of custom screens, control of the knowledge base using FCBs, calls to external programming, and the use of command files are described and explained. We shall briefly discuss certainty factors, calls to external programming, and the use of FCBs.

Certainty factors. Emphasizing that evidential reasoning using certainty factors is not derived from probability theory in that certainty factors relate to expert, developer, and user judgement, IBM's ESE allows that certainty factors may range from -1.0 to $+1.0$ where $+1.0$ means positively true and -1.0 means positively not true. Parameters with certainty values, $\geq +0.20$ or ≤ -0.2, are considered true or false relative to the associated certainty value.

Single-valued and multivalued parameters are distinguished. In the case of single-valued parameters the parameter may have a number of values assigned to it; however, when a parameter is resolved with a certainty of 1.0, all other values are discarded and the system stops trying to obtain more values. In the case of multivalued parameters any number of parameter values may be known with certainty of 1.0, but the system will continue to obtain values for the parameter until the sourcing sequence is exhausted.

Regular and fuzzy rules are distinguished. Regular rules are such that input certainty does not affect output certainty while fuzzy rules' input certainty does affect output certainty. For example, consider a regular rule referred to as an If rule:

IF income = 'high' THEN car = 'Porsche'

When 'high' is specified with a certainty of 0.8, the conclusion that the car is a Porsche has a certainty of 1.0. Similarly, when 'high' is specified with a certainty of 0.3, the conclusion that the car is a Porsche retains a certainty of 1.0.

On the other hand, if the rule is fuzzy, referred to as an "FIF" rule, the certainty of the input does affect the conclusion's certainty according to the rules of fuzzy logic that were encountered in earlier chapters. For example:

FIF income = 'high' THEN car = 'Porsche'

Here, when 'high' is specified with a certainty of 0.8, the conclusion 'Porsche' has the certainty 0.8 (0.8×1.0). The certainty of the conclusion continues to diminish with a less certain specification such as 'high' with a certainty of 0.3 when the 'Porsche' conclusion has the certainty 0.3 (0.3×1.0).

Calls to external programming and data. The capability to interface ESE with other elements of the computing environment was seriously restricted in the earlier Program Offering. The Program Product now allows the developer to interface to external procedures written in Cobol, PL/I, Pascal, Assembler, Fortran, and REXX (supported for VM only). Further, ESE allows dynamic loading of these routines at execution time, thus eliminating relinking.

ESE permits database access through SQL/DS and DB2 interfaces, and in addition, SQL or DB2 data can be created or updated from within an expert system. Graphics capability exists allowing pie charts, line charts, bar charts, and fit-curve charts to be presented during an ESE consultation, thus adding a visual interpretation to the data involved.

The use of Focus Control Blocks. ESE makes use of FCBs to partition the knowledge base into manageable units. This allows the developer to organize the problem in a heirachical manner. An FCB might represent a single unit of work and define the order of processing of parameters and rules.

Each control block is defined using an FCB control language that permits the specification of activities such as asking about initial parameter values. The FCB control language may also be used to invoke the forward or backward chaining inference engine, to display resulting screens or parameter values, to pass data to an external routine, to acquire parameter values and data from external routines, or to pass control to a different FCB.

Through the use of multiple FCBs an expert system may be structured so that irrelevant parts of the knowledge base are deactivated during a consultation such as the obtaining of male health data when the consultation is being conducted by a female. FCBs may be controlled using rules that the developer creates to explicitly direct the flow during a consultation or to eliminate the consideration of certain parameters as a result of contingent parameter resolution. The FCB is created using the same editing facility we observed in the creation of parameters and rules.

IBM, ESE, and the Future

It has become common for IBM to issue statements of direction with regard to one or another aspect of its product line. These statements are made to enlighten its customers, thus providing some sense of confidence in their planning for future data processing requirements. The IBM product line has been characterized by anything but compatibility, as we noted earlier, and these statements of direction have often not been as clear as the computer user would like them to be.

Notwithstanding, IBM has been emphatic in its insistence that expert systems, and AI in general, will constitute an important place in the future of data processing. The wary data processor would be far more at ease if IBM would tell his or her future in terms of hardware and software so that all doubt might be removed from the planning process. Unfortunately, reaching too far into the future forecloses options and reduces the competitive edge considerably. We cannot expect that IBM or any vendor, for that matter, will jeopardize its competitive position in the marketplace.

We might fabricate an illustration of the future based upon IBM's public pronouncements, comments of major customers who have been permitted to view developments just beyond the horizon, and the private comments of IBM management. That the future incorporates ESE in IBM's product line from the PC through the mid-range systems and, of course, in the major systems as we have seen, is a fact. As these pages are being written, ESE executes ensconced in a System/36-38 "successor machine" that will, in time, become the backbone of IBM's mid-range systems. Although there will still be some systems overlap, the ultimate goal is a computing environment supported at the low end by personal computers with a mid-range architecture fashioned after IBM's System/38 for ease of use, while the major mainframes will be found to conform to the MVS/XA ideal.

Some professional data processors may scoff at the possibility of this kind of IBM future being within the realm of achievement given so long a period of potpourri systems in both hardware and software. Suffice it to say that some IBM customers have defected— a fact attested to by several depressing IBM financial reports. IBM has listened and learned. The future will not mirror the past, according to IBM authorities.

In the midst of the rush to develop mainframe resident expert system shells, Cullinet acquired DMS and its Application Expert and is ready to market it for the IBM mainframe. A consortium has been formed by Artificial Intelligence Corporation that includes Liberty Mutual Insurance Company, Southern California Edison Company, and Transamerica Insurance Company, among others, to develop an expert system shell (KBMS) that will execute on IBM mainframes under teleprocessing monitors such as CICS. Clearly, IBM is feeling the heat of competition and can be expected to respond, as it has promised.

None of this will eliminate the restlessness of, and criticism by, the AI developers for whom no known level of speedy improvisation has been satisfactory. And this is as it should be for we would be condemned to a lackluster tomorrow if it were not for the restless among us who insist upon running to meet the future on its own turf.

A Summing Up

The professional data processor employing IBM as a major vendor is faced with a number of immediate choices:

1. Retain a major consulting group to develop a needed application

2. Create mainframe expert systems from scratch using LISP or Prolog

3. Implement stand-alone AI workstation applications

4. Obtain Aion's ADS and begin mainframe expert system development

5. Obtain Cullinet's Application Expert and begin mainframe development

6. Obtain IBM's ESE and begin mainframe expert system development

7. Create expert systems using a PC-based shell

8. Use PC mainframe emulation to upload or download CPU data when needed

9. Do nothing in the conviction that the technology is not yet mature

Clearly, choice no. 9 has prevailed in the vast preponderance of cases, for professional data processors have not rushed to acquire an understanding of expert system technology. The fallacy of this choice is manifest in the rapid proliferation of expert system options that are available to the data processing community.

Returning to the premise that we agreed to embrace at the beginning of this chapter, "that expert systems will not play an important role in data processing until mainframe expert system shells are available," we see that, indeed, the time has come and passed. The appropriate choice from among the remaining eight options is dictated by the circumstances with which the individual data processing installation is faced. The prerequisite is an understanding of the technology—something that only the resolve of the professional data processor can supply.

The following chapter illustrates the manner in which one company's introduction to expert systems was accomplished. While the company is a synthesis, the experiences are very real.

Let's Build
an Expert System

In this chapter we will follow the development of an expert system
from the initial introduction of AI technology in a company to the final implementation of the resultant system. In order to avoid embar-
rassment to any of the parties involved, the company will be called the
Mythical Insurance Company (MIC). The expert whose services are
portrayed, Mrs. June Donath, is a real expert in her domain. She practices her expertise daily and has for a number of years. At the outset
it is important to note that MIC is not a pseudonym for her real em-
ployer. MIC is a synthesis of several insurance companies whose ex-
ecutives were, at one time or another, interviewed and presented with
the materials that appear in this chapter either by the authors or by
intermediaries acting on the authors' behalf. Consequently, with the
exception of the expert, all the names of individuals appearing in this
saga are fictitious—any similarity to real persons is purely coinciden-
tal. The involvement of vendors is factual although it too is a synthesis.

The Decision to Act

John Rogers, director of MIS for MIC, had become interested in AI and
expert systems as a result of the publicity given the subject at the National Computer Conference (NCC) and in the trade press. John has
subsequently read a number of books dealing with expert systems and
AI. Beyond his reading, John has reviewed a number of demonstration
disks that were offered at no charge by various of the expert system
shell vendors. Generally, John is considered above average in his
knowledge of expert system technology.

John's department has a considerable backlog of users' requests, and keeping up with the development of new insurance products is already straining his personnel resources. He has followed the events of recent months that saw reports of competitive insurance companies' uses of expert systems in both underwriting and claims departments, but he felt that his company's management was too sales oriented to be interested in a back office improvement as avant-garde as expert systems. Still, at least one of his acquaintances in similar circumstances has implemented such a system.

Naturally, John's interest was piqued when he learned that a forthcoming insurance association meeting featured a presentation by a Digital Equipment Corporation (DEC) knowledge engineer. He attended the meeting and learned that, indeed, the speaker had created a number of expert systems that were successfully functioning on VAX computers in companies similar to his own. His misgivings were further diminished when he learned that an expert system could be developed using a PC-based shell and later ported to the VAX if desired. John's actuarial department was using a VAX, and so he arranged for the DEC representative to attend the next meeting of the DP steering committee in order to present the fundamentals of expert systems to his management. John felt that a professional third party might help sell the idea.

John's next step was to seek out a candidate expert system. He was led to a consideration of the claims operation since it seemed that a number of insurance companies had started there. Phil Connors, the vice president of claims, was responsible for more than a few items in John's backlog, and John saw him as a potential sponsor. Phil's annual bonus is, in large part, determined by the company's claims experience and any facility that would reduce claims expense was certain to get his attention if not his full support. The key was to locate a sufficiently restricted domain within the claims area.

John reviewed the claims experience report and noted the annual claims expense displayed for Medicare Supplement policies: $1,500,000. A 10 percent savings from the development of an expert system here did not seem extravagant. To be safe he telephoned the DEC knowledge engineer to learn that he was being quite conservative with a 10 percent estimate considering the experience in other companies.

John knew nothing about claims other than that the chief claims examiner was Mrs. June Donath who he had frequently seen at departmental meetings and with whom he had a passing acquaintance. John felt it wise to hedge his bets by engaging her in an informal conversation during a coffee break in the lunch room. His objective was to determine the extent to which real savings might be developed through the implementation of the candidate expert system he had chosen. Because this was to be a first system, if the idea survived the DP steering committee meeting, he wanted to be certain that his candidate expert system offered serious potential for savings. If that turned out not to be the case, John knew that it might be wiser to rethink his choice of a candidate system since he wanted to be able to show significant savings. The claims experience report carried a good deal of data, but he had no way to determine how MIC was really doing in the Medicare Supplement claims area when compared to industry standards.

In the lunchroom during coffee break one morning, John casually asked June, "How's the claims department doing these days?"

She responded without hesitation, "If we don't get more talent or fewer claims, we'll either wind up giving the farm away or we'll be backed up for a year. We're working on Saturdays as it is."

John opted to inquire about the Medicare Supplement. "I've been reading about the rapid growth of the senior citizen market. How is this affecting our Medicare Supplement?"

"Severely," she responded, "You know that our underwriters don't examine applications for those policies and so there is no investigation of the physical condition of the applicants. We're committed to paying any claim that occurs after the policy has been in force 6 months regardless of the preexistence of the condition. That makes the claims effort simpler on older policies—we need only verify that Medicare has paid their share and then we simply settle the claim according to the particular policy's schedule. It's the new policies whose claims can be really difficult, and they're selling like popcorn. Right now we're seeing 50 percent of our Medicare claims coming from policies that have just been issued. A large number of our people are brand new to the insurance business. With our present level of personnel experience, we're just not able to take the time we should to thoroughly isolate preexistent conditions."

John felt relieved even if he had apparently touched upon a sensitive issue. June was very forthcoming, but then again, she was noted for calling a spade a spade and it was because of this approach that she had become MIC's chief claims examiner.

John, in an attempt to terminate the brief meeting, offered, "What with the backlogs that we have in DP, it seems that we've been branded with the same iron." Glancing at his wrist watch, John promised, "We'll have an opportunity to discuss this further, I'm certain. Right now I have a budget to massage—see you soon, June."

Armed with the reassurance he was seeking—there was a need—John exited the lunchroom and headed for his office.

Preparing the Presentation

John knew that it was time to work up the necessary figures showing the return on investment. If he was to enlist Phil Connors' support as a sponsor, it would be completely necessary to show Phil that there were savings to be gained. John sat staring at that $1,500,000 claims expense for Medicare supplement policies realizing that $150,000 in annual savings was meaningful only if he had some idea of the costs involved. The DEC knowledge engineer had mentioned that companies like DuPont had claimed a 10 to 1 payoff from PC-based expert systems that they had implemented, but they were not in the insurance business. John picked up the telephone and once more got in touch with the DEC knowledge engineer.

John explained that he had, indeed, isolated an excellent candidate expert system but that it looked as though the maximum dollar commitment he could ask for was no greater than $15,000 considering that this was a first attempt. Could he achieve a 10 to 1 payback on that kind of budget?

The DEC knowledge engineer pointed out that there were a number of PC-based expert system shells available that could be used that were well within this limit although it was DEC's belief that their OPS, a language for writing expert systems, was the best tool. Yes, the savings were there.

John emphasized that an initial success at the $15,000 level with a 10 to 1 payback would probably open the door to a more serious commitment by the company. The DEC engineer agreed but explained that not all PC-based shells could be ported to the company's VAX.

John quickly asked, "Are there any inexpensive PC-based shells that can be ported to the VAX?"

"Yes," was the the knowledge engineer's answer, "And we can cross that bridge when we come to it, John. Work with the $15,000 figure, and we'll discuss the tools when we get the project off the ground."

The telephone call ended with John feeling that he had headed off a potential bid to sell an expensive tool that could stall a decision by management. Further, the knowledge engineer now realized that he was going to be doing missionary work with his presentation rather than selling a major investment.

John saw the ingredients of a simple presentation. He was essentially asking for a maximum of $15,000 for the implementation of an expert system that he would support as a 1-year payback investment. He would allow the knowledge engineer to describe the 10 to 1 potential based upon other implementations of expert systems. John felt that he would come out appearing as an arch conservative and that he quite probably would get the go-ahead on the project.

Selling the Idea to the Sponsor

Armed with what he felt would be sufficient data to get Phil Connors' interest, he telephoned Phil to set up a meeting. "Phil, I have something that I think will reduce your claims expense. If you have about half an hour, I can come over to your office and explain it."

"John, if you have anything that will reduce my claims expense, I'll be in your office in 5 minutes. I was just sitting here looking at the most recent claims experience report and we have to be paying out more than we should—see you shortly."

Phil arrived 3 minutes early. "Here I am. You're going to get some of my backlog requests moved up the priority list at the next steering committee meeting. Right?"

"Better than that. I was at the last industry association meeting and heard a presentation given by a DEC representative. He described a technique that is being used by other insurance companies to cut claims expense. I've looked into the technical requirements and it looks like it will work for us as well."

John paused for Phil's response to this applicability feature. "Great! What is it, a computer-based training program for claims examiners?"

"No, even more direct, it's a technique that allows us to provide each claims examiner with the computer-captured expertise of your claims expert. Other insurance companies that have used this technique have experienced some considerable savings in claims expense. The application I worked up for your department indicates that we can realize about $150,000 the first year with more to follow."

John again paused, turning over in his mind the practicality of going into the technical ramifications of the expert system environment. He decided not to, opting for sponsorship based on benefits.

"It sounds good, John, but how are you going to get June Donath's smarts into general distribution? We're thin on experience now and if this is going to take June off the job and place her in DP for any time at all, things will get worse, not better."

John was aware that he was facing an objection that could derail the whole effort. He recalled the knowledge engineer's comments that where an expert system is needed most, it is most difficult to get a commitment for the expert's involvement. Somehow he had to turn this objection into an asset.

"Phil, the beauty part of this is that we can do it with only a few hours of June's time and she needn't leave your department—we can build the system using the PC right in her office."

Phil settled back in his chair. "I know you guys over here are bright and you do what you do very well, but you can't possibly get her whole head into that PC in a couple of hours."

Again John was faced with an honest objection but this one was based upon a lack of communication. The scope of involvement had not been adequately described.

"I agree, but we're only looking at a very restricted area of your total claims operation—the Medicare Supplement. Your annual claims expense there is $1,500,000 and it's realistic to expect a 10 percent reduction with the system I'm proposing. We can get that expertise in a few hours of interviewing with June."

Phil looked somewhat surprised. "I thought you were looking for the $150,000 from the whole operation. You actually believe we can get 10 percent from the Medicare operation alone? I believe it's there but can you get it?"

"Others are doing it, Phil. We're as good as anybody."

"OK! Let's say that I'm in favor of this thing. What do I have to do?"

"At the next steering committee meeting I plan to ask for $15,000 seed money for the project, with a 1-year payback. The Digital Equipment representative will be at the meeting to explain the way this technique is applied and to talk about the results that other companies have experienced. All you have to do is agree to give me your support for the few interview hours I'll need with June Donath. Once we have an opportunity to see the savings, we can move on to other areas. What do you say?"

"Nothing ventured, nothing gained, John. You're making an offer I can't refuse. But why don't you ask for more than $15,000 since there's $150,000 to be gained?"

"Honestly, I think I can do it for less than the $15,000. Asking for more might not get the nod. As far as the $150,000 is concerned, we both agree that there is that much to be gained from claims conservation in the Medicare area but will the other members of the committee be willing to believe that? Further, if I use a number like $150,000 for a first system and they do believe it, they might back off on the $15,000 investment and ask you to go after at least part of those savings alone."

"You've got a point. Being conservative has its virtues. You can count me in. See you at the steering committee meeting tomorrow afternoon."

Phil returned to his office, leaving John to dictate the agenda for the DP steering committee meeting scheduled for the following afternoon. John also prepared his $15,000 budget which allowed $1000 for software and $9000 for three PCs, with the remaining $5000 earmarked for programming expenses, all of which would be expended within 4 months. His estimates were developed from parameters he recalled from a conversation with a fellow MIS director who had implemented

a similar first expert system. John simply doubled the time estimates—his friend had, in fact, implemented the system in 2 months.

The Decisive Meeting

DP steering committee meetings usually consisted of progress reports on
those projects in process, the introduction of new requests, and a review
of the backlog and its priorities. Sometimes things could get a little testy
when a recently implemented system would begin to grow warts. John
had picked this meeting for his introduction of AI because there was
nothing recently implemented that could disrupt the atmosphere. In fact,
things were going pretty well—always a good time to move ahead.

Having gotten the usual business at hand completed, John introduced the speaker's topic: Artificial Intelligence and Expert Systems.
Bob Haynes, the Digital Equipment Corporation knowledge engineer,
was escorted into the conference room by John's secretary and John
introduced Bob to each of the members of the steering committee.

Bob began his presentation, "The last few years have seen some
amazing improvements in computer hardware capability. Larger
memories, faster execution speeds, and smaller physical size have
been developed by the manufacturers almost simultaneously. We now
have desk top computers that would have required an entire room
only a few years ago. It is only natural to expect that software too
should undergo some major improvements. I would like to introduce a
major software improvement to MIC this afternoon. I am not bringing
you news of an untried or untested technology but of one that has been
applied at the Digital Equipment Corporation, saving us millions of
dollars annually."

Bob Haynes verbally walked the steering committee through DEC's
use of XCON, the widespread use of financial advisory expert systems,
underwriting expert systems, and finally, he discussed the use of expert systems in claims examination. He named insurance companies
currently implementing expert systems and closed his presentation,
"John Rogers asked me to explain all of this because he has developed
a proposal for the implementation of an expert system here at MIC. I
think John's proposal is certainly appropriate and I know that its success will open the door to your aggressive application of expert systems on your currently installed VAX. I think John's proposal is very
conservative, and although it does not directly address the use of the
VAX, I am certain the experience it will provide will find us in a future meeting discussing far more ambitious undertakings."

After a round of applause, Bob Haynes departed leaving John to
present his proposal. Sensing the tempo of the environment, John re-

alized that a lengthy presentation could be a negative in the face of Bob's excellent delivery.

He simply explained, "We can begin to realize savings in the claims area in 4 months or less. Preliminary analysis of the requirements indicate that a total investment of $15,000 will be paid back within 1 year and, as Bob Haynes has pointed out, quite possibly the payback will be much greater than my conservative figures indicate. I ran all of this past Phil Connors yesterday. What is your take on this Phil?"

True to his word, Phil looked around the table and said, "John explained yesterday that he was aiming only at our Medicare Supplement claims. As you know, this is the area where we assign our new claims examiners. It's obviously a limited effort offering limited exposure with a disproportionate opportunity for return. More importantly, it's MIC's opportunity to get a start in expert systems. After discussing this with John, I reread some of the recent journal articles on expert systems—I think we should give it a try."

The vice president in charge of policy issue responded, "That's all fine, but aren't we really talking about juggling the backlog priorities? The $15,000 is a drop in the bucket, but putting our backlog requests further down the priority list can cost us some real dollars."

John quickly explained, "This will not affect the backlog. I plan to handle the design, creation, and implementation of this system myself. It is pretty nearly a requirement. If we are going to realize the savings I believe we will achieve here, it's important that I get a personal handle on the requirements for future reference."

"OK! I have no objection then," was the reply.

As it developed, everyone was in favor of the venture and the $15,000 was granted for the project. John had distributed copies of his proposal to each of the members. The only jolt was that John was told to take the expense against his software and hardware budgets with the promise that everything would be reviewed at midyear. The meeting broke up with John making an appointment with Phil to introduce the project to June Donath first thing in the morning.

Interviews with the Expert

It was eight o'clock in the morning when John and Phil walked into June's office. Her desk was piled high with claims folders.

Phil began, "June, you've met John, haven't you?"

"Sure I have. You're going to give me a system that will clear up this claims backlog. Right?" June apparently recalled their conversation.

"Pretty close, June. You see, we have a new system in the works that will require your assistance for maybe an hour or two about 2 days a week. I can see that you're pretty busy but the finished system should reduce your problems. The question this morning is what 2 days are the best?" John sensed that June was too alert to countenance pussy footing.

John's judgment was right. She fired back, "Wednesdays and Thursdays. The gates of hell don't open until about ten o'clock on those days. Monday is the worst day—the phones start ringing 2 hours before the company opens on Mondays. Tuesdays the new claims examiners bring in all their problems from the previous Monday. Friday I spend staging the work for Saturday. What will we be doing?"

"I'll be interviewing you to find out how you settle claims for Medicare Supplement benefits. We plan to incorporate your expertise in an expert system and then make it available as a guide for your Medicare claims examiners." John looked at her desk and continued, "This might not eliminate all of those new claims examiners' problems, but it should reduce the number of them and at the same time reduce the claims dollars we're paying."

June frowned. "That sounds great but we get claims for everything from cataracts to carcinoma on the Medicare Supplements and sometimes without a properly completed claim form. Then we have to send out letters asking for more information and more letters to get an EOMB—it can get pretty involved. Do you think it can be done?"

John realized that a true salesperson never rests. "A number of insurance companies both smaller and larger than ours have created this kind of an expert system and they report success and savings, and they have gone on to build additional systems for underwriting and financial applications. It will be a first for MIC and we can't think of a more expert expert than you, June."

"What price glory? Let's get together next Wednesday at 8 A.M. and I'll keep the invaders out until 10. I'll tell you everything you want to know—well, almost everything. A girl has to have some secrets—I'll just keep the ones that don't have anything to do with claims. OK?"

Phil, feeling a little extraneous, moved toward the door, "Great June. We really appreciate it."

The first interview

It was the appointed Wednesday morning when John appeared in June's office, tape recorder and note pad in hand—eight o'clock sharp. "I brought along a tape recorder so I will be able to refer to the details if I miss something in my notes."

"Good idea! Here's a copy of the Medicare Supplement policy. It describes the 6-month exclusionary period prior to issue. Any medical conditions that the insured is diagnosed for, receives treatment for, or receives professional medical advice for during that 6-month period prior to the policy's issue is excluded from benefits until the policy is at least 6 months old." John was still looking for a place to set his tape recorder and June was off and running.

"Here, just pull over that chair and put in on the seat. I'm afraid you'll have to take notes in your lap—this desk is a mess. Now then, what would you like to know?"

"How do you handle Medicare claims?"

"Well, the first thing we like to ascertain is that any policy for which we receive a claim has reached the effective date, is in force, or that it is lapsed but is still within the grace period. If the grace period hasn't expired, we can still pay a valid claim, but we deduct the premium owing from the claim payment, taking the policy out of its lapsed state. Hard as it may be to believe, history will show that we have, in fact, paid claims on policies not yet at the effective date, not in force, or lapsed and beyond the grace period."

"How can that happen?"

"New claims examiners in a hurry to settle a claim just forge ahead. When they see that the policy is issued, they often miss the fact that it won't be effective for, say, another week. They check on the EOMB to see that Medicare has paid the insured's claim. If Medicare has paid, they just go ahead and issue the settlement. The same kind of sequence follows for policies that have lapsed and are beyond the grace period. Don't misunderstand, it's a rare event but even one a month is too much."

"What is an EOMB?

"Oh, that's the Explanation of Medicare Benefits. It's the documentation that we can request from Medicare that indicates that Medicare has paid a benefit for an illness. If Medicare hasn't paid a benefit, we're off the risk. Our policy is designed to supplement the Medicare payment, but we don't pay a benefit during the first 6 months of a policy's life if the ailment existed during the 6 months prior to the policy's issue. You see, John, these people are old and sickness strikes and suddenly they're informed that they need supplemental coverage and that Medicare just won't pay the total cost of their treatment. Often they just apply for a supplemental policy and then submit a claim for benefits as soon as the policy is delivered."

"Right ..." John was now scribbling trigger words on his pad and realizing that June was being forced to repeat herself. "So the EOMB tells you that the condition existed within the 6 months prior to the policy's issue as well as informing you that Medicare is paying for the current treatment."

"Not really. The EOMB simply verifies that Medicare paid a benefit for the treatment. It's our job to verify that the condition wasn't pre-existent."

"Can you give me an example?"

"Sure. Mr. Doe has chest pains and visits his physician. The examination reveals that he has angina. The physician prescribes nitroglycerin pills but explains that an angiogram is needed to determine the operability of the condition. Maybe a by-pass operation will remedy the situation. In the course of the discussion, Mr. Doe learns that Medicare will only pay a part of the possible expense. Mr. Doe applies for a supplemental policy and as soon as it is issued, he is hospitalized for the angiogram. They discover that a by-pass operation is needed right away. The operation is performed and, bingo, we get a claim. Pretty big dollars are involved, and we want to determine that we're not dealing with a preexisting medical condition."

"What are big dollars, June?"

"Well, anything in excess of, say, $200 is subject to scrutiny. Amounts less than that really don't justify the additional time required to make a determination."

"How do you determine that Mr. Doe was diagnosed or treated less than 6 months prior to applying for the policy?"

"When Mr. Doe applied for the policy, he completed an application and signed it, giving us the right to obtain his physician's records. We're also going to have a copy of the physician's bill for fees. Somewhere in that information we're going to find that he received a prescription for nitroglycerin pills, received a positive stress test, or whatever. If we find that the condition is preexistent, we will deny any related claim placed during the first 6 months of the policy's life."

John decided to see if he could elicit June's heuristics, "Gee, how do you know what to look for in these claims? It seems that you nearly have to be a physician."

"Not really. After you get enough experience, you develop a feel for what to expect. Take a claim for diabetes, you look for a prior FBS or a glucose tolerance test or perhaps a prescription for insulin. In other cases it's a prescribed sugarless diet that tips you off to the fact that the condition was preexisting."

"What's an FBS?"

"Oh, that's a fasting blood sugar test. Each claims condition identifies its own set of possible prior diagnostic events."

"What are some of the ..." June's phone began ringing and John stopped short. June grabbed the receiver.

"Hello, claims, June Donath. Okay, I'll be right there."

June looked at John apologetically, "I really have to get over to Phil's office. The state insurance commissioner is paying us a visit and Phil wants me to answer some questions. We can take up again tomorrow."

John felt almost relieved. "No problem. Tomorrow, same time, same place." John picked up his tape recorder, turned it off, and departed for his office.

Settling into his office chair, John looked over his scribbled notes, glanced at his wrist watch, and concluded that he still had an hour to spend reviewing the interview. It became more and more apparent that he could use the simplest confidence factor rating for the rules of this expert system—boolean probability (1, 0). The conditions were such that claims were either paid or not paid. None of June's judgments involved standard probability theory—there was no case wherein there was a 9 in 10 probability that a claim would be paid. Certainly, fuzzy logic was ruled out too. John began to itemize the possible outcomes or choices that the expert system could select:

1. Deny the claim because of policy lapse and grace period expiration.
2. Deny the claim because the policy is not yet in force.
3. Deny the claim because of lack of Medicare involvement.
4. Pay the claim, less any premium owing.
5. Pay the claim in full.
6. Deny the claim because of preexistence of the insured's condition.

Logically, it seemed that there must be an avenue of action if the claims examiner's information was indeterminant. John elected to employ a seventh choice pending tomorrow's interview when he could get a clarification from June:

7. Refer the claim to the chief claims examiner.

Using these conclusions, John realized that he would have to build a taxonomy that would classify the conditions related to each of the possible outcomes or conclusions. He quickly sketched out the beginnings of the taxonomy:

A. The policy is lapsed and beyond the grace period.
    A.1 Deny the claim because of lapse and grace period expiration.
B. The policy is issued but not yet at the effective date.
    B.1 Deny the claim because the policy is not yet in force.
C. Medicare has not paid the claim as evidenced by a received EOMB.
    C.1 Deny the claim because of lack of Medicare involvement.
D. The policy is lapsed but within the grace period.
    D.1 Medicare has paid the claim as evidenced by a received EOMB.
        D.1.1   The policy's age is 6 months or more.
            D.1.1.1 Pay the claim, less any premium owing.
        D.1.2   The policy's age is less than 6 months.
            D.1.2.1 The claim's value is less than $200.
                D.1.2.1.1 Pay the claim, less any premium owing.
            D.1.2.2 The claim's value is $200 or more.
                D.1.2.2.1 The condition is not preexisting.
                    D.1.2.2.1.1 Pay the claim, less any premium owing.
                D.1.2.2.2 The condition is preexisting.

        D.1.2.2.2.1 Deny the claim because of preexisting.
        D.1.2.2.3 The condition is indeterminant.
        D.1.2.2.3.1 Refer the claim to the chief examiner.
E. The policy is in force.
  E.1 Medicare has paid the claim as evidenced by a received EOMB.
    E.1.1 The policy's age is 6 months or more.
    E.1.1.1 Pay the claim in full.
    E.1.2 The policy's age is less than 6 months.
      E.1.2.1 The claim's value is less than $200.
      E.1.2.1.1 Pay the claim in full.
      E.1.2.2 The claim's value is $200 or more.
        E.1.2.2.1 The condition is not preexisting.
        E.1.2.2.1.1 Pay the claim in full.
        E.1.2.2.2 The condition is preexisting.
        E.1.2.2.2.1 Deny the claim because of preexisting.
        E.1.2.2.3 The condition is indeterminant.
        E.1.2.2.3.1 Refer the claim to the chief examiner.

John sat staring at his results, realizing that he was looking at what would constitute the core of the expert system. The rules could be written directly from the taxonomy. He quickly wrote a few, reviewing his understanding of the claims processing procedures:

IF A., THEN A.1.
IF B., THEN B.1.
IF C., THEN C.1.
IF D. and D.1 and D.1.1, THEN D.1.1.1.
IF D. and D.1 and D.1.2 and D.1.2.1, THEN D.1.2.1.1.
IF D. and D.1 and D.1.2 and D.1.2.2 and D.1.2.2.1, THEN D.1.2.2.1.1.

The four policy conditions, lapsed but within grace period, lapsed and beyond the grace period, in force, and issued but not yet effective, were all addressed by the taxonomy in conjunction with the claim's critical value—under or over $200—as was the nature of the insured's condition, preexisting, indeterminant, or not preexisting. All of the possible choices were applied as well.

John realized that his taxonomy did not address any of June's heuristics. If he didn't create rules that would derive information identifying the insured's condition as preexistent, indeterminant, or not preexisting, the system's user would be asked. John knew that the completion of the system would see him providing a number of rules whose objectives would be the identification of an insured's condition as preexisting, indeterminant, or not preexisting. June's heuristics would be involved. The taxonomy provided a good basis for the prototype, but there was a good deal more to accomplish after that.

John felt that what he needed right now was that expert system shell that Bob Haynes had promised. He reached for the telephone.

After two rings, there was a familiar voice, "Hello, system development, Bob Haynes here."

"Hi, Bob. This is John Rogers over at MIC. Say, I conducted the first interview this morning for the claims system we discussed. It looks like a no-probability yes or no system with backward chaining. Tell me about that PC-based expert system shell that will port to the VAX."

"Great, John. You have some of the rules outlined already?"

"Yes, I have the guts of the conditions and conclusions and I would really like to start getting familiar with the tool."

"If I recall, John, you're working on a pretty tight budget. I would recommend that you take a walk at lunch time. Go over to the Expert Software Sales Company on River and Oak. Buy a copy of Exsys for about $400. Follow the tutorial and read the manual. You'll find that shell not only provides an expert system that you can port to the VAX, but it allows you to execute your own programs from within the expert system. It will do both forward and backward chaining. You're sure that you don't see any frames in this layout eh?"

"No, Bob, this looks like a rule-based job."

"I'm glad to hear you say that. Most systems of that nature are rule based. I just wanted to be sure that you're on the right track. Now be aware that the $400 will buy the system for one user. If you want to distribute to more than one PC user, you're going to have to pay an extra $600 for what amounts to a site license. After that, the VAX version will cost a bit more. I think you can get into that later when you have this thing up and running. Give me a call if you have any questions, OK?"

"OK. You're pretty familiar with this shell?"

"I've done a few demo systems with it and the Canadian Pacific Railway, among others, is currently saving some big dollars with it. I have confidence that it will meet or exceed your requirements."

The second interview

It was Thursday morning and John again arrived at June's office at the stroke of eight. "How did your meeting with the insurance commissioner turn out yesterday?"

"Oh, no problem. He was just in on a routine visit, and Phil thought it would be good for me to give him an idea of how we handle claims on a new policy we just brought out. What are we going to do today?"

"I have a couple of preliminary questions. First, what procedure is followed if the claims examiner feels that a preexistence determination can't be made on a particular new policy claim? Let's say that the available records just don't indicate a clear yes or no." John quickly sat his tape recorder on the empty chair and brought his pad to the ready.

"A situation like that is usually indicative of the insured's having switched doctors or moved to a new part of the country. If a patient stays with the same physician, patient records can become quite extensive. Further, most physicians will have a given patient visit the same hospital each time hospitalization or outpatient treatment is required and the hospital's records will show each such event. Quite often even if the patient does switch doctors, the patient will be visiting the same hospital that his or her former physician designated because of the location of his or her home. If that patient has relocated, we have ways of going after prior records.

"There is one thing that you should know, John. The overriding philosophy in this department is that when in doubt, that is, when there's no glaring evidence of preexistence, we want to pay the claim. We are a service to the insured. We have to balance claims examinations with good sense. We just have to be more thorough than we have been.

"To answer your question, if the findings are really indeterminant, the claim joins the pile here on my desk. The trouble is that too many claims get into this pile. If I only got the toughies, I wouldn't mind, but the new examiners either bring them in for fear of making a mistake or they just go ahead and pay. I guess it's the claims that I don't see that are costing us unnecessary expense. When it's all said and done, I'm just not seeing the right claims."

"The second question has to do with the patient conditions. What are some of the conditions for which claims are submitted?"

"Well, there are the big three, cardiac conditions, carcinoma, or cancer, and diabetes. Strokes don't permit us to do much background work because they strike suddenly and we can't point to a preexistent condition when the aliment is acute such as in the case of a sudden stroke. When any diagnosis involves the words "chronic" or "severe" they're like red flags. These words imply that the condition has been previously diagnosed and is now getting more serious."

"Do the Medicare Supplement claims involve a well-defined set of ailments or do new conditions continue to appear?"

"Five years ago I would have said that the conditions were pretty standard, but today we're seeing AIDS, contracted through previous blood transfusions, parasitic conditions, salmonella-related conditions—just about the full gamut of the medical dictionary. That's the reason that I questioned the possibility of squeezing all of these conditions into a computer."

"I have a plan that will take care of the rapidly expanding set of medical conditions. What I would like to do is get a list of the more frequently encountered ailments. We can build up our collection from there."

"OK, let's let the list begin with anemia, any cardiac condition, arthritis, bronchitis, diabetes, gout, hypertension, osteoporosis, rheumatism, ulcers, and of course, carcinoma. Then there are cataracts,

Alzheimer's disease, arteriosclerosis, kidney stones or any form of nephritis or dialysis involvement, a back or spinal disc ailment, and God knows how many others that I might have left out."

One of June's claims examiners suddenly appeared in the doorway, "June, I know we're not supposed to bother you until 10, but the system just quit on us. My terminal is as dead as a door nail."

Before June had the opportunity to reply, the telephone began to ring, "Hello, claims, June Donath. Yes, he's right here. Just a minute. It's for you, John."

John took the receiver, "Hello. Yes, OK, I'll be right over." John hung up. "June, it's my turn this time. The system is down and I have to get back to the department right away. Next Wednesday, same time, OK?"

"Take care, John. And get us back up. We've got a ton of claims to work on as you know."

John grabbed his tape recorder, turned it off, and headed for his office to learn that the 3370 housing Sys Res had just crashed. The CEs were already called and they were bringing out a new HDA. The system had only been up 30 minutes, and so it was just a matter of waiting until the hardware was restored. The system programmer was ready to restore last night's backup. John instructed his secretary to call all departments to explain the problem and that any transactions would have to be resubmitted when they came up again. John sank into his chair to review his notes.

Building the Prototype

John knew that his decision to include the seventh choice dealing with the indeterminant finding in his taxonomy was valid. June had accepted it. He also had a list of patient conditions that frequently appeared on various of the Medicare Supplement claims forms. He began to make a list of outstanding requirements in preparation to creating the prototype.

Because Exsys would allow him to call a program during a user's session, John elected to write a file update program that would be called if a claims examiner encountered a patient condition not on the list of ailments. The program requested the new ailment's name, thus allowing John to modify the ailment list after auditing the file. The program was MED1.EXE.

John decided to complete the taxonomy by establishing some meta rules that he would use in its design. These rules would embody June's explanation of her department's philosophy. For example, given a hospital admission, if the hospital records showed no prior activity for an ailment, that is, they went back far enough to be considered reliable, and if the doctor's records were considered indeterminant—showed nothing one way or the other—John judged the condition as not preexistent. Only if both the hospital and the physician's records were indeterminant would the case be referred to the chief claims examiner. John devised a set of these rules so that his design of the expert system rules would be consistent under all of the circumstances that might be encountered. John decided to allow the word "prior" to mean "within the exclusionary period" when the actual rules were created. He proceeded with the taxonomy:

F. The diagnosis is for one of those ailments on the list.
    F.1 The patient was admitted to the hospital.
        F.1.1 The hospital records show the ailment's prior treatment.
            F.1.1.1 The condition is preexistent.
        F.1.2 The hospital records show no prior ailment treatment.
            F.1.2.1 The physician's records show no prior treatment.
                F.1.2.1.1 The condition is not preexistent.
            F.1.2.2 The physician's records show prior treatment.
                F.1.2.2.1 The condition is preexistent.
            F.1.2.3 The physician's records are indeterminant.
                F.1.2.3.1 The condition is not preexistent.
        F.1.3 The hospital records are indeterminant.
            F.1.3.1 The physician's records show prior treatment.
                F.1.3.1.1 The condition is preexistent
            F.1.3.2 The physician's records show no prior treatment.
                F.1.3.2.1 The condition is not preexistent.
            F.1.3.3 The physician's records are indeterminant.
                F.1.3.3.1 The condition is indeterminant.
    F.2 The patient was treated during visits to a physician's office.
        F.2.1 The physician's records show prior treatment.
            F.2.1.1 The condition is preexistent.
        F.2.2 The physician's records show no prior treatment.
            F.2.2.1 The condition is not preexistent.
        F.2.3 The physician's records are indeterminant.
            F.2.3.1 The condition is indeterminant.
G. The diagnosis identifies an ailment not on our list.
    G.1 The patient was admitted to the hospital.
        G.1.1 The hospital records show no prior treatment.
            G.1.1.1 The physician's records are indeterminant.
                G.1.1.1.1 Execute MED1.EXE.
                G.1.1.1.2 The condition is not preexistent.
            G.1.1.2 The physician's records show prior treatment.
                G.1.1.2.1 Execute MED1.EXE.
                G.1.1.2.2 The condition is preexistent.
            G.1.1.3 The physician's records show no prior treatment.
                G.1.1.3.1 Execute MED1.EXE.
                G.1.1.3.2 The condition is not preexistent.
        G.1.2 The hospital records show prior treatment.
            G.1.2.1 Execute MED1.EXE.
            G.1.2.2 The condition is preexistent.
        G.1.3 The hospital records are indeterminant.
            G.1.3.1 The physician's records show prior treatment.
                G.1.3.1.1 Execute MED1.EXE.

G.1.3.1.2 The condition is preexistent.
G.1.3.2 The physician's records show no prior treatment.
G.1.3.2.1 Execute MED1.EXE.
G.1.3.2.2 The condition is not preexistent.
G.1.3.3 The physician's records are indeterminant.
G.1.3.3.1 Execute MED1.EXE.
G.1.3.3.2 The condition is indeterminant.
G.2 The patient was treated during visits to a physician's office.
G.2.1 The physician's records are indeterminant.
G.2.1.1 Execute MED1.EXE.
G.2.1.2 The condition is indeterminant.
G.2.2 The physician's records show no prior treatment.
G.2.2.1 Execute MED1.EXE.
G.2.2.2 The condition is not preexistent.
G.2.3 The physician's records show prior treatment.
G.2.3.1 Execute MED1.EXE.
G.2.3.2 The condition is preexistent.

The taxonomy for the prototype was complete. Items A through G would constitute the rule set for the prototype. John was aware that he had not yet provided for June's heuristics—the telltale specifics that could identify a preexistent condition. June had mentioned FBS (fasting blood sugar) tests as indicators that a diabetes diagnosis was preexistent, but John felt that, with the prototype created, he could go more deeply into these heuristics with June during their next meeting.

John elected not to spend time creating a decision tree since his taxonomy allowed the direct fabrication of the rules. He booted his PC and typed EDITXS to call the Exsys rule editor in order to begin the creation of the prototype. The rule editor's screen appeared requesting the name of the file. John typed MEDICARE. The screen is displayed in Figure 9.1

After he pressed the Enter key, Exsys, not finding a MEDICARE file, asked John if he wanted to create a new file. Figure 9.2 presents the screen to which John replied, yes.

A screen requesting the subject of the knowledge base then appeared as in Figure 9.3. We see that John entered a brief identifying remark that will be incorporated in the initial screen at run time.

The Enter key produced another screen requesting the author's name. Here, John entered his own name as shown in Figure 9.4.

After identifying himself as author, Exsys returned the screen that allowed John to choose the confidence factor (CF) mode that the expert system was to use. Figure 9.5 illustrates the screen. John chose the simple yes or no mode.

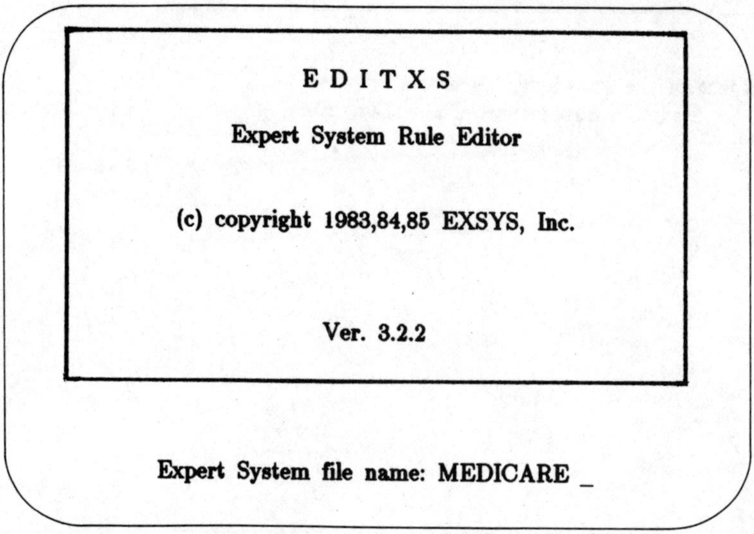

E D I T X S

Expert System Rule Editor

(c) copyright 1983,84,85 EXSYS, Inc.

Ver. 3.2.2

Expert System file name: MEDICARE _

Figure 9.1   The initial EDITXS screen.

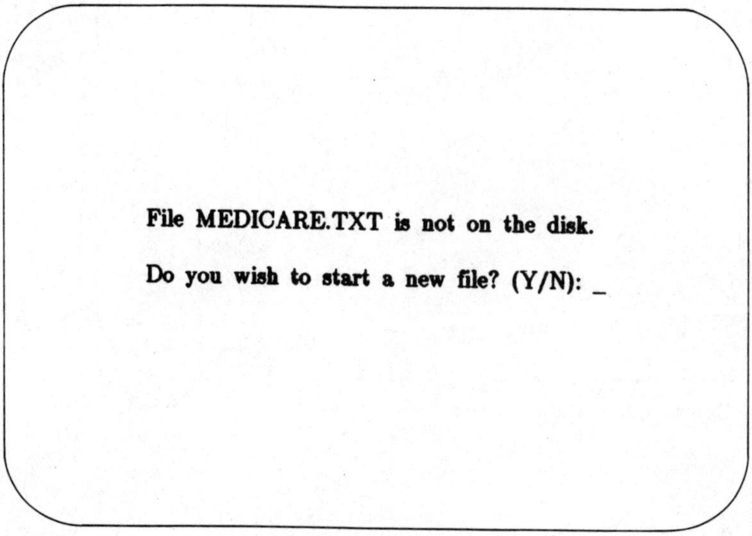

File MEDICARE.TXT is not on the disk.

Do you wish to start a new file? (Y/N): _

Figure 9.2   Exsys asks if a new file is being built.

Subject of the knowledge base:
    Medicare Supplement Claim Evaluation _

Figure 9.3   The subject of the knowledge base will be used for the initial run screen.

Author: John Rogers

Figure 9.4   Exsys requests the author's name.

How do you wish the data on the available choices structured:

1 — Simple yes or no

2 — A range of 0–10 where 0 indicates absolutely not and 10 indicates absolutely certain. 1–9 indicate degrees of certainty.

3 — A range of −100 to +100 indicating the degree of certainty

Input number of selection or <H> for help: _

Figure 9.5 The confidence factor mode is selected.

The next screen, shown in Figure 9.6, allowed John to have all rules applied in deriving data. Although this might result in the user being asked unnecessary questions, it is wiser to allow all rules to be used as an initial state. This option may be changed later if it develops that the user is being asked unnecessary questions. The default is accepted.

The screen displayed in Figure 9.7 allowed John to create the introductory text that the user will read at the beginning of a user session. As we see, John stated the purpose of the expert system rather clearly.

Similar to the introductory text is the screen that followed. Here, John entered brief concluding remarks that would appear immediately prior to the expert system's conclusion display. Figure 9.8 illustrates John's response.

John was free to choose a default condition in the screen of Figure 9.9. Here John chose not to have the rules displayed as they fire in order to avoid confusing the user. This feature may be altered during the creation of the system when it might prove useful as a debugging tool.

The screen shown in Figure 9.10 asked John if he plans to have an external program execute at the start of the user's session. As we discovered earlier, John created a program that would be called during the system's session and so he responded with an N here.

The next screen, Figure 9.11, requested that John input the choices among which the expert system will select its conclusions. These seven choices were isolated by John prior to his creation of the taxonomy.

Number of rules to use in data derivation:

1. Attempt to apply all possible rules
2. Stop after first successful rule

Select 1 or 2 (Default = 1): _

Figure 9.6   All rules will be used in deriving information.

Input the text you wish to use to explain how to run this file.
This text will be displayed at the start of EXSYS.

I am an expert system that has been designed to aid claims personnel in
determining the validity of claims for benefits payable under supplementary
Medicare policies. I specifically seek to identify claims for benefits
arising from preexisting medical conditions for which professional medical
advice or treatment was given within the exclusionary period 6 months prior to
the policy's date of issue.

In order to be of assistance, I will ask you multiple choice questions such
as:
                the policy is
                1 lapsed but within the grace period
                2 lapsed and beyond the grace period
                3 in force
                4 issued but not yet at the effective date

for which only one choice should be made. A question dealing with the
insured's diagnosis will allow you to select the number of the ailment or
descriptive word that best defines the insured's condition. If there is more
than one diagnosis, I should be consulted separately for each ailment
identified. _

Figure 9.7   The expert system's introductory text is supplied by its author.

Input the text you wish to use at the end of the EXSYS run.
This will be displayed when the rules are done but before the
choices and their calculated values are displayed

Based upon the information you have given me, I find the following action
appropriate. Please press the Enter key... _

Figure 9.8 The ending text will appear before the conclusion.

Do you wish the user running this expert system to
have the rules displayed as the default condition?
(The user will have the option of overriding this default)
(Y/N) (Default = N): _

Figure 9.9 Rules will not be shown during a user session, but this may be
altered by the user.

Do you wish to have an external program called
at the start of a run to pass data back for
multiple variables or qualifiers? (Other external
programs may also be used later) (Y/N) (Default=N): _

Figure 9.10   An external program will not be called at the start of a session.

Input the choices to select among. Input just <ENTER> when done
Additional choices can be added later
   1 Deny the claim due to lapse and grace period expiration.
   2 Deny the claim because the policy is not yet in force.
   3 Deny the claim due to lack of Medicare involvement.
   4 Pay the claim, less any premium owing.
   5 Pay the claim in full.
   6 Deny the claim due to preexistence of the insured's condition.
   7 Refer the claim to the Chief Claims Examiner.
   8 _

Figure 9.11   The choices from which the expert system may select its conclusions are supplied early in the system's creation.

After providing Exsys with the necessary preliminary information, the main editor screen appeared as shown in Figure 9.12. John's familiarization with Exsys has involved his becoming acquainted with the options shown at the bottom of this screen. We will briefly review them.

We see that a rule may be added by pressing the A key or simply pressing the Enter key. In the event that we are interested in editing or changing a rule already created, the E key must be pressed. To delete a rule, the D key is pressed, while a rule may be moved by pressing an M on the keyboard. (It is sometimes beneficial to move a rule in order to have its location in the rule base changed to optimize performance.) The rules and conditions of an expert system may be printed at the printer by pressing the P key.

If we wish to leave the editor, then S must be pressed. This will provide an opportunity to either save or directly exit the editor without saving the rules that have been created in memory. The R key allows John to run the rules in a user's session in order to test the system at any stage in its development. Pressing the O key will present a menu that allows the selection of an already-completed screen, such as the introductory remarks, so that editing may be performed. The only unchangeable item is the CF mode.

John chose to press A. The screen shown in Figure 9.13 presented him with the opportunity to enter his first rule from the taxonomy.

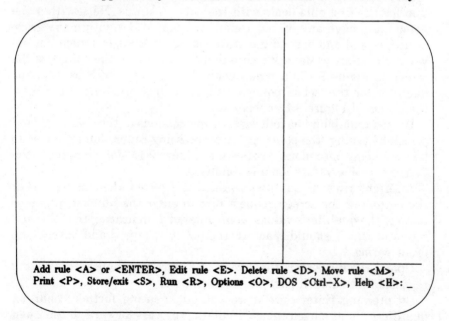

Add rule <A> or <ENTER>, Edit rule <E>. Delete rule <D>, Move rule <M>, Print <P>, Store/exit <S>, Run <R>, Options <O>, DOS <Ctrl–X>, Help <H>: _

Figure 9.12 The edit screen appears ready for the entry of the rules.

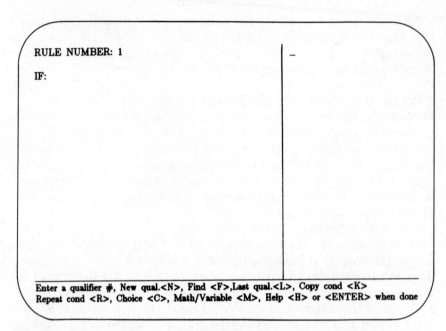

Enter a qualifier #, New qual.<N>, Find <F>,Last qual.<L>, Copy cond <K>
Repeat cond <R>, Choice <C>, Math/Variable <M>, Help <H> or <ENTER> when done

Figure 9.13   Upon pressing the A key, the system is ready for the first rule.

John referred to item A of the taxonomy and found that the condition for the first rule deals with the policy's status. He saw that the policy may have any of four conditions, lapsed but within the grace period, lapsed and beyond the grace period, in force, or issued but not yet at the effective date. We note that the options at the bottom of the screen in Figure 9.13 have now changed. John pressed N to enter the qualifier for this set of policy conditions. Upon pressing the N key, the screen of Figure 9.14 appeared.

We see that John has followed the instructions at the bottom of that screen by typing "the policy is." After pressing Enter, John referred to the taxonomy once more. As shown in Figure 9.15, John has typed the four acceptable values for this condition.

After entering the qualifier's values as directed, the instructions at the bottom of the screen request him to enter the number of one or more of the qualifier's values. John entered 2, indicating that the condition of rule 1 should read "IF the policy is lapsed and beyond the grace period."

Upon pressing Enter, the screen of Figure 9.16 appeared showing that the first rule's If part had been created.

By pressing Enter once more without creating further condition qualifiers, John moved the rule-building process forward to the Then part of the rule as shown in Figure 9.17.

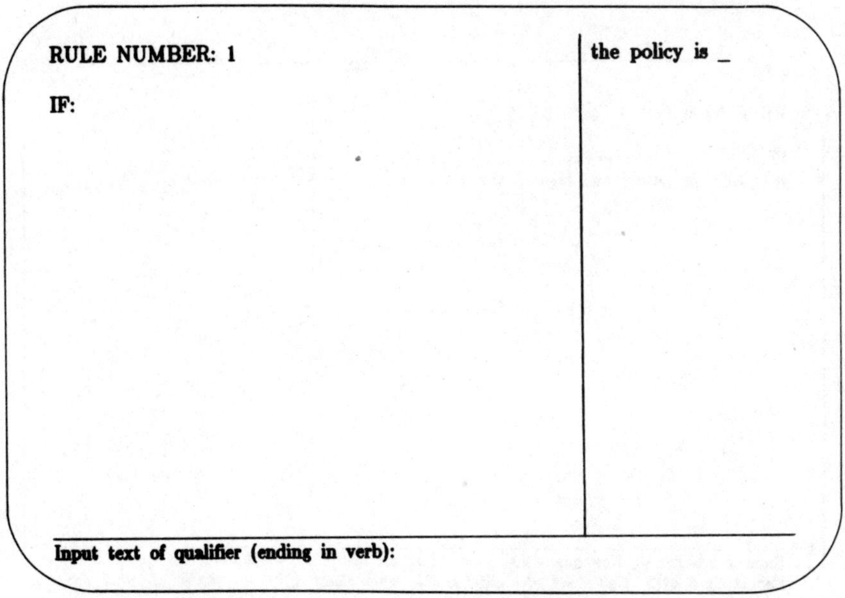

RULE NUMBER: 1

IF:

the policy is _

Input text of qualifier (ending in verb):

Figure 9.14   The first rule's If condition qualifier will be entered.

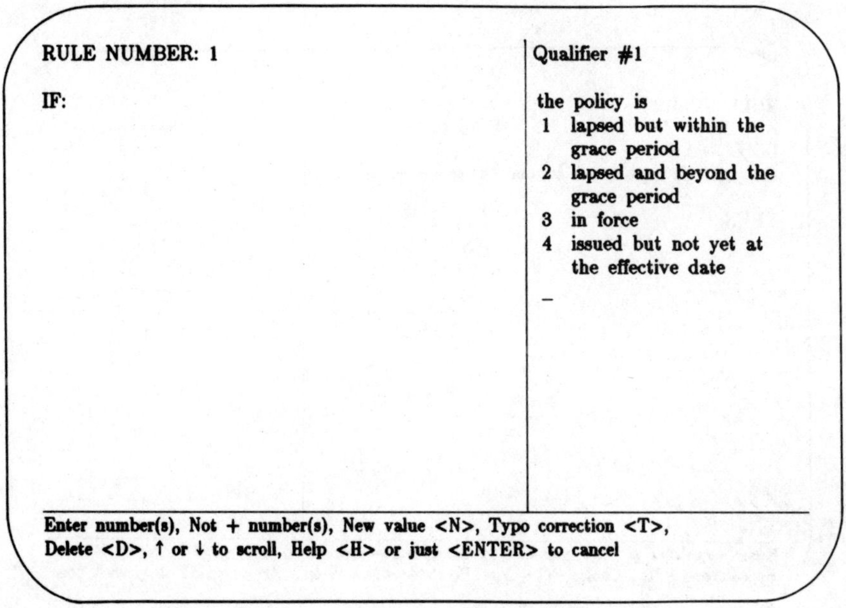

RULE NUMBER: 1

IF:

Qualifier #1

the policy is
1   lapsed but within the
    grace period
2   lapsed and beyond the
    grace period
3   in force
4   issued but not yet at
    the effective date

_

Enter number(s), Not + number(s), New value <N>, Typo correction <T>,
Delete <D>, ↑ or ↓ to scroll, Help <H> or just <ENTER> to cancel

Figure 9.15   The qualifier's values are now entered.

RULE NUMBER: 1

IF:
the policy is lapsed and beyond the grace period

Enter a qualifier #, New qual.<N>, Find <F>,Last qual.<L>, Copy cond <K>
Repeat cond <R>, Choice <C>, Math/Variable <M>, Help <H> or <ENTER> when done

Figure 9.16 The qualifier and one of its values are now part of Rule 1.

RULE NUMBER: 1

IF:
the policy is lapsed and beyond the grace period

THEN:

Enter a qualifier #, New qual.<N>, Find <F>,Last qual.<L>, Copy cond <K>
Repeat cond <R>, Choice <C>, Math/Variable <M>, Help <H> or <ENTER> when done

Figure 9.17 Upon pressing the Enter key, the Then part of the rule is ready.

The menu options at the bottom of the screen shown in Figure 9.17 are identical to those seen earlier. John pressed C to notify Exsys that he wished to have one of the system's choices appear as the Then part of this rule. Upon pressing C, the list of choices appeared as seen in Figure 9.18.

John selected choice no. 1 by entering a 1 and pressing the Enter key. The legend at the bottom of the screen then instructed John to enter his CF for this conclusion. John typed 1 as the CF and pressed the Enter key. As shown in Figure 9.19, that choice became the Then part of this rule and displays the CF value he entered.

After entering the CF for the choice, John was free to enter other choices for the Then part of the rule, but since none would apply, he again pressed the Enter key, notifying Exsys that he had finished entering the Then part of the rule. This produced the modified screen shown in Figure 9.20.

John was then able to enter an Else part for the rule. Because none of the rules in his system required an Else rule provision, he again pressed the Enter key. This produced a blank screen with NOTE: appearing in its upper left corner. This screen allowed John to enter the text of an explanatory note that will be displayed to the user should the word "why" be entered in response to a question asked by the ex-

```
RULE NUMBER: 1                                1  Deny the claim due
                                                 to lapse and grace
IF:                                              period expiration.
the policy is lapsed and beyond the grace period  2  Deny the claim
                                                 because the policy
THEN:                                            is not yet in force.
                                              3  Deny the claim due to
                                                 lack of Medicare
                                                 involvement.
                                              4  Pay the claim, less
                                                 any premium owing.
                                              5  Pay the claim in full.
                                              6  Deny the claim due to
                                                 preexistence of the
                                                 insured's condition.
                                              7  Refer the claim to the
                                                 Chief Claims Examiner.

Select choice number, New value <N> or Typo correction <T>,
Delete/reorder <D>, Find <F>, Help <H>, <ESC> or <ENTER> to cancel: _
```

Figure 9.18 From a display of the choices, the author selects the conclusion.

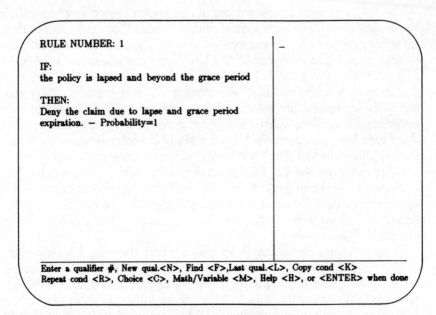

RULE NUMBER: 1   –

IF:
the policy is lapsed and beyond the grace period

THEN:
Deny the claim due to lapse and grace period
expiration. — Probability=1

Enter a qualifier #, New qual.<N>, Find <F>,Last qual.<L>, Copy cond <K>
Repeat cond <R>, Choice <C>, Math/Variable <M>, Help <H>, or <ENTER> when done

Figure 9.19   After the Enter key is pressed, the conclusion becomes part of the rule.

pert system during a user session when attempting to prove this rule.
Figure 9.21 shows the note that John supplied for this rule.

After supplying the optional informational note, John pressed the
Enter key. Another screen appeared with REFERENCE in its upper
left corner. This screen allowed John the opportunity to supply a
trustworthy reference to substantiate his earlier explanation. The object of this documentation is to allow the user to effectively interrogate the expert system during a session by entering Why in response
to a system request for information. Thus, the user is provided with
authoritative explanations rather than being forced to accept expert
system results on faith. Figure 9.22 displays John's reference to the
Medicare Supplement policy whose contractual terms support his earlier note and, of course, the conclusion of Rule 1.

John pressed the Enter key after completing the optional reference
screen. The final screen for Rule 1 then appeared for John's review
and acceptance or rejection. This screen is shown in Figure 9.23. John
pressed the Enter key accepting Rule 1.

John went on, working his way through the taxonomy, entering
each rule according to the directives at the bottom of the screen. When
he got to taxonomy item F, he entered the qualifier "the diagnosis is"
and followed it with 19 values—18 ailments or red-flag words

RULE NUMBER: 1

IF:
the policy is lapsed and beyond the grace period

THEN:
Deny the claim due to lapse and grace period
expiration. — Probability=1

ELSE:

Enter a qualifier #, New qual.<N>, Find <F>,Last qual.<L>, Copy cond <K>
Repeat cond <R>, Choice <C>, Math/Variable <M>, Help <H>, or <ENTER> when done

Figure 9.20 Pressing the Enter key once more produces an opportunity to create the Else part of the rule.

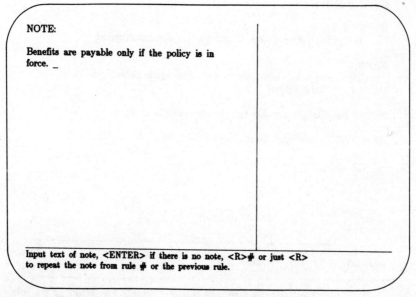

NOTE:

Benefits are payable only if the policy is in
force. _

Input text of note, <ENTER> if there is no note, <R># or just <R>
to repeat the note from rule # or the previous rule.

Figure 9.21 The author supplies a note of explanation for this rule.

REFERENCE:

Medicare Supplement Policy form 10 − 4480. _

Input text of reference, <ENTER> if there is no ref., <R> # or just <R> to repeat the reference from rule # or the previous rule.

Figure 9.22   A reference is cited in support of the note.

RULE NUMBER: 1

IF:
    (1)   The policy is lapsed and beyond the grace period

THEN:
    (1)   Deny the claim due to lapse and grace period expiration. − Probability=1

NOTE: Benefits are payable only if the policy is in force.

REFERENCE: Medicare Supplement Policy form 10 − 4480.

ALL CORRECT? (Y/N) (Default = Y) : _

Figure 9.23   The author is finally given the option of accepting or rejecting the rule.

that June had provided and a final "not on our list." When "not on our list" was chosen, John's diagnosis update program would execute just prior to the system's presentation of the conclusion. As time passed, John became quite familiar with the rule-building process and soon found that he knew enough about Exsys to no longer read the screen directives. Productivity increased rapidly as the prototype took shape.

Upon reaching the end of the taxonomy, John found himself confronting the screen shown in Figure 9.12. He pressed the R key and ran a user session to test the system. After making a minor addition to Rules 1 and 2—John elected to stop further questioning if either Rule 1 or 2 was proved—he retested the system. Everything executed as he had expected. He was ready for his next visit to June Donath. The prototype had been created after two interviews, both of which had been interrupted. John's confidence was at an all-time high.

Presenting the Prototype

It was Wednesday morning and John appeared promptly at June's office ready for their third session, pad, tape recorder, and disk in hand. "Good morning, June. This morning I have something to show you. Do you mind if I use your PC?"

"Not a bit. You've already squeezed all of our discussions onto that disk?"

"Not everything, but I think we have a start. I would like you to comment on the system as I take you through it." John quickly turned on the tape recorder, placed it on the empty chair seat and slipped the disk into June's PC drive.

After booting the PC, a batch file brought up Editxs. John turned to June, "This is what your claims examiners will see when they turn to this system for guidance in examining a Medicare Supplement claim."

June cut John off quickly, "They don't have PCs, and if they come in here to use mine, this office will turn into a thoroughfare."

"Not to worry. Part of the plan is to provide the claims examiners with one or more PCs for their use. The idea is to take the burden off your shoulders and place it upon the system."

John demonstrated his Medicare Supplement system. The first screen presented, "the policy is" and John chose, "in force." The following screen displayed "Medicare has," and John selected "paid the claim." Next John was presented with screens that allowed choices of the policy's age and the value of the claim—John chose less than 6 months for the policy's age and a claim value greater than $200. The next screen appeared displaying June's list of ailments.

John turned to June, "You see, the claims examiner is now free to choose the diagnosis for which most popular claims are submitted."

John chose "anemia" and the next screen asked him to choose the treatment mode—admitted to the hospital or treated as an outpatient, or treated in a physician's office. John chose "admitted to the hospital or treated as an outpatient." The next screen offered the options, "hospital records show ... prior treatment, ... no prior treatment, hospital records are indeterminant."

June immediately commented, "It's great, until you got to this screen. The novice claims examiner often really doesn't know what to look for in the hospital or doctor's records. It is precisely here that a claims examiner must have experience if the claim is to be examined properly."

John realized that the prototype was working. June was at the point at which she would begin to itemize the heuristics that set her apart from the average claims examiner. John turned to June and said, "We did talk about the FBS you look for in diabetes claims and a few of the other telltale indicators of the preexistence of an insured's condition. When I add those specific indicators, this type of general question will become very specific. I can change this expert system to reflect your expertise in just a few minutes. What we have to discuss today is just those items of experience that you possess."

John typed "quit" and Exsys replied asking for the name of the file in which the results gained thus far should be stored. "You see, we can quit right here and pick it up again when we have the details we need. What are some of the telltale indicators for cancer, for instance?"

Capturing the heuristics

June looked at John, "You mean that we have to go over each ailment, bit by bit, and dig up all the medical possibles associated with its pre-existence?"

John sensed that June was beginning to feel overpowered. "Not every ailment. We can pick the big three that you mentioned, carcinoma, cardiac conditions, and diabetes. Then, as we gain experience with the system, we can add others that appear to be fostering early claims."

"OK, I'll go with that approach. The cancer tip-offs include a previous positive biopsy, a positive mammogram, any chemotherapy treatment, a positive NMR scan, a positive CAT scan, a positive chest x-ray, or the appearance of the words 'melanoma, sarcoma, or leukemia' in previous treatment or consultations."

"I'm not going to ask you what an NMR is. I have a medical dictionary and I'll be using it to spell out the details. Tell me about the diabetes indicators now."

"Great, we'll make a claims examiner out of you yet. Diabetes priors often include a glucose tolerance test, an FBS, a prescription for insulin, a sugar-restricted diet, or even advice to reduce sugar intake."

"OK, June, now let's have the cardiac items."

"Heart cases might show previous prescriptions for nitroglycerin, a positive EKG, a positive stress test, a positive angiogram, or previous treatment for chest pain. You have all of that down on your note pad?"

"No, but the tape recorder has it. Now, let's call it a day and in the morning I'll have something more specific to show you. OK?"

John gathered his tape recorder and disk and was on his way.

Adding to the taxonomy and the prototype

John was back in his office listening to the tape recorder and thumbing through his medical dictionary. His thoughts turned to his relationship with June. It seemed that it was beginning to wear a bit. The prototype had helped pick up the tempo, but now there was another issue to be faced. The literature called it "technology transfer." How was he going to introduce the expert system to the claims examiners who would have to actively use it in their daily work if savings were to be realized?

Exsys has a built-in report generator that will print out the qualifiers and choices that a given session has produced if that facility is incorporated in the system's design. If the claims examiners were instructed to include that report output with their processed claims, there would be an assurance that the system was really being used. John promised himself to discuss this with both Phil and June. For now, he had to complete the taxonomy and expand the system by adding the resultant rules.

John continued the taxonomy:

H. The diagnosis is for a cardiac ailment.
    H.1 The patient is hospitalized, an outpatient, or visiting doctor.
        H.1.1 Hospital or physician's records are indeterminant.
            H.1.1.1 The condition is indeterminant.
        H.1.2 Hospital or physician's records show no prior diagnosis.
            H.1.2.1 The condition is not preexistent.
        H.1.3 Hospital or physician's records show prior nitroglycerin, positive EKG, stress test, angiogram, or chest pain during exclusionary period.
            H.1.3.1 The condition is preexistent.
I. The diagnosis is for some form of carcinoma.
    I.1 The patient is hospitalized, an outpatient, or visiting doctor.
        I.1.1 Hospital or physician's records are indeterminant.
            I.1.1.1 The condition is indeterminant.
        I.1.2 Hospital or physician's records show no prior diagnosis.
            I.1.2.1 The condition is not preexistent.

I.1.3 Hospital or physician's records show a positive biopsy, mammogram, nuclear magnetic resonance (NMR) scan, computer-assisted tomography (CAT) scan, chest x-ray, or any medical advice related to melanoma, sarcoma, or leukemia, or any other cancer-related condition during the exclusionary period.

I.1.3.1 The condition is preexistent.

J. The diagnosis is for diabetes.

J.1 The patient is hospitalized, an outpatient, or is visiting doctor.

J.1.1 Hospital or physician's records are indeterminant.

J.1.1.1 The condition is indeterminant.

J.1.2 Hospital or physician's records show no prior diagnosis.

J.1.2.1 The condition is not preexistent.

J.1.3 Hospital or physician's records show a positive glucose-tolerance test, fasting blood sugar (FBS) test, a prescription for insulin in any form, a special sugar-restricted diet, or advice to restrict sugar intake during the exclusionary period.

J.1.3.1 The condition is preexistent.

John turned to his PC, booted it, backed up his expert system Medicare files and brought up Exsys' editor, Editxs, in order to add the new rules. The process was identical to his earlier experience in adding rules, qualifiers, and their associated values directly from the taxonomy. He then tested the expert system that now contained 42 rules. Everything appeared in good order.

John decided it was time to get in touch with Phil in order to update him on his progress. He took inventory of the accomplishments thus far. John had created a program that would result in the capture of ailments not itemized by June (those not on the list) if and when they appeared on a claim. The expert system was geared for three major ailments and offered "prompts" to the novice claim examiners to at least look at the hospital and physician's records when confronted with any of the itemized or "not on the list" ailments. That covered everything that could appear on a claim.

If a claims examiner did reach a decision that the findings were indeterminant, the worst that could happen was that he or she would dump the claim on June's desk—they certainly could not go ahead and pay the claim if they were required to attach the Exsys report of their session to the paperwork.

John picked up the telephone to call Phil. He had decided to install the system the next day if it passed muster with June. It could only help. "Hello, Phil? This is John Rogers. I thought it would be good for me to get in touch and update you on the expert system's progress. Maybe it would be easier if you could attend our session tomorrow morning. Can you make it—eight o'clock sharp?"

Phil agreed that a picture was worth a lot of words and that he would be at John's fourth session with June the next morning. John ordered the required PC for June's department. He would have it later that afternoon and would be ready to install it the next afternoon at the latest if everybody was in agreement.

Technology Transfer

John arrived at June's office just as she was removing her coat. "My we're really early this morning, John. Have you got something new to show me already?"

"I do, just as I promised. I took the liberty of asking Phil to join us so he could see the results of our three sessions. I thought it would be easier to show him the system than to tell him about it. Is it OK if I get your PC booted up?"

"Sure, John. I'll be right back. My coffee maker quit and if I don't get a cup of coffee this morning, I'll die. Can I get you one?"

"No, thanks." John turned on his tape recorder and perched it on the usual chair seat. Almost immediately, Phil returned with June, coffee, and a hardy "Good morning."

"Good morning, Phil. Without further explanation, I would like to show you what a claims examiner will see when our expert system is consulted to aid in the claims processing effort." John by-passed the opening screens in favor of displaying the initial instruction screen that we saw in Figure 9.7. Pressing the space bar, he started the user session and responded to the first question as shown in Figure 9.24.

```
the policy is
    1   lapsed but within the grace period
    2   lapsed and beyond the grace period
    3   in force
    4   issued but not yet at the effective date
1 _




Enter number(s) of value(s), WHY for information on the rule,
(?) for more details, QUIT to save data entered or <H> for help
```

Figure 9.24 The first question is presented during a user session.

John's response resulted in the appearance of the screen shown in Figure 9.25. He responded as shown and pressed the Enter key.

John continued his demonstration, explaining each screen in turn. His responses are shown in the screens displayed as Figures 9.26 through 9.32. John commented at some length on the ailment options shown in the screen of Figure 9.28 and on his choice of carcinoma as an example claim's diagnosis. He explained June's cooperation in developing the possible prior diagnosis indicators displayed in Figure 9.30.

Phil and June were both impressed. John now restarted the system to demonstrate the ailment acquisition feature which incorporated the use of the program he had created to capture new diagnoses.

John's responses during the second session were no different than those of the first session, until the ailment list was again encountered. Figure 9.33 displays John's response to the second appearance of this screen, "an ailment not on our list."

In rapid order, John responded to the screens shown in Figures 9.34 and 9.35.

The appearance of the screen shown in Figure 9.36 came as a surprise when John demonstrated the program's use as a means of capturing the rapidly expanding set of diagnoses appearing in the Medicare Supplement claims. The screen shown in Figure 9.37 appeared following John's response as he pointed out that the verification

```
Medicare has
    1   paid the claim as evidenced by a received Explanation of Medicare
        Benefits (EOMB)
    2   not paid the claim as evidenced by a received Explanation of
        Medicare Benefits (EOMB)
  1 _




















Enter number(s) of value(s), WHY for information on the rule,
(?) for more details, QUIT to save data entered or <H> for help
```

Figure 9.25   Exsys asks the user for status information in order to prove a rule.

```
the policy's age is
     1   6 months or more
     2   less than 6 months
2 _
```

Enter number(s) of value(s), WHY for information on the rule,
(?) for more details, QUIT to save data entered or <H> for help

Figure 9.26 Is the policy less than 6 months of age?

```
the claim's value is
     1   $200 or more
     2   less than $200
1 _
```

Enter number(s) of value(s), WHY for information on the rule,
(?) for more details, QUIT to save data entered or <H> for help

Figure 9.27 The value of the claim is an important element.

the diagnosis includes
  1 anemia
  2 a cardiac related ailment
  3 arthritis
  4 bronchitis
  5 diabetes
  6 gout
  7 hypertension
  8 osteoporosis
  9 rheumatism
  10 ulcers
  11 chronic
  12 severe
  13 carcinoma
  14 cataracts
  15 alzheimer's disease
  16 arteriosclerosis
  17 kidney stone, nephritis, or any condition requiring dialysis
  18 back, spinal or disc ailment
  19 an ailment not on our list
13 _

Enter number(s) of value(s), WHY for information on the rule,
(?) for more details, QUIT to save data entered or <H> for help

Figure 9.28 The user now indicates the nature of the diagnosis.

the patient was
  1 admitted to the hospital or treated as an outpatient
  2 treated during visits to a physician's office
1 _

Enter number(s) of value(s), WHY for information on the rule,
(?) for more details, QUIT to save data entered or <H> for help

Figure 9.29 The patient was admitted to the hospital.

the carcinoma patient's hospital or physician's records or fees show
that the patient, during the exclusionary period, received

1   a carcinoma positive biopsy
2   a carcinoma positive mammogram
3   a carcinoma related chemotherapy treatment
4   a positive Nuclear Magnetic Resonance (NMR) scan
5   a positive Computer Assisted Tomography (CAT) scan
6   a carcinoma positive chest X–Ray
7   any carcinoma positive test results, diagnosis, or advice
    related to Melanoma, Sarcoma or Leukemia or other cancer
    related ailment
8   no diagnosis, treatment or medical advice for an existing
    carcinoma
9   treatment of an indeterminant nature

1 _

Enter number(s) of value(s), WHY for information on the rule,
(?) for more details, QUIT to save data entered or <H> for help

Figure 9.30   A biopsy was performed prior to the application for insurance.

Based upon the information you have given me, I find the following
action appropriate. Please press the Enter key...

Press any key to display results: _

Figure 9.31   The final text informs the user that a conclusion has been reached.

```
            Values based on 0/1 system                    VALUE

    1    Deny the claim due to preexistence of the patient's
         condition.                                             1
```

```
All choices <A>, only if value>1 <G>, Print <P>, Change and rerun <C>
rules used <line number>, Quit/save <Q>, Help <H>, Done <D>: _
```

Figure 9.32   The expert system has denied payment of the claim.

```
the diagnosis includes
        1    anemia
        2    a cardiac related ailment
        3    arthritis
        4    bronchitis
        5    diabetes
        6    gout
        7    hypertension
        8    osteoporosis
        9    rheumatism
       10    ulcers
       11    chronic
       12    severe
       13    carcinoma
       14    cataracts
       15    alzheimer's disease
       16    arteriosclerosis
       17    kidney stone, nephritis, or any condition requiring dialysis
       18    back, spinal or disc ailment
       19    an ailment not on our list
   19 _
```

```
Enter number(s) of value(s), WHY for information on the rule,
(?) for more details, QUIT to save data entered or <H> for help
```

Figure 9.33   The diagnosis was not on the list of ailments.

the patient was
     1 admitted to the hospital or treated as an outpatient
     2 treated during visits to a physician's office
2 _

Enter number(s) of value(s), WHY for information on the rule,
(?) for more details, QUIT to save data entered or <H> for help

Figure 9.34   The patient was treated in the physician's office.

the physician's records show
     1 medical advice or treatment for the patient's condition was
       rendered during the policy's exclusionary period
     2 medical advice or treatment for the patient's condition was
       not rendered during the policy's exclusionary period
     3 no determination may be made regarding the preexistence
       of the patient's condition
3 _

Enter number(s) of value(s), WHY for information on the rule,
(?) for more details, QUIT to save data entered or <H> for help

Figure 9.35   The records do not sufficiently inform the examiner.

The Diagnosis Adoption
A COLLECTION SYSTEM
Designed in Conjunction with the Medicare
Supplement Expert System
Author: John Rogers

You have encountered a diagnosis that is not on our list. Please enter it.
At a later date this diagnosis will be listed with others in the system.

o Please keep the wording within the line length shown on the form.

o Please press Enter when you have completed your entry.

o Finally, you will be allowed to review your entry for any
   corrections that you feel are necessary to correct spelling, etc.

ENTER DIAGNOSIS...: asbestosis_____

Figure 9.36   Because the diagnosis is needed in a future version of the aliment list, the external program is called.

The Diagnosis Acquisition
Verify Data

Medicare Expert

You have provided the following information:

Diagnosis: asbestosis

ENTER 0 TO PROCEED OR 1 FOR CORRECTION: 0 _

Figure 9.37   The external program provides an opportunity for corrections.

feature protected against gross misspellings that could result in the acquisition of an erroneous diagnosis.

Once more, the demonstration concluded with a directive for the handling of the claim as is shown in Figure 9.38. This time, however, the claim is referred to the chief claims examiner. June explained the current environment that saw her receiving examiner's claims of all kinds.

John turned to Phil to explain, "June's PC is not equipped with a printer. The one I have ordered for the claim examiner's area will have a printer attached. When the expert system is used by the claims examiner, the final disposition of a claim will not only appear on the PC's screen but will print at the printer. The printer's output will also show the conditions that led to the system's conclusion. If you direct the Medicare Supplement claims examiners to attach that printed output to the paperwork associated with each of their claims, we will have a basis for reviewing the system's performance."

Both Phil and June agreed with the idea. John then suggested that they implement the system in the morning. Not because it was a finished system but because this would allow both of them to further develop and refine the ailment list as well as the prior existence indicators for the numerous ailments. John pointed out that only three diseases, carcinoma, diabetes, and cardiac conditions, were detailed

Values based on 0/1 system	VALUE
1 Refer the claim to the Chief Claims Examiner.	1

All choices <A>, only if value>1 <G>, Print <P>, Change and rerun <C> rules used <line number>, Quit/save <Q>, Help <H>, Done <D>: _

Figure 9.38 Following the appearance of the final text, the conclusion is presented.

thus far. He further explained that he would concurrently increase the number of PCs installed in the claims area until all three systems were up and performing.

Phil noted that certainly some savings would be realized almost immediately through the expert system's application. June was interested in an early implementation in order to reduce the number of claims that find their way to her desk, or worse, are needlessly paid.

John took advantage of the positive atmosphere by arranging to install the new PC in the morning and host a brief systems introduction meeting in the claims department following the installation. After verifying his weekly appointment with June, John concluded the presentation that had resulted in immediate plans to implement MIC's first expert system.

Epilogue

As time passed, John's expert claims system expanded considerably. John came to realize that each expert system and each environment were a unique pair. Not all systems could be implemented this quickly—and MIC did develop a number of other expert systems. John's department still doesn't employ professional knowledge engineers, however. At least, the systems analysts who are today designing MIC's expert systems do not look upon themselves as knowledge engineers. They see expert systems techniques as another way to deliver results and, after all, that is what data processing is all about.

A Technical Note

The rules created from the taxonomy in this chapter were processed by Exsys' Faster to optimize performance prior to implementation. The resultant rules appear in Appendix A.

Chapter 1

Taking a Second Look

It is always beneficial to spend some time looking back over the terrain recently traversed. As well as being a review and clarification of important issues, this activity may serve as a preparation for the future.

We have seen that expert system technology is an addition to data processing and the professional data processor's armory of tools, and so it is to be expected that at some point in the not too far distant future, standard compilers will incorporate the features that are now viewed as the special province of expert system shells. Knowledge bases will be opened as are data files, to be processed, updated, or output during the normal course of data processing. In that future environment, database inquiries will result not only in the presentation of information but in the receipt of advice that will echo the expertise of long-departed experts whose many years of experience will be brought to bear upon uncounted problems.

The future will bring greater demands upon the interpersonal skill of the knowledge engineer/systems analyst who will be expected to employ a fuller understanding of analytic techniques in his or her practice. The acquisition of software packages will imply the need to make modifications not only to the standard logic of data processing but to the knowledge base and the employment of the provided inference engines as well. What indications of all of this exist today?

Portents of the Future

Syntelligence, Incorporated of Sunnyvale, California, is currently offering Underwriter Advisor which runs on IBM mainframes under MVS and CICS with a price tag in the million dollar range, depending upon the system's configuration. Underwriter Advisor generates an audit trail that allows users to determine how an underwriter reached a particular conclusion relative to the risk involved in issuing a policy. A network of users may work on the same policy simultaneously—an agent in a remote office and management in the home office may both look at the same customer file and follow the reasoning of the system.

An IBM research project, Yes/LI, involves extensions to PL/I that incorporate rules in PL/I, thus providing a closer integration between the expert system rule base and this procedural language. Clearly, IBM is directing its efforts toward integrating expert systems technology with standard programming languages. Another IBM-announced goal is the development of expert system capabilities that see the programmer developing an expert system on the PC for ultimate execution on the mainframe, and why not? Given the extensive memory capacities of the Personal System/2, distributed processing takes on a new meaning.

IBM's announcement of Common LISP opens the door to numerous developers, allowing LISP-based expert systems to be ported to the mainframe. Because of LISP's high utilization of CPU resources, the mainframe is seen as a vehicle for delivery of such expert systems rather than as a development vehicle. Thus, the means are available for the marketing of a number of expert system applications and shells that have heretofore been confined to special-purpose LISP workstations.

Digital Equipment Corporation (DEC) offers a time-sharing service through its Information Network Center that allows potential users to employ the VAX AI environment without making an extensive initial expenditure. It is to be expected that Texas Instruments will also become a vendor of mainframe expert systems applications along with a galaxy of AI software houses whose offerings have been previously confined to stand-alone environments.

Earlier chapters dealt with expert systems in use and under development. We reviewed potential systems in both the data processing department and in users' areas. We discussed the qualifications and psychology of the expert. We did not discuss hardware or the changes that may take place in computer design over the near and far term. Our assumptions were that computers would remain pretty much what they are—sequential executors of programmer-written instructions.

Current research efforts particularly in the area of AI present a picture of parallel concepts with a hardware alternative to software expert systems and AI techniques in general. The neural-network computer whose circuits are patterned after the complex interconnections among nerve cells in the human brain offers an alternative view of how artificial intelligence may present itself in future generations.

Researchers at Los Alamos National Laboratory in New Mexico have used a neural-net simulation involving a learning algorithm, called "back propagation," to solve problems in genetics. A recent problem dealt with a central question in biology: how to determine whether a particular sequence of bases in a fragment of DNA is coding for the production of a protein. While the problem has been successfully solved using statistical techniques, the procedure was limited to a strand containing at least 200 base pairs. For smaller segments with as few as one-tenth this number of bases, the conventional methods produced a correct result only half the time. It is, however, the case that fragments of approximately 30 base pairs are important. The "factories" in which proteins are constructed in accordance with the DNA blueprint are believed to work on only about 30 base pairs' information at a time. The neural net's results were 80 percent correct.

While developments involving alternative hardware design do not directly address the realm of data processing at the present, looking just over the horizon of research does afford a perspective often obscured by our daily activities. The professional data processor whose eyes are focused upon the future is certain not to be surprised by such innovations. More significant is the realization that expert system techniques are yielding important results in both hardware and software.

The Central Problem of Expert System Development

Being aware that expert systems are becoming an integral component of computer science and that the future is being rapidly painted upon a canvas of research, we are led to a closer look at the problems we confront in the adoption of the presently available technology. Without further consideration of the interpersonal skills required in expert systems development, knowledge acquisition looms as the single most difficult achievement. Knowledge acquisition has frequently been identified as the bottleneck in the development of expert systems, whether articulated in hardware or software.

Our earlier discussions touched upon this topic, offering suggestions that in dealing with the expert we might request examples of problem-solving activity in our attempt to elicit the necessary elements of expertise for incorporation in expert system rules. Indeed, in our development of an expert system in the last chapter, actual interviews were presented. In them we invoked a combination of techniques such as questioning, sampling examples, and involving the expert in the prototype.

During our review of expert system shells, we encountered one shell that makes use of Iterative Dicotomiser 3 (ID3): 1st-Class. We saw there that an expert system rule may be developed through the use of numerous examples which, in turn, are processed using the ID3 algorithm. A number of knowledge engineers employ 1st-Class and other ID3-invoking shells as a knowledge acquisition tool. Confronted with the need to elicit complex knowledge, the knowledge engineer resorts to the use of the ID3 algorithm embedded in a shell such as 1st-Class in order to build the required rules. Subsequently, the rules are input to the shell being employed as the primary development tool.

The repertory grid

The problem of knowledge acquisition can become quite unyielding when the task at hand addresses expert knowledge that, at times, may seem to border on the intuitive. It is in such instances that the repertory grid, a technique borrowed from psychology, may serve as a useful tool in stimulating the expert to view his or her knowledge from an altered perspective.

We have reviewed expert knowledge from a number of standpoints and our examples have consistently addressed heuristics that were crisply targeted. The performance of the expert was related to immediately observable phenomena. Ben, our mythical brake expert, was quickly able to describe his criteria in diagnosing brake noises in that he was dealing with a physical entity, a brake pad. The cardiologist whose heuristic addressed a relationship between gall bladder surgery and heart disease was well able to point to the common source, a high-fat diet. Mrs. Donath, our working expert, had little difficulty in pinpointing the key elements in claims processing decisions.

Numerous other experts contribute to our welfare daily, although the heuristics they employ are of a judgmental nature and, hence, more subtle and elusive when made the subject of an expert system. Under such circumstances the expert is often totally unable to articulate specific heuristics. Frequently, the knowledge engineer faces an invisible wall in a quest for such knowledge. Let us consider an example.

Mr. Personx heads the management development department of a large corporation. His department is responsible for conducting management development seminars, reviewing personnel records, and grooming candidates for management positions within the corporation. Mr. Personx's management candidates have had a 90 percent success rating in a company that prides itself on its ability to develop its own management personnel. Nothing in the corporation's management development seminars differs from the material used by other corporations whose management candidates show only a 60 to 65 percent success record. The company's top management has come to realize that it is Mr. Personx's expertise in judging management candidates that is responsible for the company's outstanding track record. Mr. Personx is scheduled to retire in

3 years, and it has been decided that capturing his expertise in an expert system in not only desirable but necessary.

The knowledge engineer assigned to the expert system development project finds, in his interviews with Mr. Personx, that the expert is able only to refer to feelings or hunches regarding the expected performance of a given candidate. Clearly, Mr. Personx is drawing upon personnel records and performance evaluations in making his judgments, but the sought-after heuristics are buried deeply in his mind, far from the level of consciousness that would permit him to crisply enumerate a series of If-Then-Else rules so necessary to the development of an expert system.

The knowledge engineer's attempts to obtain examples of Mr. Personx's judgments result in convincing narrations of one or another successful candidate's qualifications, but still the availability of clearly articulated rules eludes all efforts. The repertory grid is attempted.

Establishing the scale. The knowledge engineer proposes that the candidates currently being considered for a promotion to vice president of research and development be subjected to a rating scale whose values will be determined by the expert. The candidates are:

Jim Murphy
Bill Smith
Joan Rolf
Vera Jones
Phil Benning
Ron Prendergast
Al Carson

The expert is asked to determine from among Jim, Bill, and Joan two who are similar and different from the third.

The expert responds that Jim and Joan are similar but that Bill is different. The knowledge engineer asks the expert how Jim and Joan are similar. The expert explains that both Jim and Joan are punctual. The knowledge engineer points out that the quality of punctuality is but one extreme of a bipolar pair. What is the other extreme? The expert responds that the other extreme is tardiness. The knowledge engineer then requests that the expert rate each candidate on a scale from 1 to 3 where 3 is punctual and 1 is tardy. The ranking follows:

Tardy (1)—Punctual (3)

Jim Murphy	3
Bill Smith	1
Joan Rolf	3

Vera Jones	1
Phil Benning	1
Ron Prendergast	1
Al Carson	1

We see, from the process thus far developed, that use of the repertory grid finds the knowledge engineer choosing a scale while inviting the expert to give it meaning through the identification of quality-related similarities and differences. The scale in this case is a minimal 1 to 3. It could be 1 to 5 or 1 to 10, but once chosen it remains constant for all subsequent ratings. The expert can be expected to find similarities and differences in terms of quality ranges that are influential in the decision-making process.

The knowledge engineer continues the quest by asking the expert to now consider Vera, Phil, and Ron. What are the similarities and which is different? The expert responds explaining that Phil is more methodical than Ron and Vera and that this scale should be labeled "random—methodical." The expert proceeds to rank each candidate using the newly identified quality range on a scale of 1 (random) to 3 (methodical):

Random (1)—Methodical (3)

Jim Murphy	1
Bill Smith	2
Joan Rolf	1
Vera Jones	2
Phil Benning	3
Ron Prendergast	2
Al Carson	2

The knowledge engineer now selects Jim, Joan, and Phil. The expert responds that Jim and Phil are both excellent in delegating while Joan is not. The quality range is "retain—delegate" with delegate rated 3 and retain rated 1. The expert ranks the candidates once more:

Retain (1)—Delegate (3)

Jim Murphy	3
Bill Smith	1
Joan Rolf	1
Vera Jones	2
Phil Benning	3
Ron Prendergast	1
Al Carson	3

As the session wears on, the knowledge engineer relinquishes the choosing of candidates to the expert who proceeds to develop additional quality ranges from the specific consideration of candidate trios. In all, eight rankings are developed. The remaining five are shown below.

Loner (1)—Gregarious (3)

Jim Murphy	1
Bill Smith	3
Joan Rolf	2
Vera Jones	2
Phil Benning	1
Ron Prendergast	3
Al Carson	2

Goal Oriented (1)—Vacillating (3)

Jim Murphy	1
Bill Smith	3
Joan Rolf	3
Vera Jones	1
Phil Benning	2
Ron Prendergast	2
Al Carson	3

Innovative (1)—Hidebound (3)

Jim Murphy	1
Bill Smith	3
Joan Rolf	2
Vera Jones	1
Phil Benning	1
Ron Prendergast	3
Al Carson	1

Self-Sufficient (1)—Dependent (3)

Jim Murphy	1
Bill Smith	3
Joan Rolf	3
Vera Jones	2
Phil Benning	2
Ron Prendergast	3
Al Carson	1

Poised (1)—Self-Conscious (3)

Jim Murphy	3
Bill Smith	1
Joan Rolf	1
Vera Jones	2
Phil Benning	3
Ron Prendergast	2
Al Carson	1

It should be noted that the rating scales do not depend upon a preconception that the bipolar values represented are necessarily patterned after socially desirable values. For example, the bipolar value "poised—self-conscious" presents a scale that rates the most self-conscious individual as a 3 while the bipolar value "loner—gregarious" sees the most gregarious individual rated as a 3. From this we infer that the expert is simply supplying ratings after deriving the bipolar value from a comparison of three members of the group. The knowledge engineer is not attempting to enforce a structure that sees the values oriented in accord with generally accepted social values.

Creating the grid. The repertory grid displayed in Figure 10.1 shows the rating that each individual received on each of the bipolar value scales. At this point there has been no attempt to organize the individuals into groups or clusters according to similarities in their ratings.

Clearly, the objective is to determine the similarities that exist among the candidates. This is accomplished by analyzing the candidates into similarity clusters, a technique that involves correlating the candidates' ratings in pairs as though they were test scores. The subsequent application of factor analysis, an advanced statistical technique, divulges the commonalities. We will use a simpler approach to avoid the statistical involvement that could obscure our example.

In order to measure the distance between two candidates' rankings we will find the sum of the absolute values of the differences between the candidates' rankings. For example, the distance between Jim and Bill is:

Jim	3	1	3	1	1	1	1	3
Bill	1	2	1	3	3	3	3	1

$$2 + 1 + 2 + 2 + 2 + 2 + 2 + 2 = 15$$

Vice presidential candidates ranked 1 to 3 on bipolar value scales							
pole (1)	Jim	Bill	Joan	Vera	Phil	Ron	Al	pole (3)
tardy	3	1	3	1	1	1	1	punctual
random	1	2	1	2	3	2	2	methodical
retain	3	1	1	2	3	1	3	delegate
loner	1	3	2	2	1	3	2	gregarious
goal oriented	1	3	3	1	2	2	3	vacillating
innovative	1	3	2	1	1	3	1	hidebound
self-sufficient	1	3	3	2	2	3	1	dependent
poised	3	1	1	2	3	2	1	self-conscious

Figure 10.1   The repertory gid created from an expert's ratings of vice presidential candidates on a scale from 1 to 3.

Finding the similarities.   If we find the distance between the candidates, taking them in pairs so that each candidate is measured in relation to each of the other candidates in the group, we produce the result shown in Figure 10.2.

Now that we have found the difference measures of the candidates, we must find the percentage of similarity each bears to the others. In order to establish similarity as a percentage we use the following formula:

$$100 - 100 \text{ (difference/16)}$$

	Jim	Bill	Joan	Vera	Phil	Ron	Al
Jim	0	15	10	7	6	13	8
Bill		0	5	8	11	2	7
Joan			0	9	12	7	8
Vera				0	5	6	5
Phil					0	9	6
Ron						0	9
Al							0

Figure 10.2   The matrix displays the sum of absolute differences between vice presidential candidates, pair by pair.

Here, the difference is divided by the maximum difference that may exist between two candidates when the 1 to 3 scale is employed: 2. Because eight values were involved, the maximum difference is 2×8, or 16. If two candidates totally differ, their sum of differences would be 16 and the percentage of similarity is 0 by the formula shown above for $100 - 100(1) = 100 - 100$, or 0. If the difference between two candidates is only 1, we have $100 - 100(1/16)$ or a 94 percent similarity. Applying this formula, the result shown in Figure 10.3 is produced.

Prior to displaying the completed matrices to the expert, the knowledge engineer asks the expert who he would select for the vice presidential position. The expert explains that Jim Murphy is the choice and that he should be quite successful in this new position.

The knowledge engineer then builds the graph shown in Figure 10.4 from an analysis of the maximum percentages of similarity that appear in the matrix of Figure 10.3. The graph is developed by observing that the greatest similarity is between Ron and Bill at 88 percent. Joan bears a similarity to Bill of 69 percent. Al, Vera, and Phil all bear a 69 percent similarity while Jim's maximum similarity is to Phil at 63 percent.

At the 50 percent level of similarity we have but one group—indeed, similarity of less than 50 percent must be ignored because lower percentages than 50 will not be indicative. At the 65 percent level, however, three distinct groups emerge: Ron, Bill, and Joan in one cluster; Al, Vera, and Phil in the second cluster; and Jim, alone in the third cluster.

The knowledge engineer is aware that the expert is using a number of rules in making his judgment. Upon presenting the matrices and

	Jim	Bill	Joan	Vera	Phil	Ron	Al
Jim	100	6	38	56	63	19	50
Bill		100	69	50	31	88	56
Joan			100	44	25	56	50
Vera				100	69	63	69
Phil					100	44	63
Ron						100	44
Al							100

Figure 10.3 This matrix displays the percentages of similarity between vice presidential candidates, pair by pair.

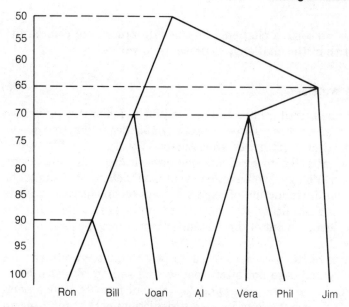

Figure 10.4　The candidates are grouped according to the similarities computed from their rankings.

graph to the expert, he too becomes conscious of his reasoning when he explains that Jim's punctuality, rated a 3 (on a 1 to 3 scale with tardy taken as a 1 and punctual taken as a 3), random approach, ability to delegate, goal orientation, innovativness, and self-sufficiency make him the ideal candidate. When asked about Jim's tendency to be a self-conscious loner, the expert points out that Jim is a researcher, not a sales type.

A summary.　The repertory grid and an application of statistical factor analysis make possible the determination of expert activity in a number of disparate environments. We did not demonstrate factor analysis nor address additional aspects of our example. Our intention was simply to illustrate two features of expert system development.

The first is that although there are expert system applications that, on the surface, may seem improbable because of the lack of a clear avenue for the development of a rule base, techniques do exist that permit the acquisition of results that would otherwise remain elusive. The second feature is that expert systems, and AI in general, call upon a number of disciplines that have often been considered too esoteric for involvement in the data processing environment. Perhaps the most unsettling aspect of the development of expert system technology is that the professional data processor is being brought face to face with the need for truly broad education in the humanities as well as the sciences. This presents a challenge to the data processing community no less great than the challenge it presents to educators.

Where Have We Been?

Our journey has introduced us to the need for a demonstrated return on investment as a prerequisite to expert system development. Indeed, we have seen that a return on investment is truly available, a fact that has been attested to by numerous organizations currently employing this technology. We have seen that basic selling skills must be exercised in the introduction of expert system technology in order to convincingly communicate its benefits to those personnel most affected by the development of the system—management, users, and experts alike.

We took note of the nature of the data processing environment, an environment which does not often sponsor the selling of ideas. Even more rarely does the data processing department form as close a partnership with talent outside of its own jurisdiction as that required in the development of an expert system. Undoubtedly, expert systems will have a moderating effect upon the data processing department and its members as both the technology and its prerequisites are developed as an integral part of existing methodologies.

We have reviewed expert system technology and have become familiar with the nature of the knowledge bases, the inference engines, and the languages that may be used in system development and delivery. As an alternative to complete expert system development, we have reviewed the numerous expert system shells that are available for the creation of the more common classes of systems. Throughout this experience there has been an emphasis upon the professional data processor's need to become more fully acquainted with subjects such as predicate logic, statistics, sales and interviewing techniques, and motivational psychology.

In the course of our journey, we took a closer look at IBM's Expert System Environment (ESE) and discussed other mainframe expert system shells as well. We developed an expert system using a popular PC-based shell in the solution of a relatively straightforward problem involving the heuristics of a working expert.

Where We Have Not Been

We have not ventured into the adjacent lands of AI to discuss the basic ingredients of expert system design at lower levels of technological detail. We have not discussed search techniques to distinguish between such concepts as depth-first search and breadth-first search, nor have we reviewed "hill climbing" as a form of heuristic search. Yet, such topics are central to expert system design as is a full understanding of conflict resolution and the use of meta rules in the knowledge base.

Our treatment of predicate logic has been, of necessity, only suggestive of the vast expanse offered by mathematical logic. The discussions of both LISP and Prolog were but a taste of the extensive powers of those languages. Similarly, we but lightly touched upon object-oriented programming, the benefits it offers, the development of object-oriented languages, and the incorporation of object-oriented programming facilities in numerous of the languages of expert systems such as Flavors in LISP.

Our treatment of sales techniques was brief and without reference to the numerous features important in sales presentations such as the use of visual aids and on-site demonstrations at current users' locations. The art and science of selling, like any other area of expertise, cannot truly be synopsized in a few pages nor even in a few chapters or books.

Finally, when we turned to psychology and the numerous techniques used in that field to apply statistics in areas most resistant to measurement, our treatment was cursory and devoid of statistical demonstration for the sake of maintaining the example at center stage. Statistical techniques are immensely powerful and factor analysis, in particular, is well suited to application in the areas indicated. Still we adverted to, but did not convey, the true techniques of statistics.

In the final analysis it must be admitted that the more that is said about many things, the less is truly said about anything. The objective here has been the sale of expert system technology to the professional data processor who has, by and large, not employed this new technology. We hope that we have demonstrated that expert systems are in use. They are not any longer in the experimental stage, although they are quite clearly still in research.

Where Do We Go from Here?

If this introduction to the application of expert systems in data processing has been instrumental in piquing the reader's interest, an application should be attempted. Despite the massive amount of technical detail that must be acquired by the practitioner hoping to become adept in the development of expert systems, hands-on involvement knows no equal in its potential for education. The following chapter provides some resources and keys to the location of others.

Again, welcome to expert systems, the future is now.

Shells, Languages, Hardware, and More

The professional data processor seeking a place to begin his or her career involvement with expert systems has, by now, become more familiar with the technology. The objective of this chapter is to present a conservative menu of the current offerings in a number of categories. The absence of one or another offering does not imply that the product, publication, or service is unworthy but rather that space is limited.

Major Mainframe Expert System Shells

Product.   Application Development System

Vendor.   Aion, Incorporated, Palo Alto, California

Hardware.   IBM mainframes and PCs

Source language.   Pascal

Inference engine.   Backward chaining, forward chaining

Certainty factors.   − 1 to +1

Database access.   Yes

External program calls.   Yes

Mathematical functions.   Yes

Development environment.   Yes

Consultation environment.   Yes

Debugging capability.   Interactive run-time debug monitor

Narrative.   Aion, Incorporated, has found that much of its market is independent software vendors and professional service firms. Very little, if any, emphasis is placed upon MIS user education, training, and support in Aion's introductory literature. Contact Aion for detailed information.

Product.   Applications Expert

Vendor.   Cullinet Software, Incorporated, Westwood, Massachusetts

Hardware.   Digital Equipment Corporation (DEC) VAX, IBM mainframes

Source language.   Cobol

Inference engine.   Backward chaining, forward chaining

Certainty factors.   IF, FIF (fuzzy logic)

Database Access.   Yes

External program calls.   Yes

Mathematical functions.   Yes

Development environment.   Yes

Consultation environment.   Yes

Debugging capability.   Trace, show cache, and structure chart, which shows the hierarchy of knowledge base variables

Narrative.   Cullinet has used Application Expert in the development of its EXL series of applications including Order EXL and Voice EXL. Application Expert's price ranges from $35,000 to $95,000, depending upon the configuration.

Product.   Expert System Environment

Vendor.   International Business Machines, Armonk, New York

Hardware.   IBM mainframes

Source language.   Pascal

Inference engine.   Backward chaining, forward chaining

Certainty factors.   IF, FIF (fuzzy logic)

Data base access.   Yes

External program calls.   Yes

Mathematical functions.   Yes

Development environment.   Yes

Consultation environment.   Yes

Debugging capability.   Trace, store/rerun, find, to locate where objects or character strings are used, and cross-reference lists

Narrative.   IBM earlier offered Expert System Environment as a program offering. It is now available as a program product. Contact IBM for pricing.

Additional Mainframe Shells (Contact Vendors for Information)

Product.   MIS Ex

Vendor.   MIS Expert Systems, Oakbrook, Illinois

Hardware.   IBM VM/CMS, MVS/TSO, DEC VAX.

Product.   Twaice

Vendor.   Logicware, Incorporated, New York, New York

Hardware.   IBM VM/CMS, MVS/TSO, DEC VAX

Source language.   MPROLOG.

Personal Computer Expert System Shells

Product.   Arity/Expert Development Package

Vendor.   Arity Corporation, Concord, Massachusetts

Hardware.   IBM PC, XT, AT, Personal System/2, and compatibles

Knowledge base.   Frames and rules

Inference strategy.   Backward chaining

Certainty factors.   Called confidence factors (CF), they may be applied to rule antecedents and consequents. Fuzzy logic, probability, and a standard method are supported

Database access.   Yes

External program calls.   Yes

Mathematical functions.   Yes

Development environment.   Yes

Consultation environment.   Yes

Debugging capability.   Debugging predicates, concept classifier, error messages

Narrative.   Arity/Expert Development Package interfaces with Arity Prolog, thus providing an extremely powerful system. The resultant expert system may be compiled or executed under an interpreter.

Product. Exsys

Vendor. EXSYS, Incorporated, Albuquerque, New Mexico

Hardware. DEC VAX, IBM PC, XT, AT, Personal System/2, and compatibles

Knowledge base. Rules

Inference strategy. Backward chaining, forward chaining

Certainty factors. 0 to 1, 0 to 10, and −100 to +100

Database access. Yes

External program calls. Yes

Mathematical functions. Yes

Development environment. Yes

Consultation environment. Yes

Debugging capability. Trace, rule display, and error messages

Narrative. EXSYS, Incorporated, has introduced an upgrade to Exsys as well as a new product and Unix versions. An IBM mainframe version is in development. Contact EXSYS for the current status of this product.

Product. 1st-Class

Vendor. Programs In Motion, Incorporated, Wayland, Massachusetts

Hardware. IBM PC, XT, AT, Personal System/2, and compatibles

Inference strategy. Decision Tree Search

Certainty factors. 0 to 100

Database access. Yes

External program calls. Yes

Mathematical functions. No

Development environment. Yes

Consultation environment. Yes

Debugging capability. Review screen, trace, and include statistics

Narrative. Programs In Motion has introduced an upgrade to 1st-Class as well as a new product, 1st-Class Fusion. Neither of these were available at this writing.

Product. Insight 2 +

Vendor. Level Five Research, Incorporated, Indialantic, Florida

Hardware. IBM PC, XT, AT, Personal System/2, and compatibles

Knowledge base. Rules

Inference strategy. Backward chaining, forward chaining

Certainty factors. Per rule and per fact

Database access. Yes

External program calls. Yes

Mathematical functions. Yes

Development environment. Yes

Consultation environment. Yes

Debugging capability. Error checking compiler

Narrative. Insight 2 + was designed for use without the services of a knowledge engineer and thus lacks some of the flexible features found in the more sophisticated shells.

Product. Intelligence Compiler

Vendor. IntelligenceWare, Los Angeles, California

Hardware. IBM PC, XT, AT, Personal System/2, and compatibles

Knowledge base. Frames and rules

Inference strategy. Backward chaining, forward chaining

Certainty factors. 0 to 1, 0 to 100 (fuzzy logic)

Database access. Yes, via a Pascal interface

External program calls. Yes, via a Pascal interface

Mathematical functions. Yes

Development environment. Yes

Consultation environment. Yes

Debugging capability. Trace, syntax checking, spell checking, execution speed control

Narrative. Intelligence Compiler brings with it an outstanding tutorial that incorporates extremely effective graphics.

Product. Personal Consultant Series

Vendor. Texas Instruments, Incorporated, Dallas, Texas

Hardware. IBM PC, XT, AT, Personal System/2, and compatibles; TI Explorer workstation; and TI Professional Computer family

Knowledge base. Frames, rules, procedures (for algorithmic knowledge), and meta rules

Inference strategy.   Backward chaining, forward chaining

Certainty factors.   − 100 to +100 (fuzzy logic)

Database access.   Yes

External program calls.   Yes

Mathematical functions.   Yes

Development environment.   Yes

Consultation environment.   Yes

Debugging capability.   Trace

Narrative.   The TI Personal Consultant Series consists of two separate offerings, Personal Consultant Easy and Personal Consultant Plus, which is supported by AT-class computers. Upward compatibility allows uninterrupted growth in application development and delivery. Contact Texas Instruments for pricing and information.

Product.   RuleMaster

Vendor.   Radian Corporation, Austin, Texas

Hardware.   IBM PC, XT, AT, Personal System/2, and compatibles and DEC VAX

Knowledge base.   Rules

Inference strategy.   Backward chaining, forward chaining

Certainty factors.   Boolean, probability, and fuzzy operators

Database access.   Yes

External program calls.   Yes

Mathematical functions.   Yes

Development environment.   Yes

Consultation environment.   Yes

Debugging capability.   Example checking, syntax checking, file and module tests

Narrative.   RuleMaster employs a modified Iterative Dicotomizer 3 (ID3) algorithm which induces rules from input examples. The knowledge engineer has the option of writing rules directly. Also, the resultant expert system may be generated in C code for subsequent compiling. RuleMaster is a highly sophisticated expert system shell. Contact Radian Corporation for pricing.

A Unique Knowledge Acquisition Tool

We discussed knowledge acquisition techniques in the last chapter and introduced the use of the repertory grid. A recently announced knowledge acquisition tool-expert system shell, Auto-Intelligence, is available from IntelligenceWare, Incorporated, of Los Angeles, California.

Auto-Intelligence employs repertory grid techniques as well as an induction algorithm to elicit expert knowledge. Although this shell is designed for the direct use of an expert without the aid of a knowledge engineer, it may be used quite profitably by the knowledge engineer in those instances in which expert knowledge acquisition is problematical.

Shells—A Summary

It is doubtful that any one person or organization is capable of listing a complete collection of the available expert system shells. We have cited only a very few of those available. Our choices have been heavily weighted in favor of those shells that are moderately priced and have withstood the test of time, although we have noted new entries in the mainframe area. There can be little doubt that, as occurred in the word processing market, there will be a massive reduction in the number of offerings as the expert system shell market matures.

The very few shells that we have cited certainly do not, by any stretch of the imagination, constitute the core of those that may be considered "old timers." There are many other deserving products that have been omitted in the interests of space and time. To those vendors we offer our apologies.

Languages

The languages that may be employed in the development of expert systems are many. Some of them are:

For the IBM mainframe

Common LISP. Available from IBM Corporation, Armonk, New York, and Intermetrics, Incorporated, Cambridge, Massachusetts

Prolog. Available from IBM Corporation, Armonk, New York

MPROLOG. Available from LOGICWARE, Incorporated, Wellesley, Massachusetts

Lattice C Compiler. Available from SAS Institute, Incorporated, Cary, North Carolina

For the PC and compatibles

Actor (object oriented). Available from The Whitewater Group, Evanston, Illinois

KNOWOL. Available from Intelligent Machine Company, New Port Richey, Florida

LISP. Available from ExperTelligence, Incorporated, Santa Barbara, California; Gold Hill Computers, Incorporated, Cambridge, Massachusetts; Integral Quality, Seattle, Washington; Northwest Computer Algorithms, Novato, California; Pro Code, International, Watchung, New Jersey; Sapiens Software, Santa Cruz, California; Soft Warehouse, Incorporated, Honolulu, Hawaii; Solution Systems, Norwell, Massachusetts; and Texas Instruments, Incorporated, Dallas, Texas

OPS83. Available from Production Systems Technologies, Incorporated, Pittsburgh, Pennsylvania

PROLOG. Available from Applied Logic Systems, Mountain View, California; Arity Corporation, Concord, Massachusetts; Automata Design Associates, Dresher, Pennsylvania; Borland International, Incorporated, Scotts Valley, California; Chalcedony Software, Incorporated, La Jolla, California; Expertelligence, Santa Barbara, California; Logicware, Incorporated, New York, New York; Micro-AI, Rheem Valley, California; Rational Visions, Phoenix, Arizona; and System Designers International, Falls Church, Virginia

Smalltalk AT (object oriented). Available from Softsmarts, Incorporated, Woodside, California

Smalltalk/V (object oriented). Available from Digitalk, Incorporated, Los Angeles, California

Languages—A Summary

Many of the PC-based languages cited above are also available in versions for the Digital Equipment Corporation's VAX, Xerox Corporation's computers, and various of the Texas Instruments Corporation's workstations and personal computers. We have not attempted to sort all of the versions out with information relative to the various systems in the belief that the computer vendors mentioned would prefer that a prospective user consult with them in choosing a suitable expert system language. Certainly, the computer vendor is then able to advise a prospective user regarding the best fit for the intended application within the scope of the particular computer's capabilities.

Hardware

The hardware vendors listed below are primarily suppliers of specialized AI workstations that may be employed in the development of stand-alone expert systems in a dedicated environment. Additionally, such workstations may be used as development vehicles for systems that will later be ported to the mainframe. The chief characteristics of these workstations are their speed and memory capability which, in the case of some vendors' workstations such as Texas Instruments, are augmented by specially designed chips to support the AI programming environment. Again, our apologies to those vendors who may have inadvertently been omitted.

Digital Equipment Corporation, Concord, Massachusetts

International Business Machines, Incorporated, Armonk, New York

LISP Machine, Incorporated, Andover, Massachusetts

Sun Microsystems, Incorporated, Mountain View, California

Symbolics, Cambridge, Massachusetts

Tektronix, Incorporated, Wilsonville, Oregon

Texas Instruments, Incorporated, Dallas, Texas

UMECORP, Larkspur, California

Xerox Corporation, Palo Alto, California

Training and Education

It is obvious that education and training are the pillars of technology. Each advance in technique would be shelved for an undetermined period if we were to rely upon our national system of formal education as our sole support. Clearly, it will be the vast army of data processing professionals that will build the expert systems of the next several years and quite possibly even beyond. To facilitate that end, the following organizations and systems offer insight to the novice expert system developer:

Active Prolog Tutor. Solution Systems of Norwell, Massachusetts, offers an extremely reasonably priced Prolog tutorial program for implementation upon a PC. Active Prolog Tutor comes highly recommended.

Complete multimedia curriculum. The Digital Equipment Corporation offers a wide selection of educational programs which may be presented on site or at one of the DEC education centers. For further information and a complete description of the offerings, contact your local DEC office

Complete multimedia curriculum. Unisys Corporation, Princeton, New Jersey, offers a comprehensive program addressing topics from the introductory level through LISP training and workstation-based development and delivery of expert systems. For further information, contact your local Unisys office.

Experteach. IntelligenceWare, Incorporated, of Los Angeles, California, offers a quite complete software program complete with manual. The set addresses AI history and fundamentals as well as expert system development, LISP, and Prolog. The complete educational program is executed using a PC.

LISP-ITS. Advanced Computer Tutoring, Incorporated, of Pittsburgh, Pennsylvania, offers "the first commercially available intelligent tutoring system." LISP-ITS is a full-semester LISP course. The program employs AI techniques to teach AI programming.

Precision Knowledge Acquisition (workshop). Expert-Knowledge Systems, Incorporated, of McLean, Virginia, presents a workshop that addresses methods for knowledge acquisition, management, and implementation of expert systems.

Video Courses. The Minerva Group of Amherst, Massachusetts, markets video tape courses entitled "Artificial Intelligence in Depth," "Expert Systems: Theory and Practice," and "Programming in Common LISP." Each of the programs is authored by a recognized authority in the area addressed.

Staying Informed

As we have mentioned, the application area of expert systems is alive with change and development. New concepts, shells, and languages are exploding upon the scene with such frequency that staying current is a challenge in itself. One of the best ways to guard against intellectual obsolescence is to become active as a reader, as a member of a users' group, and by joining an AI organization such as the American Association for Artificial Intelligence (AAAI). Membership in the AAAI offers solid benefits for the expert system practitioner in that he or she is exposed to the leading ideas as well as the leading thinkers in AI. AAAI may be contacted at 445 Burgess Drive, Menlo Park, California 94025.

Depending upon one's interests, two magazines offer an excellent exposure to expert systems. Computer Language (P.O. Box 11333, Des Moines, Iowa 50347) addresses the broader area of programming with frequent articles dealing with AI topics as well as a specialized column, AI-eye, that deals with various topics in AI on a regular basis. AI Expert: The Magazine for the Artificial Intelligence Community (P.O. Box 10953, Palo Alto, California 94303) is, as its name implies, a magazine dedicated to expert systems.

The Consultants

The professional data processor interested in obtaining outside help in the development of expert systems may turn to the services of one or another consulting group. We have chosen not to enumerate those organizations that offer this service. Rather, we offer a few words of advice.

The best place to begin a search for expert system development consulting is with your firm's auditors and/or your computer vendor. They have a vested interest in your company's success and satisfaction and will rarely jeopardize their relationship with a valued client by making a careless referral if they do not have the in-house expertise to be of immediate personal assistance.

In any event, be prepared for an expensive experience, the success of which will be totally dependent upon the effort expended in assessing both the domain to be addressed and the track record of the consulting group. The reasons for this warning are obvious. There are not enough experienced knowledge engineers to satisfy the needs of interested clients. As expert system development gains momentum in MIS quarters, some consultants will resort to "hot house" personnel development techniques in order to take advantage of a rapidly growing practice. All too often this results in expenditures that serve to develop the consultant's expertise while a similar expenditure made to develop in-house talent would offer a far more lasting benefit for the company. It remains true that "He who chops his own wood is twice warmed."

Bibliography

The following books are listed according to the level of sophistication expected of the reader. Some assume a specialized language or educational background. As far as possible, we note the requirements in our comments. Again, the list is partial in that the attempt is to provide a point of departure for the professional data processor interested in expert system development. These books, in turn, offer bibliographies that will lead the reader to further publications.

Introductory

Turner, M.: *Expert Systems: A Management Guide,* PA Computers and Telecommunications, London, England, 1985. Comment: A light treatment of expert systems complete with Dick Tracy cartoon illustrations. An excellent "quick read" for the harried manager interested in gaining a superficial acquaintance with expert systems.

Mishkoff, H. C.: *Understanding Artificial Intelligence,* Texas Instruments Information Publishing Center, Dallas, Texas, 1985. Comment: A broad introductory coverage of AI in general. This book was employed in conjunction with Texas Instruments' first symposium.

Xerox: *The Keys to Artificial Intelligence are at Xerox,* Xerox Corporation, Pasadena, California, 1985. Comment: Xerox oriented.

Levine, R. I., D.E.Drang, and B. Edelson: *A Comprehensive Guide to AI and Expert Systems,* McGraw-Hill Book Company, New York, New York, 1986. Comment: An excellent introduction oriented to the PC. For those conversant with BASIC and having access to a personal computer.

Sawyer, B. and D. L. Foster: *Programming Expert Systems in Pascal,* John Wiley & Sons, Incorporated, New York, New York, 1986. Comment: An experience in programming rule-based expert systems in Pascal (USCD or Turbo Pascal). For the reader with access to a PC, this book offers an opportunity to the Pascal literate programmer to become familiar with rule-based expert system architecture.

Intermediate-Advanced

Waterman, D. A.: *A Guide to Expert Systems,* Addison Wesley Publishing Company, Reading, Massachusetts, 1986. Comment: Academically oriented, this book examines much of the early research work in expert systems as well as a number of the systems in current use. More meaningful to a reader at the second-year college level.

Jackson, P.: *Introduction to Expert Systems,* Addison Wesley Publishing Company, Reading, Massachusetts, 1986. Comment: A college-level introduction to expert systems of benefit to the reader conversant with symbolic logic or willing to undertake prerequisite reading in computer science.

Barr, A., and E. A. Feigenbaum: *The Handbook of Artificial Intelligence, Volume I,* William Kaufmann, Incorporated, 1981.

— and —: *The Handbook of Artificial Intelligence, Volume II,* William Kaufmann, Incorporated, 1982.

Cohn, P. R., and —: *The Handbook of Artificial Intelligence, Volume III,* William Kaufmann, Incorporated, 1982. Comment: These three volumes are the definitive works in artificial intelligence. They are definitely not light reading for the individual with a casual interest in AI or expert systems. Written at the college-graduate level, they deal with AI research and are intended for the serious student.

Prolog and Logic Programming

Clocksin, W. F., and C. S. Mellish: *Programming in PROLOG,* Springer-Verlag, New York, New York, 1984. Comment: The original textbook of Prolog programming. For the serious student of Prolog programming this book is a must.

Marcus, C.: *Prolog Programming,* Addison Wesley Publishing Company, Reading, Massachusetts, 1986. Comment: Written by a member of the Arity Corporation, this book is an excellent companion to Arity's Prolog.

Hogger, J. C.: *Introduction to Logic Programming,* Academic Press, Incorporated, Orlando, Florida, 1984. Comment: An excellent treatment of logic programming for the reader versed in symbolic logic and familiar with a logic-based language such as Prolog.

LISP

Winston, P. H., and B. K. P. Horn: *LISP,* Addison Wesley Publishing Company, Reading, Massachusetts, 1984. Comment: The text introduces the reader to LISP proceeding from the basic LISP primitives to the implementation of frames. This text is best employed in conjunction with a LISP interpreter using a PC or workstation.

Background Material

For the professional data processor interested in gaining the necessary background without the aid of formal classes, Dover Publications, Incorporated, New York, New York, is recommended as an excellent source of paperbacks dealing with symbolic logic, statistics, and mathematics. The more serious seekers of knowledge are urged to contact their local community college or university to inquire about the availability of classes that address these areas. A wise person once said "Chance favors the prepared mind."

Artificial Intelligence and expert systems in particular are part of our lives, for better or worse. Good luck and a successful future.

Medicare Supplement Claim Evaluation Rules

Author:
John Rogers

RULES:

RULE NUMBER: 1

IF:
       the diagnosis includes an ailment not on our list
and the patient was treated during visits to a physician's office
and the physician's records show no determination may be made
regarding the preexistence of the patient's condition

THEN:
       RUN(MED1)
and the condition is indeterminant

RULE NUMBER: 2

IF:
       the diagnosis includes an ailment not on our list
and the patient was treated during visits to a physician's office
and the physician's records show medical advice or treatment for the
patient's condition was not rendered during the policy's exclusionary
period

THEN:
       RUN(MED1)
and the condition is not preexisting

RULE NUMBER: 3

IF:
        the diagnosis includes an ailment not on our list
and the patient was admitted to the hospital or treated as an outpatient
and the hospital records show that medical advice or treatment for the patient's condition was not rendered during the policy's exclusionary period
and the physician's records show no determination may be made regarding the preexistence of the patient's condition

THEN:
        RUN(MED1)
and the condition is not preexisting

RULE NUMBER: 4

IF:
        the diagnosis includes an ailment not on our list
and the patient was admitted to the hospital or treated as an outpatient
and the hospital records show that no determination may be made regarding the preexistence of the patient's condition
and the physician's records show no determination may be made regarding the preexistence of the patient's condition

THEN:
        RUN(MED1)
and the condition is indeterminant

RULE NUMBER: 5

IF:
        the diagnosis includes an ailment not on our list
and the patient was admitted to the hospital or treated as an outpatient
and the hospital records show that no determination may be made regarding the preexistence of the patient's condition
and the physician's records show medical advice or treatment for the patient's condition was not rendered during the policy's exclusionary period

THEN:
        RUN(MED1)
and the condition is not preexisting

RULE NUMBER: 6

IF:

        the diagnosis includes an ailment not on our list

and the patient was admitted to the hospital or treated as an outpatient

and the hospital records show that no determination may be made regarding the preexistence of the patient's condition

and the physician's records show medical advice or treatment for the patient's condition was rendered during the policy's exclusionary period

THEN:

        RUN(MED1)

and the condition is preexisting

RULE NUMBER: 7

IF:

        the diagnosis includes an ailment not on our list

and the patient was admitted to the hospital or treated as an outpatient

and the hospital records show that medical advice or treatment for the patient's condition was not rendered during the policy's exclusionary period

and the physician's records show medical advice or treatment for the patient's condition was rendered during the policy's exclusionary period

THEN:

        RUN(MED1)

and the condition is preexisting

RULE NUMBER: 8

IF:

        the diagnosis includes an ailment not on our list

and the patient was admitted to the hospital or treated as an outpatient

and the hospital records show that medical advice or treatment for the patient's condition was not rendered during the policy's exclusionary period

and the physician's records show medical advice or treatment for the patient's condition was not rendered during the policy's exclusionary period

THEN:
      RUN(MED1)
   and   the condition is not preexisting

RULE NUMBER: 9

IF:
      the diagnosis includes an ailment not on our list
   and   the patient was treated during visits to a physician's office
   and   the physician's records show medical advice or treatment for the
         patient's condition was rendered during the policy's exclusionary
         period

THEN:
      RUN(MED1)
   and   the condition is preexisting

RULE NUMBER: 10

IF:
      the diagnosis includes an ailment not on our list
   and   the patient was admitted to the hospital or treated as an outpatient
   and   the hospital records show that medical advice or treatment for the
         patient's condition was rendered during the policy's exclusionary
         period

THEN:
      RUN(MED1)
   and   the condition is preexisting

RULE NUMBER: 11

IF:
      the diagnosis includes a cardiac related ailment
   and   the patient was admitted to the hospital or treated as an outpatient
         or treated during visits to a physician's office
   and   within the six months prior to policy issue either hospital or
         physician's records or fees show that the patient received treatment
         of an indeterminant nature

THEN:

the condition is indeterminant

RULE NUMBER: 12

IF:

the diagnosis includes anemia or arthritis or bronchitis or gout or hypertension or osteoporosis or rheumatism or ulcers or chronic or severe or cataracts or alzheimer's disease or arteriosclerosis or kidney stone, nephritis, or any condition requiring dialysis or back, spinal or disc ailment

and the patient was treated during visits to a physician's office

and the physician's records show no determination may be made regarding the preexistence of the patient's condition

THEN:

the condition is indeterminant

RULE NUMBER: 13

IF:

the diagnosis includes anemia or arthritis or bronchitis or gout or hypertension or osteoporosis or rheumatism or ulcers or chronic or severe or cataracts or alzheimer's disease or arteriosclerosis or kidney stone, nephritis, or any condition requiring dialysis or back, spinal or disc ailment

and the patient was treated during visits to a physician's office

and the physician's records show medical advice or treatment for the patient's condition was not rendered during the policy's exclusionary period

THEN:

the condition is not preexisting

RULE NUMBER: 14

IF:

the diagnosis includes anemia or arthritis or bronchitis or gout or hypertension or osteoporosis or rheumatism or ulcers or chronic or severe or cataracts or alzheimer's disease or arteriosclerosis or kidney stone, nephritis, or any condition requiring dialysis or back, spinal or disc ailment

and   the patient was admitted to the hospital or treated as an outpatient
and   the hospital records show that medical advice or treatment for the
       patient's condition was not rendered during the policy's exclusionary
       period
and   the physician's records show no determination may be made regarding
       the preexistence of the patient's condition

THEN:
       the condition is not preexisting

RULE NUMBER: 15

IF:
       the diagnosis includes anemia or arthritis or bronchitis or gout or
       hypertension or osteoporosis or rheumatism or ulcers or chronic or
       severe or cataracts or alzheimer's disease or arteriosclerosis or
       kidney stone, nephritis, or any condition requiring dialysis or back,
       spinal or disc ailment
and   the patient was admitted to the hospital or treated as an outpatient
and   the hospital records show that no determination may be made regarding
       the preexistence of the patient's condition
and   the physician's records show no determination may be made regarding
       the preexistence of the patient's condition

THEN:
       the condition is indeterminant

RULE NUMBER: 16

IF:
       the diagnosis includes anemia or arthritis or bronchitis or gout or
       hypertension or osteoporosis or rheumatism or ulcers or chronic or
       severe or cataracts or alzheimer's disease or arteriosclerosis or
       kidney stone, nephritis, or any condition requiring dialysis or back,
       spinal or disc ailment
and   the patient was admitted to the hospital or treated as an outpatient
and   the hospital records show that no determination may be made regarding
       the preexistence of the patient's condition
and   the physician's records show medical advice or treatment for the
       patient's condition was not rendered during the policy's exclusionary
       period

THEN:
>   the condition is not preexisting

RULE NUMBER: 17
IF:
>   the diagnosis includes anemia or arthritis or bronchitis or gout or
>   hypertension or osteoporosis or rheumatism or ulcers or chronic or
>   severe or cataracts or alzheimer's disease or arteriosclerosis or
>   kidney stone, nephritis, or any condition requiring dialysis or back,
>   spinal or disc ailment

and
>   the patient was admitted to the hospital or treated as an outpatient

and
>   the hospital records show that no determination may be made regarding
>   the preexistence of the patient's condition

and
>   the physician's records show medical advice or treatment for the
>   patient's condition was rendered during the policy's exclusionary
>   period

THEN:
>   the condition is preexisting

RULE NUMBER: 18

IF:
>   the diagnosis includes anemia or arthritis or bronchitis or gout or
>   hypertension or osteoporosis or rheumatism or ulcers or chronic or
>   severe or cataracts or alzheimer's disease or arteriosclerosis or
>   kidney stone, nephritis, or any condition requiring dialysis or back,
>   spinal or disc ailment

and
>   the patient was admitted to the hospital or treated as an outpatient

and
>   the hospital records show that medical advice or treatment for the
>   patient's condition was not rendered during the policy's exclusionary
>   period

and
>   the physician's records show medical advice or treatment for the
>   patient's condition was rendered during the policy's exclusionary
>   period

THEN:
>   the condition is preexisting

RULE NUMBER: 19

IF:

the diagnosis includes anemia or arthritis or bronchitis or gout or hypertension or osteoporosis or rheumatism or ulcers or chronic or severe or cataracts or alzheimer's disease or arteriosclerosis or kidney stone, nephritis, or any condition requiring dialysis or back, spinal or disc ailment

and   the patient was admitted to the hospital or treated as an outpatient

and   the hospital records show that medical advice or treatment for the patient's condition was not rendered during the policy's exclusionary period

and   the physician's records show medical advice or treatment for the patient's condition was not rendered during the policy's exclusionary period

THEN:

the condition is not preexisting

RULE NUMBER: 20

IF:

the diagnosis includes anemia or arthritis or bronchitis or gout or hypertension or osteoporosis or rheumatism or ulcers or chronic or severe or cataracts or alzheimer's disease or arteriosclerosis or kidney stone, nephritis, or any condition requiring dialysis or back, spinal or disc ailment

and   the patient was treated during visits to a physician's office

and   the physician's records show medical advice or treatment for the patient's condition was rendered during the policy's exclusionary period

THEN:

the condition is preexisting

RULE NUMBER: 21

IF:

the diagnosis includes anemia or arthritis or bronchitis or gout or hypertension or osteoporosis or rheumatism or ulcers or chronic or severe or cataracts or alzheimer's disease or arteriosclerosis or kidney stone, nephritis, or any condition requiring dialysis or back, spinal or disc ailment

and   the patient was admitted to the hospital or treated as an outpatient

and　the hospital records show that medical advice or treatment for the
patient's condition was rendered during the policy's exclusionary
period

THEN:
the condition is preexisting

RULE NUMBER: 22

IF:
the diagnosis includes a cardiac related ailment
and　the patient was admitted to the hospital or treated as an outpatient
or treated during visits to a physician's office
and　within the six months prior to policy issue either hospital or
physician's records or fees show that the patient received no cardiac
related treatment or advice

THEN:
the condition is not preexisting

RULE NUMBER: 23

IF:
the diagnosis includes a cardiac related ailment
and　the patient was admitted to the hospital or treated as an outpatient
or treated during visits to a physician's office
and　within the six months prior to policy issue either hospital or
physician's records or fees show that the patient received a
prescription for nitroglycerin or a positive EKG or a positive
angiogram or a positive stress test or treatment for chest pain or
any cardiac treatment or advice

THEN:
the condition is preexisting

RULE NUMBER: 24

IF:
the diagnosis includes carcinoma
and　the patient was admitted to the hospital or treated as an outpatient
or treated during visits to a physician's office

and   the carcinoma patient's hospital or physician's records or fees show
that the patient, during the exclusionary period, received a
carcinoma positive biopsy or a carcinoma positive mammogram or a
carcinoma related chemotherapy treatment or a positive Nuclear
Magnetic Resonance (NMR) scan or a positive Computer Assisted
Tomography (CAT) scan or a carcinoma positive chest X-Ray or any
carcinoma positive test results, diagnosis, or advice related to
Melanoma, Sarcoma or Leukemia or other cancer related ailment

THEN:

the condition is preexisting

RULE NUMBER: 25

IF:

the diagnosis includes carcinoma
and   the patient was admitted to the hospital or treated as an outpatient
or treated during visits to a physician's office
and   the carcinoma patient's hospital or physician's records or fees show
that the patient, during the exclusionary period, received no
diagnosis, treatment or medical advice for an existing carcinoma

THEN:

the condition is not preexisting

RULE NUMBER: 26

IF:

the diagnosis includes carcinoma
and   the patient was admitted to the hospital or treated as an outpatient
or treated during visits to a physician's office
and   the carcinoma patient's hospital or physician's records or fees show
that the patient, during the exclusionary period, received treatment
of an indeterminant nature

THEN:

the condition is indeterminant

RULE NUMBER: 27

IF:

the diagnosis includes diabetes
and   the patient was admitted to the hospital or treated as an outpatient

or treated during visits to a physician's office

and The diabetes patient's hospital or physician's records or fees show that the patient, during the exclusionary period, received a positive glucose tolerance test or a positive fasting blood sugar test (FBS) or a prescription for insulin in any form or a special sugar restricted diet or advice to restrict sugar intake or a diagnosis, treatment for, or advice, regarding diabetes

THEN:

the condition is preexisting

RULE NUMBER: 28

IF:

the diagnosis includes diabetes

and the patient was admitted to the hospital or treated as an outpatient or treated during visits to a physician's office

and The diabetes patient's hospital or physician's records or fees show that the patient, during the exclusionary period, received no diagnosis, treatment, or advice, relative to diabetes

THEN:

the condition is not preexisting

RULE NUMBER: 29

IF:

the diagnosis includes diabetes

and the patient was admitted to the hospital or treated as an outpatient or treated during visits to a physician's office

and The diabetes patient's hospital or physician's records or fees show that the patient, during the exclusionary period, received treatment of an indeterminant nature

THEN:

the condition is indeterminant

RULE NUMBER: 30

IF:

the policy is lapsed and beyond the grace period

THEN:
    Deny the claim due to lapse and grace period expiration. -
    Probability=1
and stop

RULE NUMBER: 31

IF:
    the policy is issued but not yet at the effective date

THEN:
    Deny the claim because the policy is not yet in force. -
    Probability=1
and stop

RULE NUMBER: 32

IF:
    Medicare has not paid the claim as evidenced by a received
    Explanation Of Medicare Benefits (EOMB)

THEN:
    Deny the claim due to lack of Medicare involvement. - Probability=1

RULE NUMBER: 33

IF:
    Medicare has paid the claim as evidenced by a received Explanation Of
    Medicare Benefits (EOMB)
and the policy is lapsed but within the grace period
and the policy's age is less than 6 months
and the claim's value is $200 or more
and the condition is not preexisting

THEN:
    Pay the claim, less any premium owing. - Probability=1

RULE NUMBER: 34

IF:

Medicare has paid the claim as evidenced by a received Explanation Of
Medicare Benefits (EOMB)
and   the policy is lapsed but within the grace period
and   the policy's age is less than 6 months
and   the claim's value is less than $200

THEN:
Pay the claim, less any premium owing. - Probability=1

RULE NUMBER: 35

IF:
Medicare has paid the claim as evidenced by a received Explanation Of
Medicare Benefits (EOMB)
and   the policy is lapsed but within the grace period
and   the policy's age is 6 months or more

THEN:
Pay the claim, less any premium owing. - Probability=1

RULE NUMBER: 36

IF:
Medicare has paid the claim as evidenced by a received Explanation Of
Medicare Benefits (EOMB)
and   the policy is in force
and   the policy's age is less than 6 months
and   the claim's value is $200 or more
and   the condition is not preexisting

THEN:
Pay the claim in full. - Probability=1

RULE NUMBER: 37
IF:
Medicare has paid the claim as evidenced by a received Explanation Of
Medicare Benefits (EOMB)
and   the policy is in force
and   the policy's age is less than 6 months
and   the claim's value is less than $200

THEN:
>
> Pay the claim in full. - Probability=1

RULE NUMBER: 38

IF:
>
> Medicare has paid the claim as evidenced by a received Explanation Of
> Medicare Benefits (EOMB)
>
> and the policy is in force
>
> and the policy's age is 6 months or more

THEN:
>
> Pay the claim in full. - Probability=1

RULE NUMBER: 39

IF:
>
> Medicare has paid the claim as evidenced by a received Explanation Of
> Medicare Benefits (EOMB)
>
> and the policy is in force
>
> and the policy's age is less than 6 months
>
> and the claim's value is $200 or more
>
> and the condition is preexisting

THEN:
>
> Deny the claim due to preexistence of the insured's condition. -
> Probability=1

RULE NUMBER: 40

IF:
>
> Medicare has paid the claim as evidenced by a received Explanation Of
> Medicare Benefits (EOMB)
>
> and the policy is lapsed but within the grace period
>
> and the policy's age is less than 6 months
>
> and the claim's value is $200 or more
>
> and the condition is preexisting

THEN:
>
> Deny the claim due to preexistence of the insured's condition. -
> Probability=1

RULE NUMBER: 41
IF:

      Medicare has paid the claim as evidenced by a received Explanation Of
      Medicare Benefits (EOMB)
and the policy is lapsed but within the grace period
and the policy's age is less than 6 months
and the claim's value is $200 or more
and the condition is indeterminant

THEN:

      Refer the claim to the Chief Claims Examiner. - Probability=1

RULE NUMBER: 42

IF:

      Medicare has paid the claim as evidenced by a received Explanation Of
      Medicare Benefits (EOMB)
and the policy is in force
and the policy's age is less than 6 months
and the claim's value is $200 or more
and the condition is indeterminant

THEN:

      Refer the claim to the Chief Claims Examiner. - Probability=1

QUALIFIERS:
1 the policy is

lapsed but within the grace period
lapsed and beyond the grace period
in force
issued but not yet at the effective date

Used in rule(s):	30	31	33	34	35	36
	37	38	39	40	41	42

2 Medicare has

paid the claim as evidenced by a received Explanation Of Medicare
Benefits (EOMB)

not paid the claim as evidenced by a received Explanation Of Medicare Benefits (EOMB)

Used in rule(s):	32	33	34	35	36	37
	38	39	40	41	42	

3   the policy's age is

6 months or more
less than 6 months

Used in rule(s):	33	34	35	36	37	38
	39	40	41	42		

4   the claim's value is

$200 or more
less than $200

Used in rule(s):	33	34	36	37	39	40
	41	42				

5   the condition is

preexisting
not preexisting
indeterminant

Used in rule(s):	(1)	(2)	(3)	(4)	(5)	(6)
	(7)	(8)	(9)	(10)	(11)	(12)
	(13)	(14)	(15)	(16)	(17)	(18)
	(19)	(20)	(21)	(22)	(23)	(24)
	(25)	(26)	(27)	(28)	(29)	33
	36	39	40	41	42	

6   the diagnosis includes

anemia
a cardiac related ailment
arthritis
bronchitis
diabetes
gout
hypertension
osteoporosis
rheumatism
ulcers
chronic
severe
carcinoma
cataracts
alzheimer's disease
arteriosclerosis
kidney stone, nephritis, or any condition requiring dialysis
back, spinal or disc ailment
an ailment not on our list

Used in rule(s):	1	2	3	4	5	6
	7	8	9	10	11	12
	13	14	15	16	17	18
	19	20	21	22	23	24
	25	26	27	28	29	

7   the patient was

admitted to the hospital or treated as an outpatient
treated during visits to a physician's office

Used in rule(s):	1	2	3	4	5	6
	7	8	9	10	11	12
	13	14	15	16	17	18
	19	20	21	22	23	24
	25	26	27	28	29	

8   the hospital records show that

medical advice or treatment for the patient's condition was rendered
 during the policy's exclusionary period

medical advice or treatment for the patient's condition was not
rendered during the policy's exclusionary period
no determination may be made regarding the preexistence of the
patient's condition

Used in rule(s):	3	4	5	6	7	8
	10	14	15	16	17	18
	19	21				

9   the physician's records show

medical advice or treatment for the patient's condition was rendered
during the policy's exclusionary period
medical advice or treatment for the patient's condition was not
rendered during the policy's exclusionary period
no determination may be made regarding the preexistence of the
patient's condition

Used in rule(s):	1	2	3	4	5	6
	7	8	9	12	13	14
	15	16	17	18	19	20

10 within the six months prior to policy issue either hospital or
physician's records or fees show that the patient received

a prescription for nitroglycerin
a positive EKG
a positive angiogram
a positive stress test
treatment for chest pain
any cardiac treatment or advice
no cardiac related treatment or advice
treatment of an indeterminant nature

Used in rule(s):	11	22	23

11 the carcinoma patient's hospital or physician's records or fees show
that the patient, during the exclusionary period, received

a carcinoma positive biopsy
a carcinoma positive mammogram
a carcinoma related chemotherapy treatment
a positive Nuclear Magnetic Resonance (NMR) scan
a positive Computer Assisted Tomography (CAT) scan
a carcinoma positive chest X-Ray
any carcinoma positive test results, diagnosis, or advice related to
    Melanoma, Sarcoma or Leukemia or other cancer related ailment
no diagnosis, treatment or medical advice for an existing carcinoma
treatment of an indeterminant nature

        Used in rule(s):   24   25   26

12 The diabetes patient's hospital or physician's records or fees show
    that the patient, during the exclusionary period, received

a positive glucose tolerance test
a positive fasting blood sugar test (FBS)
a prescription for insulin in any form
a special sugar restricted diet or advice to restrict sugar intake
a diagnosis, treatment for, or advice, regarding diabetes
no diagnosis, treatment, or advice, relative to diabetes
treatment of an indeterminant nature

        Used in rule(s):   27   28   29

CHOICES:

1 Deny the claim due to lapse and grace period expiration.
2 Deny the claim because the policy is not yet in force.
3 Deny the claim due to lack of Medicare involvement.
4 Pay the claim, less any premium owing.
5 Pay the claim in full.
6 Deny the claim due to preexistence of the insured's condition.
7 Refer the claim to the Chief Claims Examiner.

Index

ABOUT THE AUTHORS

JEROME T. MURRAY is presently director of management information services for a leading international food processing firm. An alumnus of Loyola University, Chicago State University, and the Illinois Institute of Technology, Mr. Murray's academic background is in mathematics and clinical psychology. He is a member of the Mathematical Association of America (MAA) and the American Association for Artificial Intelligence (AAAI). He had been employed in the Government, Education, and Medical Region of IBM and has served as the Chicago director of Honeywell's Institute of Information Sciences and as director of the Computer Center at Roosevelt University. Mr. Murray also spent several years as a computer systems consultant, both in private practice and with a major international consulting firm.

MARILYN J. MURRAY, an alumna of Butler University, is presently vice president, renewal processing, for the North American Company for Life and Health Insurance, where she previously served as project leader in the installation of insurance industry software. She is currently active in the areas of proprietary software testing, new product evaluation, commissions, and premium billing. Ms. Murray has also held management positions with the Indianapolis Life Insurance Company and the Globe Life Insurance Company of Chicago.